THE *FAST* TRACK

Inside the Surging Business of Women's Sports

THE *FAST* TRACK

Jane McManus

TEMPLE UNIVERSITY PRESS
Philadelphia / Rome / Tokyo

TEMPLE UNIVERSITY PRESS
Philadelphia, Pennsylvania 19122
tupress.temple.edu

Published 2025

Library of Congress Cataloging-in-Publication Data

Names: McManus, Jane, 1971– author.
Title: The fast track : inside the surging business of women's sports / Jane McManus.
Description: Philadelphia : Temple University Press, 2025. | Includes bibliographical references and index. | Summary: "This book looks at the business of women's sports, including broadcasting, pay, unions, merchandising, leagues, investments, and endorsements, to document ways that it has been undervalued relative to its potential and identify areas for improvement. The author interviews stakeholders across the industry and presents data"— Provided by publisher.
Identifiers: LCCN 2024039608 (print) | LCCN 2024039609 (ebook) | ISBN 9781439925089 (cloth) | ISBN 9781439925102 (pdf)
Subjects: LCSH: Professional sports—Economic aspects—United States. | Sports for women—Economic aspects—United States. | Mass media and sports—United States. | Women athletes—United States—Social conditions.
Classification: LCC GV716 .M44 2025 (print) | LCC GV716 (ebook) | DDC 796.04/40820973—dc23/eng/20240925
LC record available at https://lccn.loc.gov/2024039608
LC ebook record available at https://lccn.loc.gov/2024039609

♾ The paper used in this publication meets the requirements of the American National Standard for Information Sciences—Permanence of Paper for Printed Library Materials, ANSI Z39.48–1992

Printed in the United States of America

9 8 7 6 5 4 3 2 1

This book is dedicated to Nadgia James.

CONTENTS

Introduction *1*

1. A Dollar and a Dream *17*
2. Pay Equity *31*
3. The Body *45*
4. Know Your Audience *62*
5. Broadcasting Gatekeepers *77*
6. Broadcasting: *The Road Forward* *96*
7. The Future of Sports Commerce *109*
8. Investing in Women: *The Set-Up for League Success* *121*
9. Finding Allies *138*
10. Negotiating Value *149*
11. Taking a Stand *159*

Conclusion: *Passing the Torch* *172*

Acknowledgments *185*

Notes *189*

Index *195*

THE *FAST* TRACK

INTRODUCTION

"We've had cinderblocks tied to our feet for all these years."
—Megan Rapinoe[1]

In 1967, an enthusiastic runner named Kathrine Switzer made sports history simply by registering for the Boston Marathon and showing up at the starting line. To elude the race's ban on women—a restriction that would last until 1972—Switzer signed up with her first initial instead of her full name and wore baggy sweatpants to cloak her gender.

But her shoulder-length brown bob was clearly feminine. And trouble came quickly.

Jock Semple, a race official, spotted Switzer in the stream of runners and tried physically to pull her off the course. Her boyfriend, Tom Miller, roughly pushed Semple out of the way. The photos of that scene went nationwide—Semple's angry grimace; Miller's protective shove.

Switzer finished the race and kept on running. She won the New York City Marathon in 1974 and in 2023 was honored by the Women's Sports Foundation for her continued advocacy in sports. Switzer was radiant that night. A brand ambassador, she wore a brightly colored Adidas dress as she walked the red carpet. Her hair was blond and styled, her walk confident, and she warmly greeted old friends as the night went late.

All these years later, I asked: Why do you think Jock Semple tried to pull you from the course?

"He thought that wasn't the place for women. I mean, he was a product of his time," Switzer said. "I've thought about it so often, and he was just so angry."

When we talk about women in sports overcoming adversity, Switzer is an excellent example. But it's important to name the adversity. In the case of the Boston Marathon, adversity had a well-designed set of rules, unwritten expectations, and gatekeepers. There were plenty of structures in place designed to keep Switzer off the starting line well before Semple made his last-ditch attempt to pull her out.

History of a Moral Panic

What was it that was really the issue with a woman wanting to run?

An article published in 1898 in the *German Journal of Physical Education* claimed—without any evidence—that vigorous physical activity could dislodge a woman's uterus and make her sterile.[2] The unsupported conclusion became accepted wisdom in parts of the Western world, a convenient story at a time when women were making strides outside the home.

Becoming a mother was still the assumed purpose of womanhood, so anything that might disrupt a woman's reproductive system posed a threat to gender itself. Sports for women were subsequently restricted to the least strenuous activities or completely discouraged.

A race of 26.2 miles was out of the question.

The mid-1800s in the United States were also marked by concern that women were starting to take leadership roles, particularly in the church, which men wanted for themselves. In response, church leaders encouraged men to hone their physical strength to further distinguish the sexes from each other.[3] You don't have to look far to see some of today's men following the same playbook. Think of the ads for testosterone supplements on sports talk radio, or Meta's founder, Mark Zuckerberg, and the SpaceX tycoon Elon Musk floating the spectacle of a martial arts bout in some sort of alpha male showdown.

In the 1800s, the movement was called Muscular Christianity. It's why we have YMCAs all over the country, and it's how football came to American colleges before the turn of the twentieth century.

Today's women have been living with the legacy of these social assumptions for so long they've forgotten the reactionary moments that sparked them. Generations have been raised and lived their lives with these notions. They've passed these myths on in the way they have encouraged some of their children to play sports and others to cheer from the sidelines. These ideas had a wide impact on what women could do with their own bodies for decades.

It's time we understand the adversity.

Running took off in the 1980s, and we no longer humor superstitions about sports uniquely harming women's bodies. But we've retained a bit of this myth of delicacy even as we've moved past medical advice from the era of high-dose mineral poisons.

The countless women around the world who run competitively serve as a refutation of bad science, but gatekeepers—whether figures such as Semple or the faceless rules and expectations behind the scenes—haven't gone away entirely. With just 5 percent of media coverage on televised news and highlight shows between 1989 and 2019 and as little as 1 percent of sponsorship dollars, by some estimates, going to women's sports, it's clear that celebrating stories of individual success, on which much of the media dedicated to women's sport has focused, has not made much of a dent in larger cultural assumptions about who should be supported in sports.[4]

Over the course of a thirty-year career in sportswriting, I've written plenty of stories about women in sports. And when I played roller derby in the 2010s, our league's coverage was mostly limited to the occasional feature on the subversive nature of a full-contact sport for women, with bonus points for the mom angle.

It's time to take a larger focus, beyond individual stories, on systems of adversity and systems of advancement.

Not One Bad Guy, Not One Hero

The adversity in "overcoming adversity" comes in many forms: the decades of discouragement; the arguments over times to train and facilities in which to do so; the threat of physical violence against women such as Switzer, who break rules written and unwritten. The structural impediments don't all exist in the same way for kids growing up today, but we are barely two generations away from women being allowed to race in Boston.

Sometimes, the obstacles *are* individuals with systemic power.

You will meet dozens of people in the pages of this book who are creating and quantifying the momentum around women's sports at this very moment. The pitch to investors is about patient capital and return on investment rather than an appeal to charitable impulses with "It's the right thing to do."

You'll learn from women and men who were the decision makers, analysts, and newsmakers or who had a front-row seat as surge and stagnation tugged at our subject.

One of those people is Molly Tissenbaum, a twenty-nine-year-old data analyst and consultant for Sports Innovation Lab. Tissenbaum played ice hockey at Harvard, but as we spoke, she also revealed she'd been denied a spot on the youth baseball team on which her brother played when the coach told her he didn't take girls. And that coach's individual preference was the final decision for her and others like her.

"That's something that has obviously stuck with me," Tissenbaum said. "It's what I wrote my college admissions essay about. That was the moment where I realized, even if mom and dad see me and Max the same way, perhaps there are other people who don't."

For Tissenbaum, what seemed like an individual obstacle in the person of one baseball coach was merely the beginning of a larger world of "other people" dismissing women's participation in sport, despite its value to her and many others. Individual efforts cannot always overcome systemic problems, particularly when they are merely alluded to and not formally challenged. So today Tissenbaum's work at Sports Innovation Lab shows sports leagues, media companies, and sponsors the value of systemic investment in women's sports. A systemic problem requires a comprehensive response, and that's the sort of struggle that needs its story told.

The 1967 Boston Marathon was the story not of one woman's defiance but of decades of oppression of women and girls in sports. The cheerleading for individual girls and women is a hedge against the larger impediments—they serve as role models and create permission for others—but in ignoring the structural issues, each woman who wants to play sports, each Molly Tissenbaum, is often challenged to scale the mountain anew. The story of women's sports is filled with such redundancies. There has been much written about the boost women in sports got from Title IX, a federal law mandating greater equity in institutions that accept federal funds, in 1972. And there were gains—one in twenty-seven girls played sports in the United States before Title IX, according to research by the Women's Sports Foundation, and now one in three girls play. But to focus only on the gains is to leave part of this story untold.

Title IX was passed to allow women equal access to graduate schools and universities, but the way it was written, it applied to playing fields, too. That interpretation was vehemently opposed at first. With so few women playing at the time, it was seen as ridiculous that they would be entitled to half of anything in that space. Athletic scholarships for women? There were lawsuits for decades. As late as 2002, George W. Bush commissioned a panel to look at the issue with an eye toward weakening the statute.

Instead, that commission affirmed it.

Yet the impediments don't disappear. They just pack up their bags and migrate. Where once the argument was that women wouldn't want to play college sports, not that the opportunities weren't available, those assumptions of interest and affinity have also been applied in the area of investment for women's sports and athletes.

Is This a Moment?

This book is a snapshot of where women's sports as an industry and investment stand at this moment. Many of the numbers and anecdotes will be superseded in the months and years ahead. And yet the attention on women's sports is actually quite cyclical and tied to how women are seen culturally in a moment. As we've seen when it comes to the loss of ground in reproductive rights, progress does not continue in a single direction, and the rights one generation's women gained can be denied to their daughters.

I've spent my career as a woman in this space experiencing a kind of Groundhog Day. I experienced the shock of watching a colleague turned away from a professional locker room early in my career and chalked it up to retrograde thinking, only to see again the veteran journalists Lisa Olson and Tara Sullivan later blocked from locker rooms in Major League baseball and professional golf. These were mistakes each time, of course, but mistakes that are never made when the reporters are male.

You could choose to tell this story from the vantage of those who have broken though, ignoring the stories of women who didn't find the intersection of talent and opportunity. You could tell this story with the surety of an equity that is just around the corner or the cynicism that nothing has changed. But the truth is in between. Women's sports have been a cyclical venture in the past one hundred years, with incredible moments and demonstrable interest.

Professor Victoria Jackson is in Canada, but only barely. It's summer, and she's escaped the heat around Arizona State University for a more traditional summer north of Michigan. Jackson is an academic but she's also an athlete, as her Twitter handle @HistoryRunner blends. She's got the lean limbs of a person accustomed to endurance sports, but she spends her days researching issues such as how the arrival of sovereign wealth funds might change the business of soccer.

She has also spent time abroad studying the women's soccer leagues that existed across the world well before the Women's World Cup was established in 1991. Some teams—notably, in Mexico and the United Kingdom—drew enormous crowds to watch games.

"I think [interest in women's sports has] always been there because there was a women's World Cup in Mexico, before it could actually be called a Women's World Cup, that is still technically the attendance record," Jackson said. "And it was, like, 110,000 in 1971. That has always been there. And it's not like, 'Oh, we've arrived.' It's like, 'Oh, the lid that has been pushing us down has been taken off again.'"

Serena and Venus Williams underwrote a documentary about the Cup titled *Copa 71*. I say more about their work in this space later, but women's sports deserve to have their origin stories well-documented because too often the history has been discarded.

"I think there's almost, like, an eagerness to continue to prove that women will never be as good as men in sports; that the market will never be the same as the market for men's sports," Jackson said. "And we gave you a chance and it failed again. And we'll see you in another generation when we allow you to rise to this level again. By contrast, the equity in the structures built into American college sports show that if you think something is going to exist forever, you will allow it to."

Economics is a science, but not in the way that chemistry is, and you can't take cultural values such as identity out of the equation. There is a saying in politics that a budget is a statement of values. Likewise, our values help determine what we spend money on, as individuals and as a society. Men and women as categories have a different set of historical values associated with them, and the values we give to sports tend to be associated with men.

They need not be. But women looking to raise the value of their play face layers of complication. We will get into the issue of equal pay later, but when league salaries are based on revenue, most athletes in women's sports won't see pay that approaches that of their male peers. How can women earn more until their leagues earn more? How can their leagues earn more until sports fans change their habits? Why should sports fans change their habits unless the coverage or the level of play changes? Why should the level of play change if the league won't invest in athletes? Where does the buck stop?

"If all professional men's sports teams had to be profitable in the first ten years their leagues existed, we would not have any men's professional sports leagues now," said David Berri, a professor of economics at Southern Utah State University. "When men say they expect this of women's teams, what they are really saying is they don't want to invest in women."

As a sports journalist on social media, I've seen the comment "No one cares about women's sports" under virtually every piece about women's sports. It's time we understand that's not an expression of apathy. It's hostility.

For example, let's say you don't care for broccoli. You wouldn't order it. When it is served to you, you might put broccoli to the side of your plate. It probably wouldn't garner another thought. Most people wouldn't march into the kitchen and yell at the chef for making the broccoli. They wouldn't mock fellow diners for ordering it or demand that the restaurant take it off the menu.

But that's what happens with women's sports. Its mere existence can ignite a vocal group of people who very much care about women's sports—so much so that they rail against broadcasters and degrade athletes and fans. They will say women's voices are too high to call games or make any number of other gendered criticisms.

The hostility isn't limited to social spaces. It can find purchase in media and in business. I've seen producers cut a women's sports story from a show rundown out of concern that the discussion might alienate viewers. Even if the producer didn't dislike women's sports, the mere awareness that the conversation might trigger a segment of the sports audience was enough to shape coverage.

Women's leagues have also been wary of these fans and worked to win them over by emphasizing the "athlete" in women's athletics. You'll read stories in these pages of players being asked to tone down their comments or present more femininely in photo shoots. Pregnancy, abortion, and periods have been off-the-table topics when it comes to media coverage of professional women's leagues.

Even in sports broadcasts, the visible roles for women have been limited—mainly to host and sideline reporter—and the women hired are often young and conventionally attractive. This gives women an approved lane in coverage without challenging sports viewers' gender expectations. As women take on roles as analysts and in the front office, they might still face scorn and abuse.

Alexis Ohanian, the founder of Reddit and an investor in women's sports (he's also the tennis champion Serena Williams's husband), has told conference audiences about behind-the-scenes conversations with men who invest in women's sports as owners but don't value that investment in the same way they do other properties.

These attitudes have combined to create inertia in the space around women's sports and investment. So women's leagues aren't just fighting for fan bases and broadcast windows and sponsorship; they are also working against the drag of that reluctance to disrupt a sports framework that has functioned well for men's sports and the fans of men's sports.

Ellen Staurowsky, a professor in sports media in Ithaca College's Roy H. Park School of Communications and the author of *Women and Sport: A Continuing Journey from Liberation to Celebration*, is clear-eyed about this history when she assesses a rising tide in the women's sports space.

"When we get to this moment, while there is absolutely no doubt in my mind that we are in a moment of momentum in terms of women's sports, I'm actually not sure if we are moving forward or if this moment is actually signaling that this is the amount of work that it takes just to keep the small portion of what we've got in place," she said. "And that's a very grim thought."

This web of inertia is not a single lack of opportunity. This isn't something that one plucky girl can solve. It's something that has to be met and assessed and addressed, and then met and assessed and addressed again.

There have been three major peaks in the momentum around the modern women's sports movement in the United States in my lifetime. We are living in the third peak now, spurred by new ways for audiences and athletes to connect. The first came in the early 1970s, when Title IX became law and Billie Jean King defeated Bobby Riggs. The second came in the late 1990s, as American women took gold medals in basketball, soccer, gymnastics, and softball at the 1996 Atlanta Olympics, which ultimately birthed two professional basketball leagues. The U.S. Women's National Team (USWNT) win in the '99 World Cup in front of a crowd of 90,185 at the Rose Bowl spawned a pro soccer league named the Women's United Soccer Association (WUSA) just a few years after the 1996 start of the men's Major League Soccer (MLS).

Within five years, the only league left standing was the NBA-backed Women's National Basketball Association (WNBA), and it was struggling.

Karen Weaver, graduate faculty and academic director at the University of Pennsylvania who has done research into college and women's sports, witnessed the turn.

"I was in Atlanta for that enthusiasm that burst around the women's games," Weaver said. "There was a moment—the personalities of the women's soccer players—you could feel the excitement. Something happened, and the air went out of the room by the time it hit 2000."

Brandi Chastain, after making the penalty kick to give the USWNT the gold medal in 1999, was on the cover of *Sports Illustrated* and *USA Today* when, in a moment of triumph, she tossed off her jersey in the sport's celebratory gesture. Twenty years later, the National Women's Soccer League (NWSL), the third of the major pro women's leagues to give it a go in the United States, was launched.

That's a long runway to something that is starting to look like sustainable success.

Part of the issue has always been the media coverage of women's sports. Estimated to be 4–5 percent of the total TV broadcast sports highlight show coverage by an ongoing study by Cheryl Cooky at Purdue University, and without a network of its own to make up for the fickleness of mainstream storytelling, women's sports struggled for visibility once Chastain's triumphant—and jersey-less—image faded.

You will see in the pages that follow the creative approaches that are being taken and the new entities that are springing up to capitalize on and measure fans' interest. There is the Women's Sports Network led by ESPN's Carol Stiff and the website Just Women's Sports, started by the former All-Pac-12 midfielder Haley Rosen when she was just twenty-six years old.

The current momentum is real, but historians such as Ithaca College's Staurowsky are still aware of the cyclical nature of interest and are cautious in distinguishing that from a true breakthrough of acceptance.

"When we have less than 1 percent of the global marketing budget and we're still at 1950 levels in terms of actual coverage of women's sports, and maybe just a little bit above that," Staurowsky said, "as much as all of this activity is very exciting and the Women's Sports Network and the stuff that Carol Stiff is doing and all of the things that Billie Jean King has been doing both in front [of] and behind the scenes, it may all be signaling that a major shift has occurred. But we're still not even yet at 20 percent, which would at least say that there's actually a strong foothold there."

In 2022, Jessica Berman was brought in to be the commissioner of the National Women's Soccer League. She came from a front office career in men's sports, where she got a primer on the structural issues that make success more challenging for women's leagues.

"It's not to attribute blame to anyone," Berman said. "It's just human nature that we default to certain behaviors that are rooted in us from, like, the day of our birth. And it's generational. So you have to, like, be committed to it. It's a daily practice of saying, 'That's not serving me. I'm going to change the future.'"

And so, to the future.

Building a New House

When Rosen was making the rounds looking for seed investors for a media start-up called Just Women's Sports, she had a conversation with the USWNT star Abby Wambach. There is an informal network of women in sports spaces who lean on one another to try to better understand the challenges that keep coming up.

Rosen was in her early twenties when she noticed that women's sports weren't covered with the same seriousness, humor, or consistency as men's sports. Rosen was getting a lot of skepticism about the concept of a separate network, and it's hard to clear the persistent doubts out of the way to make change. Why wasn't this idea as obvious to everyone?

Wambach encouraged Rosen to think about her pitch in another way.

"I have no interest in breaking the glass ceiling," Rosen recalled Wambach saying. "I want to build a new house."

"When she said that, it just, like, really succinctly captured the feeling of, like, I don't feel the need to fight," Rosen said. "It feels like there are systems that are just fundamentally not set up for women's sports. And a lot of times, for women to succeed, let's just go build new systems. I like that."

So, a new house.

Athletes such as Wambach are using their own money on the lumber. Let's take a look around the NWSL to start. In Washington, DC, the gymnast Dominique Dawes and the WNBA's Elena Della Donne joined Alex Ovechkin of the National Hockey League (NHL) in an investment group. Sarah Spain, the sports broadcaster, and the soccer player Kendall Coyne Schofield invested in Chicago's Red Stars. In Los Angeles, Serena Williams; Julie Foudy and Mia Hamm of the 1999 gold medal–winning USWNT, nicknamed the 99ers; and the actress Natalie Portman are part of the investment group. The tennis star Naomi Osaka has taken on the North Carolina Courage.

"It's a watershed moment," Economics Professor Andrew Zimbalist at Smith College told me. "It's been almost fifty years since the passage of Title IX, and some of these women athletes have enough money to make that investment."

Like a mortgage payment on a new house.

It's very disruptive, this nontraditional capital coming in. Owners such as Clara Wu Tsai at the Liberty and Nadia Rawlinson in Chicago, and a group of investors in the NWSL's Los Angeles Angel City franchise, are loud and involved and very different from the suited billionaires who make up ownership groups in men's sports.

"It's a different mindset than anything I've ever been a part of," Foudy said about the group investing in Angel City on the *Ladies Room* podcast I co-hosted with the sports journalist Julie DiCaro.[5] "It's always been more 'You should be grateful we have a team,' and this is 'Let's kick some ass. Let's go!'"

Women in sports are social media influencers in the truest sense of the word.

Foudy and company are spending their cultural capital on women's teams. As the sportswriter and podcaster Kate Fagan put it: Why should a women's sports celebrity sit courtside at a Lakers game? The Lakers don't need her cultural capital. Neither does a Marvel movie; plenty of people will find that compelling and buy tickets. But if a women's sports celebrity can make it cool to go to an NWSL game—now, that's changing the game.

And if you sit at a WNBA Chicago Sky game, you might see the team's owner, the NBA player Dwyane Wade; or if you sit at an NWSL Gotham FC game, you might see the former Giants quarterback Eli Manning.

"What's also interesting is, now I have a ton of companies calling [and saying], 'Do you want to come be an owner investor with us? We want more female athletes. Can you help us get there?'" Foudy said. "It certainly has been contagious. . . . There is a blueprint and a road map for how we can think differently about this. And clearly our sponsorship numbers— We haven't revealed all of them publicly, but we're crushing it with sponsorship in a way that will again be a road map for how we should be doing and thinking about this."

A. New. House.

Change Is Here

The path that women have charted in sports—whether on the field, on the sideline, or in the front offices—has not been easy. Or even fair. It's a lot to take in. Once you understand the structural inequities that women have been confronting for decades, it can feel like women's sports are permanently stalled.

And yet women who have been swimming against the current for decades see the change in the environment, Stacey Allaster, former chief executive of the Women's Tennis Association (WTA) and current tournament director for the U.S. Open, said. She has been up against that wall for nearly three decades, but even she said it feels as if there is a moment here for women's sports.

"We've been stuck for twenty years," Allaster said. "It feels like there's some momentum here. There's been an unlocking of the code, and the value to the brand to associate themselves with Serena, with Coco [Gauff], with Venus is immense. We're seeing this whole influencer world change, which is, in essence, what these professional female athletes are, and that will come with a new business model. The reality of it is [that] linear TV is now going to be analog, almost. Streaming is going to be the gift to women's sport and to all sports that aren't in the big leagues."[6]

The technology to make women's sports more accessible, with high production values and high quality, is in streaming broadcasts. Viewers, particularly young ones, are adapting streaming platforms quickly.

Women's leagues won't need a conventional broadcast network in the same way that men's leagues did in their growth years; the financial model can be more like buying a ticket for an event than having cable subscribers and advertisers pay the costs. The newest iPhone might not be so far removed technologically from a few generations of television cameras, and that means the ability for a league to produce its own broadcast, that looks and sounds professional, is at hand.

The most conventional measures of interest—attendance at games and television viewership—have been rising. By a lot. The backstory is this: both the WNBA and the NWSL opted to play early in the COVID-19 pandemic as other professional sports were paused. They created closed systems: players and personnel had to test and quarantine to get in, and they played without crowds.

In mid-June 2021, after the success of the NWSL and the WNBA broadcasts during the pandemic, ESPN put out a press release to announce that the Women's College World Series finals averaged a best ever 1.8 million viewers over three games. National Collegiate Athletic Association (NCAA) women's volleyball was up 29 percent over the 2019 broadcast year. As for the women's NCAA tournament, the final drew four million viewers.

The WNBA was up 25 percent, as well, with 605,000 viewers for the first doubleheader on ABC. But the real breakthrough came with the 2023 Women's NCAA Basketball Tournament. In the first year it was able to use the term "March Madness," the women's final on ABC and across ESPN's networks drew nearly ten million viewers.

Even better, those fans tended to be younger and more technologically savvy than the fan bases for more established sports, such as baseball.

"I think it's a huge opportunity for us to, really, kind of full circle, go back to Abby's idea of building our own house," Rosen said. "I think that is the opportunity to go build the infrastructure of women's sports the same way that there's a whole infrastructure set up for men's sports to do super, super well. That's the opportunity in women's sports, but we need to go build it, and every piece of it needs to get built, from media to the advertising side to betting. I think that's a really, really exciting opportunity. I also think there's just the right momentum; there's the right culture of women's sports. It feels like the key leagues are in good spots. Stuff like NIL [name, image, and likeness rights]. It just feels like so much is coming together to make this the moment in women's sports. But we got to take our moment, because how many do you get?"

If you build it, they will come. It's something I heard repeated over and over. But it took a pandemic to disrupt the entire sports broadcasting landscape, to create the willingness to showcase these leagues accordingly.

Women are now taking the lead to grow these numbers and the popularity of their sports.

"Sometimes you need a couple of false starts to move the ball forward in an incremental way," Chicago Sky's Operating Chairman Nadia Rawlinson told me. "But now I think both for women's sports overall and for the

WNBA and women's soccer, and then even some of the other leagues that are out there, this is a critical moment."

This isn't meant to be the definitive book on this subject; the terrain is simply too vast. I lamented the scope of it to Sue Anstiss, whose 2021 book *Game On: The Unstoppable Rise of Women's Sport* detailed the same phenomenon and the impact it is having on women's sports in the United Kingdom.[7] I promise, I told her, I wrote the proposal before I read your book. She laughed and said there should be shelves of books on women and sports and that we can see this as a collaboration rather than a competition.

As her book published, Anstiss received a congratulatory card from a friend.

"He said he feels like I've been paddling behind the wave, trying to get on for all these years," she said. "And actually, the wave is coming up behind me. It's finally come, but it's come because I've been behind and waiting to get on it. I love that analogy."

In this book, I often refer to women and women's sports. This is how women's leagues have identified themselves and allows a historical tracing of the category. However, there are athletes who play in professional women's leagues who identify differently, so I know the terms don't fit everyone, and I endeavor to use inclusive language when possible. It's also important to acknowledge that race plays a huge role in how athletes are perceived and discussed and, importantly for the purposes of this book, paid.

Our cultural ideas about gender and identity are in motion, and I imagine that well-intended phrases may fall awkwardly at some point after this is printed. I am also aware that the structural inequities that have disadvantaged athletes in women's sports don't care for these subtleties, and those who oppose women's sports altogether are often the most rigid in enforcing gender categories.

As I wrote this book, people wanted to talk about the issues arising as transgender women compete in women's sports. I look at that subject in Chapter 3, but as someone who played against transgender skaters in roller derby bouts sanctioned by the Women's Flat Track Derby Association (WFTDA), I saw firsthand the value of inclusiveness, even in a full-contact sport. My perspective comes from playing sports and seeing how they connect people who feel on the margins in other ways and seeing the banner of "women's sports" cover many kinds of bodies.

"Here we have what's supposed to be this zenith moment for women athletes and their successes, and arguably the biggest story is the policing of women's sports and supposed fairness for women athletes," Staurowsky said. "I don't think it's accidental that these two things are running at the same time."

People who never supported women's sports have used this and other issues to divide those who love and play women's sports. When colleges were cutting men's Olympic sports, some administrators pointed the finger at Title IX. At the same time, the arms race around college football was the elephant in the locker room.

We can understand this moment only by seeing the forest and the trees, with the full breadth of hope and adversity as the two weave competing narratives anew each generation.

"I am seeing a macro shift in the way the whole society and culture feels about women's sports," said Donna Orender, who was a commissioner of the WNBA and is now the chief executive of the consulting firm Orender Unlimited, in an interview for a *Sports Business Journal* event in New York.

"By the way, we should have done it twenty years ago," Orender added. "I mean, we should have done it twenty-five years ago, but the fact it's finally happening is incredibly encouraging."

When I was eleven, my mom and I moved from Harrisonburg, Virginia, to Lincoln, Nebraska. It was culture shock. I still remember my sixth-grade teacher passing around a sheet of paper where we guessed the final score of each weekend's Cornhuskers football game. The winner would receive a Herbie Husker pencil. Downtown on Saturdays, the sidewalks were overrun with red sweatshirts and scarves before Lincoln became a ghost town between the whistles.

Memorial Stadium, where the University of Nebraska Cornhuskers played, was the third-largest city in the state on game day, with more than 85,000 fans. Without professional leagues nearby, Nebraska football's hold on the culture was second only to religion. And even then, I sometimes wondered which one would come out on top if you really forced people to make the choice.

In the summer of 2023, I got a call from the reporter Aaron Bonderson at Nebraska Public Radio. The University of Nebraska was planning something different for the preseason Volleyball Day: it was going to build a court for Memorial Stadium and have a four-team tournament.

Women's volleyball is another incredibly popular sport at the university and routinely sells out its eight thousand–seat Bob Devaney Center. Up to that summer, the team had sold out 306 consecutive games. By some measures it was the only profitable women's sport in the NCAA.

The university put the tickets on sale. Within three days, all 82,900 had been sold. The university reconfigured the seating and printed more tickets. On August 30, 92,003 fans filed into the stands for Volleyball Day, making it the most attended women's sporting event in the United States.[8] In second place: the 90,185 who watched the Women's World Cup final in 1999.

Volleyball Day, which took place as I was writing this book, really brought things home for me.

If my hometown in Nebraska, where football always felt like the only game in town, can find creative ways to showcase volleyball, can turn a nearly sacred football palace into a spectacle for the fans of a women's sport, this can be done anywhere. It's easy to focus on the biggest market, but nothing that happened on August 30 in any way diminished what Nebraska football means to that state.

But administrators, sponsors, leagues, and broadcasters have to be willing to adapt.

"When I look at what Nebraska did recently with the announcement about their volleyball day, then I do wonder whether or not, in terms of the decision makers and gatekeepers, . . . they finally have really gotten the message that they're leaving money on the table," Staurowsky said.

"It's like, 'Oh, OK. Embarrassing. We've been leaving money on the table.'"

1

A DOLLAR AND A DREAM

How to turn a buck into $94 million.

Billie Jean King blazed into the packed auditorium at Seton Hall University, in South Orange, New Jersey, wearing a bright red jacket and white pearls, and spontaneously offered her hands to high-fives as she walked up the center aisle to the stage on a mild mid-February day in 2023. Those who had gathered for an event billed as a conversation about equity and influence turned the moment into a celebration. After all, there are few people who hold such a foundational place in the modern American sports story.

It was hard to believe that, as she neared her eightieth year, King was once polarizing. But the truth is, she was a hero and a villain as the women's rights movement forced a dramatic reorientation of gender roles in American society in the 1970s and beyond. In many ways, King is the progenitor of the modern professional sports movement for women. On this day, as a woman whose nimbleness and activism defied age, she was appreciated.

The Yogi Berra Museum in Montclair, New Jersey, was exhibiting photographs from her long and successful tennis career; the nearby U.S. Open, in the New York City borough of Queens, had renamed itself the Billie Jean King National Tennis Center a decade earlier, and just two days earlier she'd had a cameo role in one of the National Football League's (NFL's)

Super Bowl commercials. King even had a line after she opened a car door to help the running back Diana Flores avoid a defender in a flag football game that had escaped the stadium.

"Oops," she landed, with a bemused look at the camera.

King and her longtime partner, Ilana Kloss, a former tennis player who now spearheads the couple's business ventures, had made the journey at my request. They were onstage; the Super Bowl commercial played on a large screen at the front of the room; the audience quieted; and the lights went up.[1]

In the chapters that follow, I give the full context behind my question for her. But here are some of the highlights: the years of success and suppression of women's sports, of "You go girl!" and "Go make me a sandwich." From failed soccer leagues to expansion of the WNBA and NWSL and the Professional Women's Hockey League about to debut. All since the moment in 1973 that King herself defeated Bobby Riggs on a regulation tennis court in the Houston Astrodome, broadcast live on network television, with 30,472 in attendance. It's still the largest crowd to watch a tennis match in the United States.

More important, that win staked new ideological turf for the growing women's liberation movement: a woman could beat a man in a sport. Even if Riggs, at fifty-five, was a fading player while King was at the top of her game, it wasn't just the skill needed to take him down—it was the chutzpah. King succeeded where another great player of the time, Margaret Court, failed, in part because King relished the moment. She was carried in on a feathered board by four bare-chested men. An estimated fifty million people watched the ABC broadcast.

Women could play sports, and everyone saw it.

There were some in the room at Seton Hall who could remember that day firsthand, but even the students too young to bear witness knew King was a change agent, a barometer of progress. She had remained at the forefront of the discussion of women and sports, and in the late winter of 2023, there was a burst of investment as ratings and interest surged. And King still had a hand in all of it, in front of the camera and behind the scenes. If anyone was poised to understand the distance traveled and the potential on the horizon, it was King.

"When you see this movement and enthusiasm, is this the moment?" I asked her.

King was quick to respond.

"No, we're not even started—we're just getting started," she said, amending her answer on the fly. "We're always so far behind. I think companies should ask themselves, 'Do you spend as much on women's sports as you do on men's sports?' That's the one I want to see."

Kloss looked up from her notes to add a more optimistic data point.

"If you invest in women—give them the same kind of emotional investment, financial investment, and time commitment—then judge, and you have to look at men's sports and how long they've been around, and they don't really give women's sports the same opportunities," she said. "And I think that's starting to change. I think you're starting to get, I call them the B guys—mostly, and women—billionaires involved in owning women's sports to round out their portfolios. And I think that's really significant."

Tennis Paved the Way

Change isn't always evident when you look year to year, but when you check back over a few decades, it's easier to see.

It was 1970, and Jack Kramer, executive director of the Association of Tennis Professionals (ATP), announced he wanted to pay the winner of the women's draw of the Pacific Southwest Open $1,500, a fraction of the $12,500 the men would get. The paycheck was not just an insult in King's mind; again, it was a statement of values. Kramer clearly valued the men's game, and he merely *allowed* the women to play.

Gladys Heldman, who at that time was a tennis promoter and the publisher of *World Tennis Magazine*, told King not to get angry but to start her own tournament.

Nine players signed on with Heldman to play that tournament under its historic $1 contract, despite threats from what is now the United States Tennis Association that the women would be barred from future Grand Slams should they break away from the traditional format. Led by King, those women—Peaches Bartkowicz, Rosie Casals, Judy Tegart Dalton, Julie Heldman, Kristy Pigeon, Kerry Melville Reid, Nancy Richey, and Valerie Ziegenfuss, collectively known as the Original 9—declared their independence from the decision makers in tennis and staked a claim to their own economic potential when few in professional sports cared much about what women were doing.

"That is the birth of women's professional tennis," King said. "This was 1970. We played an eight-woman tournament at the Houston Racquet Club. Fast forward to 1971. We had our tour, the Virginia Slims."

The risk of failure was very real, and the women needed money to make this work. Player Kristy Pigeon wrote a letter to Philip Morris asking the company to sponsor the event, leveraging Chief Executive Joe Cullman's desire to capitalize on the women's movement with a brand of cigarettes aimed at the newly liberated. Pigeon ended the letter to Cullman, "Joe, show us some dough!"

He did, and the Virginia Slims tour was born.

"Tennis was run by men, the good ol' boys club," another of the nine, Valerie Ziegenfuss, told the Associated Press for a retrospective look at the pivotal moment.[2] "Our tennis tour was dominated by male promoters who didn't really believe in women's tennis."

If it took marketing cigarettes to feminists to get this new league off the ground, so be it, and King has defended the decision with a matter-of-factness. The respectable sponsors were tied up with other leagues and tournaments; this new league needed cash and didn't have the luxury of choice.

What it did have was an idea of why this women's league would be different.

"Here's the three things we decided on. We were willing to give up our careers," King recounted to *PBS NewsHour* in 2021. "And there are the three things: any girl, if she's good enough, that she would finally have a place to compete. Number two, that she be appreciated for her accomplishments and not only for her looks. And number three, and the most important thing, to be able to make a living. That's why we are the leader in women's sports today. Every time a woman tennis player gets a check or makes money off of the court, that is because of that moment in time."[3]

High risk, but look at the rewards.

In 1971, prize money on the new WTA Tour was more than $300,000. In 2019, before the pandemic altered schedules, the WTA's total prize money was $146 million. Roughly 2,500 athletes were competing for a share of it.

In 2021, Naomi Osaka became the highest-paid female athlete ever by earning $60 million in twelve months, according to *Forbes*. Osaka was twelfth on the list of all athletes, regardless of gender, and the top-earning woman. The bulk of her earnings, $55 million, came from endorsements.

The only other woman in the top fifty was Serena Williams, with $41.5 million in earnings. This was not unusual. On *Forbes*'s list of the highest paid female athletes of 2018, eight of the top ten were tennis players, and most of their earnings came from endorsements:

1. Serena Williams, $18.1 million, 99 percent from endorsements
2. Caroline Wozniaki, $13 million, 46 percent from endorsements
3. Sloane Stephens, $11.2 million, 49 percent from endorsements
4. Garbine Muguraza, $11 million, 50 percent from endorsements
5. Maria Sharapova, $10.5 million, 90 percent from endorsements
6. Venus Williams, $10.2 million, 59 percent from endorsements
7. P. V. Sindhu, $8.5 million, 94 percent from endorsements
8. Simona Halep, $7.7 million, 19 percent from endorsements
9. Danica Patrick, $7.5 million, 60 percent from endorsements
10. Angelique Kerber, $7 million, 57 percent from endorsements[4]

"The New Economy of Sports," a 2023 data set by the Wasserman Collective, compared men's and women's playing salaries across four professional sports in 2022: tennis (WTA and ATP), soccer (NWSL and MLS), golf (Ladies Professional Golf Association [LPGA] and Professional Golfers' Association of America [PGA]), and basketball (WNBA and National Basketball Association [NBA]). Men earned 1.2 times what women earned in tennis, $335,000 to $280,000 per year.[5] In basketball, where there was the largest discrepancy, men earned 108 times what the women did. Women in tennis earned twice the average wage as the next-best sport for women, golf, where the average earnings for women were $142,000 per year.

And here's something less expected: the more equal the prize money, the more equal the endorsement opportunities, according to the Wasserman research. Tennis had the smallest advantage for men on the ATP Tour—just one-and-a-half to four times what WTA players earned in endorsements, with soccer coming in second, at two-and-a-half times what women earned.

Women's tennis has been by far the most lucrative sport for women, with that fifty-year head start, as King puts it.

The Original 9 are all now in the International Tennis Hall of Fame (although even that didn't happen without some grousing from the traditionalists). Their accomplishment has become an origin story in women's sports, the first great heroic tale of the modern era in women's sports. But as much as it is a story of women risking everything for the opportunity to be true professional athletes, it is also the story of how men's sports don't want to cede any power: in this case by a difference of $12,500 to $1,500.

Keeping Up the Momentum

To understand women's sports is to be a historian, a sociologist, a sports fan, an athlete, a politician, and a prognosticator. Most important, it is to witness the way that women have been shut out; how gender has been strictly enforced; and how those stories reflect the larger plight of people entering the workforce while King was swinging her racket and had to negotiate with a less endearing Jack Kramer for her salary.

Early on, King approached the ATP, the men's tennis association, and asked it to create a women's division. That made sense: men and women both played four Grand Slam events each year, and fans of tennis were accustomed to watching men's and women's matches at the same time. The ATP wasn't interested at that time and, despite the possibility being raised a few more times in the intervening half-century, the tours remain separate.

King and Kloss have since consulted with numerous leagues and businesses about how to strategize around women's sports, such as the NHL after the success of the U.S. Women's Ice Hockey Team at the Nagano Olympics in 1998. King was on speed dial for Mia Hamm and Julie Foudy during the 1999 World Cup campaign, when the event was moved to the United States and U.S. Soccer put the women's matches in small venues.

Ultimately, those 99ers fronted money to get into bigger stadiums and filled the Rose Bowl before a record TV audience to win the gold. As detailed in the ESPN documentary *The 99ers*, they needed to hustle, because they believed in the power of their game more than anyone else.

"The epiphany for me as a professional athlete was that I would still have to be selling, selling, selling the game every single day," the veteran basketball player and men's basketball coach Nancy Lieberman said on Kate Fagan's *Through the Looking Glass* podcast.[6]

Nine women working toward financial equity have sparked a movement across women's sports, leading us to the current moment.

As executive vice president at The Collective, a part of the Wasserman agency that focuses on representing women, Thayer Lavielle is in charge of an effort to connect today's professional athletes with compensation and sponsorships. She shares King's assertion that the fifty years since the beginning of the WTA Tour are a start, but there is still much work to be done. She's in meeting rooms advocating for those players to be recognized.

"To have been Billie Jean King or some of these women who really, like, were fighting for Title IX. What an uphill, lonely road to have paved, and how fearless they must have been, and relentless they must have been," Lavielle said. "To now come to a place where it feels like there's so much great noise around women in sports and women's sports— How do we maintain the growth and investment into just the fundamental ecosystem to make sure that there will always be a place for the next Sue Bird to play and to shine and to have all the assets that they need and whatever those things are? But also there's continued awareness and kind of drum banging around it, because we also can't just be like, 'Well, thanks. We're OK, thanks. Now we're ready to take more crumbs.' We have to keep going, and we're not going to stop until this playing field is just more equal, period. And it's so much nicer to do with other people around you."

Cultural Expectations Make Progress Difficult

So much cultural change has been witnessed through sports, from Jackie Robinson's breaking of the color barrier in Major League Baseball in 1947 to Carl Nassib's becoming the first openly gay player in the NFL in 2021. Yet in some ways sports have also shown us how strong the opposition to true progress is. In 2020, Kim Ng was celebrated as the first woman to be named a general manager in baseball, but you could just as easily have tipped your cap to how long baseball had managed to keep women out of top jobs until then.

These achievements are milestones because it is so difficult to disentangle the cultural expectations we have of people from their value in the workplace. Thus, the qualities associated with excellence on the playing field are often male, as John Amaechi once explained to me, and might not be associated with a man who is gay. Amaechi came out in 2007, after his career as a professional NBA player ended.

"None of the stereotypes about gay people suggest they would be good at sports," Amaechi told me for an ESPN story in 2011. The reason—or one of them, he said—was that men who are gay have been perceived as more feminine than men who are not, and misogyny is a subtext in homophobia.

Associations between people's occupations and the value correlated with their identity have had an economic impact on women in sports. As female tennis players appear on lists of top-earning athletes and earn salaries comparable to those of male tennis players, minds open anew to the possibilities for other female athletes. But thanks to the cultural meaning of the high-earning female tennis player, people wonder how far to extend that economic potential into the category of female athletes generally. Were female tennis players doing well because the Original 9 in tennis took an independent stand early? Or because women's tennis coincided with other values associated with femininity?

For many years, the top sports for women were the ones in which they could wear skirts or makeup as part of their performance: think of tennis, gymnastics, and ice skating. In the first year of the WNBA, promotional shots of the league's original three athletes—Sheryl Swoopes, Lisa Leslie, and Rebecca Lobo—emphasized their femininity along with their skills. Women's team sports have not been able to reach the escape velocity to clear these cultural dynamics.

This workplace expectation isn't unique to women who play sports. It's just a bit clearer there. Charlotte Burrows is the chair of the Equal Employment Opportunity Commission, where she frequently sees labor-related issues such as this one in fields that have homogeneous workforces.

"We've had these genderized and racialized norms about caregiving, on the one hand, and housekeeping, and then, on the other hand, things like sports and heavy lifting and construction," Burrows said. "So, when you're talking about a job that's disproportionately been performed by women and women of color, these have been some of the lowest-paid, lowest-status jobs, even though they're hugely important in the economy. And, on the other hand, when women go into some of these other [high-]status jobs, it's almost like they are seen as not really able to fully do it at the at the top level and therefore are not needing or deserving the compensation at the top level based on nothing more than the fact that they are women.

"And so we see those stereotypes persist in sports where women athletes are just perceived to be less skilled or not aggressive enough or not dedicated enough, particularly if they have family obligations, and so aren't given the same compensation or promotions or media opportunities or access to sponsorships."

It's this context that makes what has happened in women's tennis even more of an outlier.

Tennis's Advantages

Tennis had a few things going for it as a sport that helped it overcome the cultural expectations that hold other sports back from progress or even use them to their advantage.

One advantage was the uniform. Women in tennis adopted short skirts quite early to be able to move better on a court. Wimbledon, the British Slam, mandated all-white attire, including underpants, for women, which were often visible during play. The look was feminine and fashionable, which was in keeping with traditional expectations of women.

In addition, there were four Grand Slam tournaments a year that hosted men's and women's tournaments. There were also doubles and mixed-doubles draws at each Grand Slam. These traditions had their origins in genteel club rules, but the evolution into the professional sports meant that having skilled women as partners was valuable to the men in the sport, as well.

Because men played, media outlets would have reporters on-site. King made a point of learning their names and being friendly with them, and Slams became a place where outlets might send women to report. These four built-in media opportunities for women were more regular opportunities for coverage than the Olympics or the World Cup.

Andrew Zimbalist, the Robert A. Woods Professor Emeritus of Economics at Smith College, has long studied the intersection between sports and markets and notes that women's tennis has been an outlier because of a structure that showcases the men's and women's tournaments at the same time. Other sports, such as the NCAA basketball tournaments or soccer World Cups, host their men's and women's tournaments at separate times and venues.

"If you want to watch women's golf, you can't turn on the U.S. Open and see the men and the women on the same golf course, or World Cup," Zimbalist said. "So the cultural prejudice is highlighted for these other sports where the women are not getting promoted and the men are getting promoted. But what's true in tennis—and it's been true for at least, I think, going to the back to the Open Era in the 1960s—is that the men and the women play in the majors at the same time in the same place. It still might be the case that the men get a little bit more news coverage, but instead of the differential being 99 percent for men and 1 percent for women, now it's more, whatever, 52 percent and 48 percent in terms of the resources that are being used to promote the two sports."

So, when the conditions of coverage and the promotion was for one tournament with both draws, rather than a men's or women's event, it completely changed conditions for the health of the women's version of the sport.

"It's because of this historical accident," Zimbalist said, "So I think that that's wonderful evidence [of] . . . the culture holding down, holding back, the progression."

Ultimately, women's tennis grew so popular that ratings for women's tennis can eclipse those for the men's game. For example, the 2023 U.S. Open final with the American Coco Gauff defeating Aryna Sabalenka drew 3.4 million viewers to ESPN on Saturday, while the Sunday men's final between Novak Djokovik and Daniil Medvedev pulled 2.3 million in the United States. The men's final is traditionally programmed against the first week of the NFL season, but Djokovic won his record twenty-fourth Grand Slam title, so it was a compelling final for tennis fans. The audience for Gauff's first U.S. Open win was the largest ever for a women's Grand Slam final, according to ESPN.

As an international sport, if tennis waned in popularity in one place, it could be sustained by growing interest elsewhere. This happened in the mid-2010s when a player named Li Na captivated fans in her native China, which soon began hosting more tournaments and, eventually, the year-end final before COVID. More important, WTA sponsorships can come from major multinational corporations, keeping prize money high. The raw prize money was not as high as it was for the ATP tour, but a woman who was a mid-tier player could make a living professionally as a tennis player, which was not true in other women's sports. Because tennis is an individual sport, players paid their way to tournaments and hired their own coaches and staff, for the most part. Costs that other leagues might have to bear for team travel instead fell on the player, but the amount of prize money and endorsements now keeps tennis lucrative, despite these expenses.

Since players travel around the world, and tennis is seen as an aspirational community, luxury brands such as Rolex sponsor individual players to wear their products and appear in advertisements.

The project begun by the Original 9 has yielded sports stars who have become household names and gotten progressively richer from their efforts. Martina Navratilova, Chris Evert, Steffi Graf, Martina Hingis, and then, in the late 1990s, two young players named Venus and Serena Williams would further question the traditional underpinnings of tennis.

Richard Williams taught his young daughters to play tennis because he saw the kind of money they could make in the professional ranks. Tennis is an individual sport, so, as the apocryphal story goes, he picked up coaching tips from a videocassette and taught his daughters on the courts in Compton, California, where they lived at the time.

Venus Williams won ten Grand Slam singles titles, half of them on grass at Wimbledon, and has earned $42 million on the WTA Tour. Serena Williams played for twenty-seven years, winning twenty-three Grand Slam singles titles and, at the time of her retirement, had earned $94,816,730 on court and many millions more in endorsements. They both competed for titles into their forties. As impressive as those numbers are, their influence on the game was far greater.

A decade into Venus and Serena Williams's careers, American women's tennis was filled with women and girls of color, many of whom went on to success on the tour. Gauff, Taylor Townsend, Madison Keys, and Sloane Stephens have origin stories that include seeing someone playing tennis on television, someone who looked like them. It was a notable impact and one based on their advocacy within the U.S. Tennis Association (USTA) for grassroots tennis programs outside the club systems. Although Tiger Woods was dominating golf at roughly the same time that the Williams sisters started winning tennis tournaments, his career didn't change the face of golf in the same way.

The Williams sisters played during an era when players' careers across sports were extended through advancements in training and medicine. Women began to have children and then continue with their careers. Kim Clijsters, Serena Williams, and Victoria Azarenka have all played Grand Slams with their toddlers in the stands.

Attitudes shifted around sexual orientation such that, unlike during the era in which King and Navratilova played, LGBTQIA players didn't have to hide their identities to have access to endorsement opportunities and wider cultural acceptance.

Both Venus and Serena Williams have also had a lasting impact on the economic success of tennis. After years of advocacy on many fronts for equal pay for men's and women's champions at all four majors, Venus wrote a pivotal op-ed for the *Times of London* that I discuss in a later chapter. Serena Williams has gone on to speak about racial injustice; after the birth of her first daughter, Olympia, and life-threatening complications, she also raised the issue of disparities in maternal health care. Serena Williams and her husband, Reddit's founder, Alexis Ohanian, have invested heavily in the future of women's sports such as the NWSL.

A New Era?

At Seton Hall, we commissioned a You.gov poll, timed for the visit with King and Kloss, to gauge fans' thoughts on women's sports. I'd asked Dan Ladik, professor at the Stillman School of Sports Management, to include a question on men and women playing together and against one another. The results showed 57 percent of avid sports fans wanted to see more competitions with men and women.

The men's and women's events at the Grand Slams make them more lucrative events for organizers, players, and sponsors. The same is true of the Olympics. The NCAA tournament could do something like that with its championships, and the International Federation of Association Football (FIFA) might look at the World Cup competition schedule and have some events coincide. I relayed the poll results and those thoughts to King and Kloss.

"From your lips to God's ears," King said. "This has been my whole life. Nobody'll budge."

"Why do you think that is, then, when it would bring more money?" I asked.

"People get used to whatever *is*," King said. "They just love it; they understand it. They're losing, but they understand it. It feels comfortable."

That inertia means that King has had to work even harder to turn goodwill into action.

King conveyed that there is no rest when you are building something. And she's not done. She and Kloss are finding the "B guys," meeting them, pulling them into the conversation. She'd just spent some time with Mark Davis, the owner of the NFL's Raiders who went on to buy the WNBA's Las Vegas Aces in 2022. He hired Becky Hammon, a former Liberty point guard who was an assistant with the NBA's Spurs and had been up—and passed over—for head coaching jobs in that league. There has never been a woman hired as a head coach of an NBA team, and Hammon was the first candidate with a profile to make the case.

But Davis wanted the best coach for his WNBA team. Rather than continuing to wait it out for a glass-ceiling shot at coaching in the NBA, Hammon returned to the WNBA. Davis made a few headlines when he opted to miss a Raiders game so he could attend an Aces postseason game.

The Aces won the title that year. King and Kloss caught up with him.

"We went there and met him and had a Title IX night there and got to know him," King said. "And he just feels so strongly that the women deserve as much as the guys, but we also have to earn it. If you look at the money, it's been really a rough go.

"Here's what always used to happen: the NCAA would do the basketball contract for the men and just throw the women in for nothing. That's how it started and what happens; that sets a culture of, 'Oh they're free. Let's just worry about the guys,' instead of worrying about everyone."

King's conversation floats back and forth between what happened forty years ago and what happened last week. She's always catching people up, whether it's about the $1 contract or the 99ers and their fight to book the largest stadiums they could in the United States that summer. She is fighting to educate and empower as though she's just been given the microphone when, in reality, she's been holding it for decades. You have to learn about your past, she tells these students.

"The more you know about history, the more you know about yourself, but most importantly, it helps you shape the future," King said.

King's advocacy has helped foster a sisterhood in women's sports, starting with tennis. For years, when men held most of the keys to the purse money and platform access, these informal collaborations helped women's leagues leverage what they could. But now, as women begin to amass real wealth in sports, they are looking to reinvest some of that in the women's game.

Stacey Allaster is the chief executive of professional tennis for the USTA and the U.S. Open's tournament director. In 2023, as the U.S. Open celebrated fifty years of equal pay for the winners of the women's and men's tournaments, Coco Gauff won her first Grand Slam event in New York at nineteen. Women's tennis, and American women's tennis, was in a very good place. Allaster was at Cipriani Wall Street on a crisp October evening to pick up the annual leadership award from the Women's Sports Foundation, an organization King started a year after the U.S. Open awarded equal pay.

"I even feel more optimistic today than I did a couple of years ago," Allaster said. "I just think we have a combination of billionaires and millionaires investing in women's sport because they see the value. In the long-term opportunity, you see brands stepping up to allocate their sponsorship dollars equally, like Ally Financial, Canadian Tire. I do think this Gen Z and Gen X generation put more pressure on brands to invest in women. Let's stop talking about values of inclusiveness and equality and let's see some action. I think . . . [we're] seeing a lot of strength in our female athletes. They're leaning in, just like Billie did, like Serena and Venus. And ultimately, athlete leadership really changes the game."

So, for perspective, let's look at the bottom line.

When Serena Williams retired in 2022 at forty, she had amassed a WTA record $94,606,355 in prize money. To compare, King earned $1,966,487 playing tennis.

A $1 bet pays off, but the real money takes a few generations.

2

PAY EQUITY

Venus Williams picks up a pen for the Times of London, *and fans carry the message to soccer fields in France.*

Few people have better used their platform for change than Venus Williams.

Venus knows how to meet the moment, and her own moment came in 2006 when Wimbledon was still paying the winner of the women's draw less than the winner of the men's. Not much less, just enough to make a point about value.

It's important to understand that Venus was beloved in London. She had won the grass Grand Slam three times at that point. The length of her arms and long legs allowed her an effective reach when the ball would skip along the speedy green surface. Her demeanor and natural grace were in keeping with a particularly British sensibility. As a mature champion, local royalty welcomed her.

Her younger sister, Serena, with her language skills and her French coach, may have charmed the crowds in Paris, but Venus was the toast of London.

And sometimes it is easier to hear criticism delivered from an old friend.

The elder of the two Williams sisters who dominated tennis does not often get the credit she deserves for her advocacy behind the scenes of the

WTA that finally attained equal pay for the winners of the women's Grand Slam events. Venus has known and worked with Billie Jean King since she was a child, and King's influence means understanding the idea of value. In our capitalist society, money is how value is assessed and respect is conferred. In the early 2000s, the WTA Tour was the best avenue in women's sports for a professional athlete to earn good money. As one of the few Black women on that tour, Williams had strong role models in the legendary players Althea Gibson and Arthur Ashe.

Venus was on the player council, and even if she didn't often speak publicly, she was politically savvy. After being booed in Miami in 2001 when she played Serena—detractors said their coach and father, Richard, was deciding who would win their matches—Venus had become a more private adult. While Serena boycotted the Miami tournament for thirteen years as she went on to win twenty-three Grand Slam singles titles, it was Venus who would eventually determine what the number on her sister's checks would be: a denomination equal to that of the men's championship.

While the U.S. Open and the Australian already awarded men and women equal prize money, Wimbledon and the French Open held on to the discrepancy between the prizes.

Venus was the person, and this was the time.

Williams wrote an opinion article in the *Times of London* on June 26, 2006.[1] Here is how it concluded:

> Equality is too important a principle to give up on for the sake of less than 2 percent of the profit that the All England Club will make at this year's tournament. Profit that men and women will contribute to equally through sold-out sessions, TV ratings or attraction to sponsors. Of course, one can never distinguish the exact value brought by each sex in a combined men's and women's championship, so any attempt to place a lesser value on the women's contribution is an exercise in pure subjectivity.
>
> Let's put it another way, the difference between men and women's prize money in 2005 was £456,000—less than was spent on ice cream and strawberries in the first week. So the refusal of the All England Club, which declared a profit of £25 million from last year's tournament, to pay equal prize money wasn't about cash. It could only be trying to make a social and political point, one that was out of step with modern society.

> I intend to keep doing everything I can until Billie Jean's original dream of equality is made real. It's a shame that the name of the greatest tournament in tennis, an event that should be a positive symbol for the sport, is tarnished.

By the following year's Wimbledon, the women had equal pay.

Venus took the women's singles trophy two straight years after that, for a total of five career Wimbledon titles. Even into her forties, Venus was an excellent grass-courter and had always been a threat, no matter her seed or age. At forty-three, she was granted a Wild Card to the tournament, something usually reserved for young British players but in this case, a show of respect.

In her book *All In*, Billie Jean King recalled Venus's pitch to the Grand Slam board for equal pay in 2005: "In one of the most moving parts of her remarks to the board, Venus said, 'When your eyes are closed, you can't really tell who's next to you, who's a man and who's a woman. Think about your daughters, your wives, your sisters. How would you like them to be treated? All our hearts beat the same.'"[2]

King stood in the Royal Box at Wimbledon cheering Venus on as she won that equal champion's check.

Gendered Work, Gendered Pay

Equal pay is a concept that goes well beyond sports. The Equal Pay Act of 1963 was signed into law by President John F. Kennedy and was meant to abolish pay disparity based on sex. The Equal Employment Opportunity Commission (EEOC) celebrated the sixtieth anniversary of the act in 2023.

Charlotte Burrows was named EEOC chair in 2021 after being appointed by President Barack Obama as one of the five permanent commissioners in 2014. Burrows is a Yale University–trained lawyer who has focused on pay equity not just for women but also for demographic groups that traditionally have been paid less in the workforce.

"[The act] was really intended to address this undervaluing of women in the labor force, which had traditionally been paying them less," Burrows said. "Part of it is stereotypes. I think in sports and in other areas where you have also a lot of women of color as part of the labor force, the racial and gender stereotypes come together in terms of what people's work is worth. And so historically, women's work has not been out there on the field. It's been taking care of the home, cooking, cleaning, the family, caregiving, and teaching, which are hugely important but were not paid commensurately and still aren't—those things that were considered soft labor, emotional labor, and not really thought of even as work that should be compensated. And so as it got into the workplace, that was the same thinking that undergirded the lower pay. . . . The idea really is that you've got women suddenly in a place where they were not considered to belong."

It wasn't about measuring the dollars and cents contributed, in other words. It was about who belonged.

In 2023, Claudia Goldin, a professor of economics at Harvard University, became just the third woman to win a Nobel Prize in Economics, and the first to win it outright, for her lifetime of research into pay inequity. The pay gap at the time Goldin received the award was about twenty cents per dollar, with women earning just eighty cents to every dollar earned by men. At the risk of reducing a lifetime of research to a few words, Goldin found that women tended to earn less because they held jobs that allowed them the flexibility of caretaking.

"We see the residue of history all around us," Goldin told the *New York Times* after the announcement came from the Nobel Committee.[3]

Goldin's work on the subject goes back to the 1970s, and she has looked at the impact birth control had on women in the workplace. She was one of the first few economists to examine the wage gap and found that its history is tied not just to the economy, but also to the social expectations of women. The expectation that women would take on child care and elder care made them less able to take the categories of jobs that tend to pay more. The reverse is also true, as other economists have speculated further: some jobs may pay more out of the expectation that the women who take on child care and elder care will not be interested in them.

Anecdotally, Goldin also noted in an IMF Podcast with interviewer Rhoda Metcalfe why there aren't more women in her field: "When we ask women why they don't want to major in economics and why they want to major in psychology, which is the field that they're drawn to more, they will say economics is not about people, and psychology is about people. Well, we have to do better in teaching people that economics is about people."[4]

The EEOC deals with complaints of all kinds, from warehouse applicants who are told the company doesn't hire women, to other kinds of discrimination. It was in that capacity that Charlotte Burrows learned about the plight of the U.S. Women's National Team.

U.S. Soccer and Equal Pay

It was July 10, 2019, and the USWNT had just won its fourth World Cup title. The team was given the full New York City treatment with a parade up Broadway's Canyon of Heroes. It was fitting. Before honoring New York teams such as the Yankees, Giants, and Rangers, the route was used to honor Olympic teams and, after she became the first woman to swim the English Channel, the swimmer Gertrude Ederle in 1926.

But even in that moment of victory, there was real discord. As they had on the playing fields in France, fans had chanted "Equal Pay" on the streets of New York as the confetti flew out of the office windows.

This USWNT had been fighting in court with the U.S. Soccer Federation throughout the tournament, and well before, to raise the compensation the players received so it was equal to what the mediocre, no-gold-medal-having men's team was getting.

U.S. Soccer is the governing body for both the men's and women's national teams and operates as a nonprofit. So the argument that the men were bringing in more money—and that's an argument that could be examined more closely—isn't the same as it would be if one were comparing the pay structure in the same sport but different leagues, such as the PGA and LPGA tours in golf. With U.S. Soccer, the pay was coming from the same body for the same task.

After the march up Broadway, the players gathered at City Hall for a presentation. Then U.S. Soccer President Carlos Cordeiro took to the podium, praised the team, and promised to keep working toward equal pay. He then introduced the star player for her turn to address the crowd,

"And finally but not last, the winner of the golden boot, the tournament's top scorer and the golden ball, the best player, Megan RAP-in-oe," Cordeiro said, mispronouncing the name of the most decorated and famous member of this world-best team. Rapinoe sat there for a moment with a stunned smile on her face. Coach Jill Ellis turned and whispered to the person next to her. Rapinoe then got up and made her famous victory pose to the delight of the crowd, which started a chant that corrected her name: "Ay-ya ya ya Ra-PEA-no."

The gaffe was truly epic. This was a woman whose name was called out six times for scoring in the World Cup. She was besieged with requests to go on talk shows and podcasts, for endorsements and appearances; the most prominent member of the most beloved team in U.S. Soccer, which Cordiero oversaw. And it was a name that was appearing in court filings against U.S. Soccer that, no doubt, were part of Cordeiro's daily conversations as the USWNT sued for what it thought was fair compensation.

There are a lot of reasons why this compensation was low. Each contract in sports is negotiated from the one that came before it. So each union wants to incrementally improve the new contract, but the USWNT was limited by the inherent inequities established in the previous contract. Imagine if "no one cares about women's sports" were the lawyer drafting the first women's soccer contract: that's the foundational premise each women's team had to escape anew with each successive contract building on the prior.

The inaugural men's World Cup was in 1930. The Women's World Cup only began in 1991.

The women could never catch up this way, no matter how many World Cups and gold medals, because the premise underlying their pay structure was one that does not value women in sports. And the value attached to learning how to pronounce your star player's name apparently runs hand in hand with that monetary value. That's why the USWNT was in court; that's why it was asking publicly for equal pay. You know who understood that? Not the lawyers. Not always the judges. And certainly not the executives at U.S. Soccer or FIFA.

The fans got it.

As the U.S. women's team played its brash version of the world's game, those fans would take up chants of "Equal Pay!" on international soil. They were only demanding what sport promises: that on grass or hard court or ice or water, the rules are fair for everyone. And that means men and women.

Not everyone was on board.

President Donald Trump came at Megan Rapinoe in a series of tweets. The other half of the biggest power couple in sports, the WNBA player Sue Bird, took to the *Players' Tribune* in an op-ed titled, "So the President F*cking Hates My Girlfriend."[5]

"If you're not on the right side of this fight," Bird wrote in the piece, "and advocating fiercely for equal pay—whether it's in soccer or basketball or any other industry, and across every intersectional boundary—then I just straight up feel bad for you. Because you're sad, and you're wrong, and going down."

You know the outcome to this story. The USWNT won another World Cup title, paraded down New York City's Canyon of Heroes, and did not get invited to the White House.

But the real win was those chants of "Equal Pay! Equal Pay!" shouted by legions of fans in Lyon, France, as the U.S. team was victorious in yet another title game, and in the streets of New York as the fans, victory on the field in hand, looked to the larger fight.

Olympic Value

If you really want to get into the relationship between equity and value in women's sports, Kathy Carter wants you to think about the Olympic movement.

"It's irrefutable what the impact has been from the Olympic Games onto women's sport," said Carter, then-chief executive of LA28, the organization planning the Olympic and Paralympic events that will take place in Los Angeles in 2028.

"I think that the Olympic movement deserves a whole lot of credit for the evolution of women's sport and participation," Carter said. "And you can look back in 1984, which was the first time that the women's marathon was run, and now I look at 1996, which was the first time women's soccer was in the Olympic Games, and how and what that has meant—certainly from a United States perspective, if not globally—to acceptance and then the ongoing support around women's sport."

Carter, an American born around the same time Title IX came into existence, has a great point. Joan Benoit Samuelson, an American, won that first marathon gold in Los Angeles, but even before that, American women had donned their Team USA gear and won gold. Babe Didrickson won the javelin throw in 1932 and again in Los Angeles. Think of Wilma Rudolph winning the 100-meter race in Rome in 1960 and Florence Griffith-Joyner winning in Seoul in 1988. Peggy Fleming and Dorothy Hamill won gold in figure skating. These are just a few highlights, because the list is so long, and each athlete has a story to tell.

American audiences learned of those stories and shifted their expectations of the value of women's sports because the Olympics were on television. Men's events might have gotten a larger percentage of coverage but, as we learned in Chapter 1 through tennis, combined events such as the Olympics draw more media—media who cover both men's and women's events.

Andrew Billings, a professor and researcher at the University of Alabama, has done long-term studies of the percentage of coverage NBC gives women's and men's events during its primetime coverage every two years. In 2012, Billings's research found that women's events received more airtime than men's.[6]

This means that NBC has learned over years of televising Olympic sports that showing women is a smart business decision. Equal television coverage is not equal pay, but it, too, is a driver of value.

There are a few ways an NBC Olympics broadcast differs from the kind of coverage you might see for an NBA or NFL game. The Olympics broadcast was on network television and in prime time. That's going to be a potential audience that contains more women. Knowing that women were watching, NBC did more storytelling around events. Each Olympic Games brings a new cast of characters, so NBC introduced them in engaging ways. And, given the success American women had in international events, many commentators came from the ranks of those athletes. Donna de Varona swam in Rome in 1960 and was a commentator on ABC's *Wide World of Sports* at seventeen.

Olympic women were visible in ways women hadn't always been in sports. So when the American women won gold in softball, basketball, gymnastics, and soccer during the '96 Atlanta Games, that energy had to go somewhere. For soccer, it was channeled into the World Cup three years later.

Carter said, "I can tell you that as a girl who grows up in the soccer game and, like you, as a pure Title IX baby, 1999 does not happen if not for 1996. No question. It started with the Olympics. It started with the fact that they sold out the Athens stadium at [the] University of Georgia. And I was sitting in the stadium."

Carter paused to imagine how powerful that might have been for the soccer players who would go on to book bigger venues at the World Cup to show off the game. Many of the future 99ers were the driving force in booking football stadiums in major cities for the next North American World Cup.

She continued, '[I wonder whether] the organizers in 1999 thought to themselves, 'We sold out a stadium in the heart of Georgia for the U.S. women to win a gold medal match. I think we should blow the doors off this thing and say, 'Why don't we try to play the final at the Rose Bowl?'"

Your Budget Is Your Values

So many of the arguments that are made against pay parity in women's sports cannot be applied to the U.S. national soccer teams. The women win more than the men. They have larger television audiences. Their players are household names going back two decades—Abby, Megan, Mia, Hope, Brandi, Brianna, Alex, Julie, and more.

How is it that these champion women are consistently lowballed and underestimated by their own governing body?

Bob Ley, an ESPN journalist who anchored the premier reporting outlet *Outside the Lines* during his tenure, saw the promise and enthusiasm for this team firsthand back in 1999. That event was a wakeup call for him.

"I did several matches, including the USA's first match against Denmark at Giant Stadium," Ley said. "And it was the weirdest thing. I mean, I've been in Giant Stadium in the same announcers' booth I used to do play-by-play for the '94 men's World Cup, where I had the same press level where I was doing the [public relations] announcing for the Cosmos in the late '70s. And now we had 78,000 people filling Giant Stadium.

"But the thing was, when the team trotted out, the sound was unlike anything I'd ever heard because of the pitch. It was girls. It was women. A lot of young girls. And suddenly you realize, like, this is a different reality. Women's basketball at UConn [the University of Connecticut] had a lot of middle-aged men following them, believe it or not. But when that moment happens, like, oh my gosh! And then, of course, that spectacle unfolded for the next six weeks and just captured the country."

Was it more difficult to take the phenomenon of women's soccer more seriously because it was attracting new and female fans to the game? Families? A crowd that looked a little different from the crowd at a Giants game on Sunday?

The conversation around the NFL playoffs in 2024 offered a reprise of this reaction to the changing face of fandom. When superstar Taylor Swift's attendance at Kansas City Chiefs games to watch her boyfriend, Travis Kelce, brought more girls to football, some complained every time the camera cut to show her celebrating. The essential argument was that the games are a celebration of masculinity—like Jason Kelce's shirtless cheering in a suite during the playoffs, for instance—not a place to showcase a woman more culturally powerful than her NFL boyfriend. It's worth noting that many of the issues around gender and sports are also reflected in the music industry.

"Illuminating the challenges and paths to achieving equality is important because power and influence are still mostly held by white men," King wrote in *All In*. "I've spent my whole life watching men stick up for each other and help each other out. I've seen men—even men who otherwise have little in common *except* that they're men—actively organize with each other to shut women out. Women don't bond or organize that way."

If the Jack Kramers, Bobby Riggses, and Jock Semples of the world are setting the pay scale, women will never convince them that they are worth more.

"My major bugaboo is 'Women are making progress,'" the women's sports historian Jean Williams told me for an article I wrote for the *New York Daily News* in 2019. "The problem is not women. We've been playing football for 150 years. The fact is we've got a rigidly enforced labor market that women didn't create."

Before the 2019 World Cup, I asked a person connected with U.S. Soccer why they didn't put more effort into the women's team, given its success. The person told me that women's World Cup gold was great, but if the men won it would be "bigger than the Super Bowl."

Whomever the USWNT beat on the field, the team would never be able to top "bigger than the Super Bowl." That measure of success was unlikely to be achieved by the men's team, given that it has finished no higher than eighth since 1934, but given the scale of compensation and coverage for the women's tournament, it was altogether impossible for the women, too. Both teams could argue that what's been keeping them from Super Bowl levels of popularity (and scales of finance) is investment.

One of the legitimate critiques of the women's argument for equal pay is that they signed a contract that accepted less in wages because it risked less. Women also traded wages for investment by U.S. Soccer in the women's game. They saw it as another way of saying, "Even if you don't believe in this game, we do."

"It's been so heavily implicit for so long, the idea that we can give them less because they expect less," Lindsey Darvin, an assistant professor and gender equity researcher at Syracuse University's David B. Falk College of Sport and Human Dynamics, told me. "That's how we've been socialized."

You can't tease apart the women's soccer contract from the way women in sports are viewed by society. Before Title IX, gatekeepers in sports had valued women's sports as all but worthless. The effects of that valuation were still lingering in the USWNT contract, which first saw the women's game as a favor to players.

"It's the view that men's sport is an economic benefit, and women's sport is an economic drain, and whatever you give women is a charitable donation," Williams said. "They can't see where that value is going to come from."

In 2018, FIFA had a $400 million prize pool for the men's World Cup and $30 million for the women's.[7] The winning women made 7.5 percent of what the winning men did.

The fans, whose voices so struck Ley and whose attendance at the 1996 Olympics spurred investment in the Rose Bowl years later, took up the cause—one that was being fought not for the players on the field but for the future.

"We know it's not coming to us," Rapinoe told me during an interview for our podcast in July 2021. "We know that all the work that we're doing now, because it takes so long and it's so arduous— I mean, I'm on the eve of turning thirty-six, and I don't know how many years I have left. . . . I might get one or two years out of this new contract, or three or four years out of this new contract, but this isn't really for me. So I hope to God the next generation doesn't have to do the same stuff that we do and that hopefully they will be in a much better position. If that's the legacy we can have or the gift we can give or the work that we have to do now, I'll be jealous of them and probably bitter, but I'll be happy for them in a small part of my heart, and I'll make them pay for everything every time I see them."

Rapinoe was not being hyperbolic. When she retired in 2023, she'd made little more on the field than the average American salary during that same time. More on that later. But Rapinoe and her teammates did improve the wage and conditions of every player coming behind them.

Just being aware of the difference in pay scale in sports was an advantage women who face wage gaps don't have in other industries.

As Burrows elaborated: "I think what's important here, which is different than in a lot of instances, [is] that there was transparency about what the men were being paid and the women were being paid, to some degree.

They were actually able to find that out and to see that in black and white. Often it's not the case. So I think that there's a real importance for people to do that. And it's important to be able to build those coalitions and find that out. But a lot of times, neither the men nor the women realize that there are these huge gaps. So I think one of the challenges [is that it can be] disconcerting to have to take on your employer about something so fundamental."

Players contended that the U.S. Soccer Federation hadn't done nearly enough to maximize the revenue it derives from the women's game. For example, rather than maximizing the value for the women's games, U.S. Soccer combined the broadcast rights for the USWNT with the lower-rated domestic league, Major League Soccer, and sold them as a package. The federation thus was using the more successful women's property to leverage an investment in growing the platform and audience of the less successful men's product—exactly the sort of thinking sports organizations refuse to apply when the men's sport has the larger audience. There have been concerns about the way U.S. Soccer negotiated sponsorship and jersey deals for the women, as well. FIFA, the international governing body for soccer that hosted the World Cups, did not negotiate separate deals for that event, either.

"Imagine the story is reversed," Economics Professor David Berri of Southern Utah State University said. "The men's team is dominating the international scene, and ask then what kind of deal the men should be able to negotiate. Would you say, 'One that's as good as the women's's'?"

Less than a year after Cordeiro botched Rapinoe's name during the victory celebration, he was forced to step down due to some of the legal arguments the organization made against the USWNT, including that women's soccer was a poorer product because it was played by women.

From the *New York Times* piece by Kevin Draper and Andrew Das on the March 2020 filing: "In those documents, the federation's lawyers had argued that it required more 'skill' and 'responsibility' to play for the men's team than the women's equivalent."[8]

The outcry was swift and wide-ranging. Rapinoe said that lawsuits are contentious, but that crossed a line. Major corporate sponsors condemned the assertions in the lawsuit. But it wasn't just the wording; it was the stance that women's soccer was inherently inferior because women played it. It is impossible, players argued, to negotiate in that environment.

U.S. Soccer promoted Cindy Parlow Cone to replace Cordeiro. She was a member of the 1999 World Cup winning team, and the tone of the negotiations changed. Eventually, U.S. Soccer settled the suit in February 2022 for $24 million.

U.S. Soccer negotiated new collective bargaining agreements with both the men's and women's players' associations with equitable terms in September 2022. This could be done only because the union for the men's team agreed. It was an example of true solidarity.

A PBS story quoted Cone: "I have to give a lot of credit to everyone involved, the women's national team and their PA [players' association], the men's national team and their PA, and everyone at U.S. Soccer. There were so many people that helped, that worked together to make this happen. And it wouldn't get pushed over the line without the men jumping in and being on board with equal pay."[9]

As challenging as suing an employer is, it can be a useful instrument in changing policy and drawing a light to inequity. The players had faced legal setbacks in the case even as they won public support, so the settlement gave players what they sought while keeping U.S. Soccer from further damaging its own brand.

"I think it's enormously important to be able to hold that [leverage]—and, frankly, to create leverage—because in the end, the lawsuit came before the settlement," Burrows said. "So in terms of creating leverage, making sure that all of the right folks have the issue firmly in their sights is important, sometimes that doesn't always happen until there's a lawsuit. And that's unfortunate. But it is true."

In his famous quote, "Upon the fields of friendly strife are sown the seeds that upon other fields on other days will bear the fruits of victory," General Douglas MacArthur was referring to military success, but in this case the idea took root.

The Equal Pay for Team USA Act became law in 2023. It requires that all athletes are compensated fairly for representing the nation. It directly impacts Olympians, Paralympians, and World Cup players.

Senator Maria Cantwell of Washington State introduced the bill. "I . . . want to thank heroes like Megan Rapinoe and Alex Morgan who brought that case against U.S. Soccer," she said when it overwhelmingly passed the House and Senate. "U.S. Women's Soccer led the charge after winning the World Cup and making it clear to everyone that women athletes deserve equal pay."[10]

In April 2023, the European Union passed the Pay Transparency Directive, a measure designed to address gender inequity in compensation.

Under the act, companies must share the compensation for work of equal value, and if there is more than 5 percent difference between what men and women make, they must take action. The act includes a penalty structure.

What Rapinoe and her teammates, and Venus Williams and the women of the WTA Tour, have done is put a face on a problem that affects women around the world. Bus drivers and office managers who bear the same workplace penalties just don't have the same platform.

The USWNT planted ideas of equity on the fields of friendly strife in France, and they are already bearing fruit.

3

THE BODY

How cultural ideas about the female body impact women in sports, or "Foxes not oxes."

The 2023 World Cup final was over, and the Spanish players were celebrating their win over England. If you looked closely, you'd have noticed the schism. Many of Spain's players weren't really celebrating with their coach, Jorge Vilda, or with Royal Spanish Football Federation (RFEF) President Luis Rubiales. There was long history there—a culture of abuse and chauvinistic attitudes such that the professional women on the team were treated like girls instead of the highly skilled players they were. Fifteen Spanish players had already refused to play for these men and their federation this World Cup cycle, so even in the moment of jubilation on the field in Australia, the players had faced challenges well beyond the pitch.

And still Spain had won.

The confetti flew, the crowd cheered, and Rubiales appeared determined to celebrate this moment as though he'd earned it himself. He enthusiastically grabbed his crotch as he stood in front of Queen Letizia of Spain and her daughter Princess Sofia and, with his free hand, raised his index finger signaling victory.

But one moment of hubris stood out. When the players filed through a line on the podium to get their gold medals, Rubiales grabbed Jennifer Hermoso by the back of the head and kissed her on the lips.

The outrage came quickly. Rubiales said Hermoso clearly consented to the treatment, while Hermoso said she'd done no such thing.[1] One wonders, looking at video of the moment, how Hermoso would have had time to signal agreement.

In the week that followed, Hermoso released a statement saying she felt the contact was intrusive and violative. Her teammates backed her. FIFA opened an inquiry into the crotch-grabbing gesture. Rubiales said he would not resign in a speech to the federation, and many cheered him from their seats. But that was not the reaction writ large. Eleven Spanish team coaches resigned. Nearly eighty Spanish players said they would not play with Rubiales at the head of the RFEF. Condemnation for Rubiales's kiss and subsequent aggressive defense of it came from players and federations across women's soccer. The RFEF said it would withdraw from the Union of European Football Associations if it insisted on Rubiales's resignation. FIFA still suspended Rubiales, and in a gesture that was both alarming and operatic, his mother locked herself in a church and went on a hunger strike.

After twenty-one days of undiminished condemnation, Rubiales finally agreed to resign.

"I would be hard pressed to say ten years ago he [would have] resigned," said Professor Cheryl Cooky of Purdue University. "I don't think that's happening. I think the culture has changed in really important ways. This generation of athletes has changed. And [that's] not to suggest that athletes before were tolerant or ignorant. The climate is different now, and athletes—women athletes—are at a different point in their historical development where they can be— They can speak out, and they're speaking out collectively in ways that sort of mitigate the kind of threat they might have experienced in the past."

It is not that players' complaints over Rubiales's behavior would have been any less serious ten years ago; rather, players, fans, and entire leagues have learned to exercise their power to curb such behavior—and sponsors and league officials have learned to respect it. But why did Rubiales double down on his belligerent behavior, and more important, why did the RFEF defend him after the decades of complaints by players about the organization? It was as if the RFEF would rather take down Spanish football than censure its president for his inappropriate actions.

The RFEF's response was almost a parody of institutionalized misogyny in 2023, but nothing happens without context.

Think of how different the reaction was to the iconic photo of the sailor kissing the woman in a nurse's uniform in Times Square at the end of World War II. In *The Kissing Sailor: The Mystery behind the Photo That Ended World War II*, by Lawrence Verria, the dental assistant Greta Zimmer was identified as the woman in the photo.[2] "It wasn't my choice to be kissed," she later told an interviewer for the Library of Congress's Veterans History Project.

The sailor was in the throes of victory and Zimmer—by then, Greta Friedman—excused the tight grip on her neck and body while he celebrated the end of the war. Meanwhile, the world celebrated the *Life Magazine* photo; eventually, there was even a commemorative stamp.

The context, a great celebration, is what connects these two moments: that a celebration gives license for a nonconsensual and nonromantic kiss. The decades that separate these two moments also show how much work has been done around the idea of bodily autonomy in the past seventy years. Rubiales was not the main character in the World Cup celebration. The players were. His role as an official in the organization was to support their celebration, not take it as his own.

Hermoso's response to the moment was anchored in the present, where important work has been done to establish consent around all kinds of intimate physical contact.

Clearly, this is about more than a "kissing controversy," as headlines called it. In the pages that follow, we will learn more about historical expectations for the treatment of athletic bodies and why a playing field was not treated like a workplace in that moment.

"As somebody who studies the media, I just can't help but notice how much coverage the win and the championship garner[ed] in those mainstream spaces versus how much of the story then became in some ways, rightly so, . . . about sexual harassment and sexual assault and the kiss and so on," Cooky said. "It's like, not only did he steal this moment away from Hermosa and the team, but he stole the moment away from . . . sports fans to have an opportunity to learn about the game, to learn more about the Spanish team."

Sports Is Bodily Autonomy

You cannot understand the opposition women have faced as athletes until you look at the way women's bodies have been treated and why choosing to play professional sports has been a radical act. Even looking back over

Ancient Roman statuary of chiseled male athletes, while women were sculpted in softer and more modest poses, shows how long these expectations have been in place in the Western imagination.

Billie Jean King points out that one of the most revolutionary benefits of sports is very simple: "Girls learn to trust their bodies."

The Women's Sports Foundation tracks the good that comes from girls' playing sports, including academic success and lower rates of unwanted pregnancy in high school. The good news continues after their sports careers, as well: the consulting firm Ernst and Young collaborated with espnW in 2015 to find that 94 percent of women in C-suite-level jobs have an athletic background, and 52 percent of those women played in college.[3]

The practice, the discipline required to compete is a skill that translates into workplace success. However, playing sports is, at its very heart, fun. And fun can be revolutionary for women, too. It's sometimes infuriating, frustrating, disappointing, and all sorts of other things, but it's hard to match the feeling of training your body to do something and being able to connect it in kinetic sequence toward a desired end.

The financial success of the sports media is a testament to our ability to transmit the joy of physical victory: the smiles; the tears; the close-up shots of parents' faces; eighty thousand bouncing, jubilant fans and one athlete in the midst of the ultimate catharsis.

But there is a difference how male and female athletes have been perceived in these moments of victory.

"I often talk in class about, like, historically how a woman using her body for herself, for her own power and pleasure, is in any context transgressive, radical, challenging of authority," Professor Victoria Jackson of Arizona State University said. "Therefore, depending on that context, it might provoke varying levels of resistance."

The challenge that women's athletic achievement represents to the expectation that women must depend on men for their power, pleasure, and prosperity can affect pay and the treatment of women in sports, including incidents of sexual harassment. The resistance that some men might demonstrate to the independence of working female athletes often forgets that pro sports is a workplace, with workplace protections.

Equal Employment Opportunity Commission (EEOC) Chair Charlotte Burrows noticed that, anecdotally, sexual harassment may be associated with work spaces where the body is the focus. She also noted the prevalence of harassment toward women who model as avatars for video games.

"It is interesting to me that a lot of this, the sexual harassment in particular, is when the female body is actually the focus of the work," she said.

If you think back to the doctors we met in the Introduction—the ones who cautioned women that they would jostle themselves into sterility with activity—we have our clues to the dominant social script: what a woman's body is for, who it is destined to serve, has been a matter of infuriating debate.

Women's professional sports on such a large scale are possible only because women have a degree of reproductive autonomy in today's culture. Women can decide to postpone childbearing or return to play sports between children. They can hire a person to help with childcare or have a spouse assume responsibilities that differ from traditional gendered expectations.

The birth control pill was introduced in the United States in the 1950s but became legal everywhere in 1972, and the Supreme Court's decision in *Roe v. Wade* made it legal for women to have an abortion in 1973. It was only after women had the ability to be sexually active without an unplanned pregnancy that large-scale professional women's sports were even possible.

Harnessing the Male Gaze

Even with the greater autonomy, there are lingering expectations of women culturally that can make their way into the sports economy. Think of the backlash to NCAA athletes who are excelling in winning sponsorships now allowed through the ability to capitalize on their name, image, and likeness.

For some background, NCAA athletes have been constrained economically in ways other revenue-generating athletes haven't been due to an antiquated idea called "amateurism." Amateurism itself has roots in the exclusion of the British working class from games the nobility played on private school fields in the 1800s. When American universities fielded teams for friendly play, these exclusionary ideas of who is welcome to play came along long before anyone considered including women.[4]

We have clung to these strict ideas about who is allowed to play and how despite the century that has passed. Amateurism may exist in name only, but it's not the athletes who have changed. The institutions did.

Broadcast deals have paid the NCAA billions to beam college sports into American living rooms starting in the 1980s. Even as this money enriched colleges and sports organizers, athletes had strict rules against earning money or taking benefits. In the early 2000s, a school could be penalized if an athlete had, in addition to the sustenance of a bagel, the option of a luxurious dollop of cream cheese.

Unlike a science major, a college player didn't have the ability to take a part time job in sports or make money endorsing a product. This changed when a former NCAA basketball player named Ed O'Bannon noticed he had been written into a video game—his number, his playing style, even his face. The NCAA was making money from the rights to this video game, and he didn't benefit.

O'Bannon sued. The result was that, in 2019, California passed a law allowing college athletes to profit from their names, images, and likenesses (NIL). Other states followed suit, and the NCAA, as an organization in decline, capitulated.

The structure we have now isn't the result of careful planning. It came about because the NCAA couldn't refuse a firehose of revenue aimed at men's basketball and football or resist evolving interpretations of what athletes contribute relative to legal definitions of labor.

As a result, a chaotic new market has emerged. Since the deals athletes are allowed to take are essentially endorsement- and marketing-related, that market comes with many of the same gender biases that exist elsewhere.

And just as Maria Sharapova's endorsement income often topped Serena Williams's when they were among the best in tennis, the college women who are the best at their sport aren't always the ones making bank.

"So first of all, it's pretty clear that men's football and basketball players are getting somewhere between 80 and 90 percent of the NIL money that's out there," Smith College's Andrew Zimbalist said. "There are a small number of excellent female athletes—and maybe, in some cases, not so excellent, but they're very attractive and aggressive with their social media posts—who get some money."

On the women's side, Olivia Dunn, a Louisiana State University gymnast, has outearned her peers. She is an excellent collegiate athlete, an All-American in the uneven bars; she is also attractive in a way advertisers have used to sell products for the past seventy-five years. She is estimated to be worth $3.5 million and leading all other women in the category, according to ON3 NIL, a multifaceted college sports and recruiting company that also covers the industry.

Dunn appeared in the 2023 *Sports Illustrated* swimsuit issue. The swimsuit issue represents a formula that worked well for a long time: a gorgeous female athlete; a conventional medium for the consumption of the female form; and a few triangles of spandex. Now, with the advent of Instagram and other forms of social media, athletes can curate their own image just in the moment that magazines are struggling to fit the new media landscape. Women in sports are creating their own ways to connect to fans and capitalize. In the traditional sense, Dunn has an advantage.

"I think what it is, the controversy with Olivia Dunn and her NIL agreement and how she's sort of presenting herself on social media," Cooky said, "that's a choice, but that's a choice that's made within a larger social and cultural and economic context. Then we have to look at: Why is she making that choice, and who does it benefit, and what are the implications of that choice beyond just her? Because it's not just her as an individual that's impacted by that, but it's sort of the larger context and what that might say."

Young women in this position, such as Dunn, have as little control in their inclusion in this privileged group as those who are excluded. Capitalizing on men's desire has been one of the few means women have had to briefly exercise power in patriarchal societies. Why should they be required to forgo it?

But many are excluded from the beauty economy, and historically that's included many women of color.

"But, then, I also like to ask the question of 'Who?' when we're looking at representation and imagery like that. Who has been marginalized, and who is erased in those spaces?" Cooky said. "Certain women athletes are able to make that choice. And certain women athletes, even if they wanted to, don't or can't."

So the women who play college sports are, in the course of their sports and their conferences, getting a crash course in how they personally may be affected by these market forces. It must be jarring, at eighteen, to realize that your ability to play is only part of the equation that drives your worth to your audience; that men don't deal with the same expectations; and that the imperfect NIL is still the best way for athletes to raise financial benefit from sports in the current system.

"Athletes should be able to [take NIL deals] without polluting or changing the relationship to the university, which should be primarily an educationally based relationship," Zimbalist said. "But in terms of gender equity, more of the money is going to men. And I don't think there's anything you can do about that, except over time as the mistreatment and lesser treatment of women is attenuated and there's more equality in the promotion and the treatment of women's sports. Then women athletes will have more prominence and they'll be able to get better NIL deals. But for the time being, I think it's going to be a source of greater inequality."

Whose Bodies?

Although this attention to conventional beauty standards is not a novel understanding of the dynamics of human interest, it has implications for who is able to make money as an athlete and who is not. When 82 percent of annual earnings for female athletes comes through endorsements rather than salary, according to research by Wasserman's The Collective, an individual's appeal to sponsors can be the difference between making a living playing sports or retirement. So female athletes face a choice about how to present themselves to maximize their ability to make a living.

"If you're white and heterosexual, you can present in damn near any way and get marketing campaigns," said Amira Rose Davis, an assistant professor in the Department of African and African Diaspora Studies at the University of Texas, Austin, who specializes in American history, with emphasis on race, gender, sports, and politics. "If you're white and gay, you can present in nearly any way and get marketing campaigns. If you're a Black woman and femme-presenting, you're marketable. But if you're a Black woman and you are anything to this side of the spectrum of femme, then there's no kind of pathway for these same marketing opportunities that are coming with being the face of a league or with brand partnerships."

The only counter to that, Davis explains, is to be so great at your sport that you are *undeniable*.

"That's, like, really instructive, because it's very revealing that here's this box that you have to be in. And what can push on the sides of the boxes [is] undeniability. If you're undeniable—like Serena [Williams], like Simone [Biles]. But it doesn't leave a lot of space for people who are not undeniable but are damn good athletes to find space for themselves within the ecosystem of sports marketing and women's sports."

So what bodies aren't welcome? Often, they were more masculine-presenting bodies and nonwhite bodies. There were class signifiers, Davis said. The visibility of the bodies that play women's sports, and the lens through which we judge these bodies, has an effect on their compensation.

"Leagues are asking for continued investment and have been very good at trying to say this is not a charity," said Davis. "This is always working in tandem with this very historically based, lingering perception of what bodies should be playing, what bodies are worthy, what bodies are marketable, what bodies are consumable, and what bodies are disposable. And I think that that's what is still belaboring women's sports when it comes to marketing, investment, selling the games."

So think of this, as Davis does, through a historical lens. The sports that could be played in dresses, flashing a little ankle in the process, were allowed and then thrived. Had Billie Jean King been a race car driver or a boxer, her advocacy might have been received very differently. At that time, King was a femininely presenting woman in an individual sport filled with them.

"When we look at the evolution of this, to bring it back to, like, sports media and marketing, the money that we see going into sports now absolutely tracks along the lines of the sports that were more open and permissible to women because they emphasize femininity and didn't really disrupt it," Davis said. "Those are the clubhouse sports, golf and tennis—those individual sports where you're not in an entire team. You're an individual; you're marketable like that. You're wearing dress whites, etc. [That] is why we see those big paychecks in the tennis and golf realm."

The idea that women who played sports were tolerated as long as they weren't a threat to the larger ideals of femininity had other consequences. Women often quit playing sports if they married or, certainly, when they had children. There was no consideration of women's particular physicality when it came to sports—for example, the effect monthly hormonal changes might have on peak performance.

"[There were] a lot of those fears around the masculinizing effects of sport participation on women," Cooky said. "That's happening in the late 1800s, early 1900s in women's colleges, and women's physical educators actually were at the forefront of policing women's athleticism because they were worried that [women] were going to become too manly. That's loaded with all kinds of middle-class or Victorian values around femininity."

I certainly remember the "concern" I heard as a young reporter about teams that welcomed gay players or when a coach was rumored to be gay. Any threat to the feminine ideal could be used as a reason to keep girls out of sports. So this dance between being desired and being desirable, while also being strong enough to win, is real.

When Sheryl Swoopes became pregnant the first year of the WNBA, she may have worried that she was betraying her teammates and the young league. I discuss in a later chapter how the WNBA players' union took that issue head-on and brought change. Davis has another viewpoint. In her view, the pregnancy was important to the WNBA in another way: the league wanted to attract young families to the games, wanted those parents to see opportunities for their daughters, and did not want to challenge those families with the idea that athletic excellence requires different expressions of identity or new models of womanhood. So the silver lining of the pregnancy for how the league wanted to market itself was that it reinforced traditional expectations of gender and sexuality. While Swoopes may have felt self-conscious underlining a difference between the WNBA and men's sports as the new league established its appeal, the league may well have welcomed the chance to show that it would not be challenging a long-held social expectation about the role of women.

"The league actually loved being able to market [Swoopes's pregnancy], because it reinscribed femininity," Davis said. "And one of the things that you see in my work in the mid-century is when you have these moments where Black women are able to emerge in sports in a very visible way—whether it's the baseball women who I talked about who play in the Negro Leagues—they always have to do that image work simultaneously to assure people of their femininity and their heterosexuality."

Davis tells the story of the Tennessee State University Tigerbelles and their coach, Ed Temple. The team won thirty-four national titles while he was the track coach there, and forty of the women who played went on to compete in the Olympics.

"After a game, the Tennessee State Tigerbelles, who are producing so many of the Olympians of note in the '50s and '60s, their coach famously was like, 'I want foxes, not oxes,'" Davis said. "They weren't allowed to speak to media until they powdered their face and brushed and had their hair done after a race. And there was always this dance between wanting to show that they were desirable and dating and stuff like that and not wanting to play into any stereotypes about the sexual nature of Black womanhood."

Lest you think this was all a function of a bygone era, today's Black athletes routinely face similar scrutiny.

"Serena [Williams] as a mom had a cultural currency that she didn't have during the years of people calling her a man," Davis said. "All of a sudden, her pregnancy affords her this access to femininity in a different way."

Reclaiming the Body

When King said that sports teach girls to trust their bodies, it might not initially be clear how broad the implications of that are. Finding your physical strength is important, but for Paralympic athletes, it means something more in a world that isn't always built to fit them.

One of the roles of the Women's Sports Foundation is to make sure that athletes get the funding they need to train. As the five-time Paralympic medalist Mallory Weggemann brushed the tires of her wheelchair up the red carpet at the foundation's annual gala, her six-month-old daughter, Charlotte, smiled in the arms of her father just beyond the ropes.

Weggemann was paralyzed at eighteen, about a decade after she had taken to competitive swimming. As she learned the new parameters of her changed abilities, her athletic training and the ability to know and get to know her body helped her adjust.

"Despite all the changes, the pool was my constant," Weggemann said.

She told me that sports were part of her emotional, physical, and spiritual recovery from injury, and has never let antiquated ideas of what her body is capable of dissuade her. She went through two rounds of in vitro fertilization to conceive Charlotte with her husband, Jay Snyder, and hopes her experience as an athlete and a mother with a disability will be part of the story of women's sports writ large.

"I'm so excited to see what can happen for my daughter in the next fifty years," Weggemann said.

Barriers to participation are falling, and some subjects that were off-limits are now out in the open. Rather than apologizing for not fitting into the traditional athletic image, these athletes are reclaiming their bodies through their play.

Michelle Betos, goalkeeper for the New Jersey-New York Gotham soccer team, was standing in front of reporters having a very normal postgame press conference in June 2023. The quality of the National Women's Soccer League was so high, and Betos elaborated.

"That's where this league is at," she said. "You have players coming off the bench that a few years ago were easily starters. The talent pool is incredible. . . . This league is really something special."

Then came the kind of question you wouldn't have heard a few years ago, or from a male sports corps, about players' periods.

Some teams, and event tournaments, had begun a conversation about uniforms and dress codes—specifically, whites. As anyone who menstruates knows, you may feel more confident on those days if you wear dark or baggy clothing, particularly if you are doing something that doesn't allow you unfettered access to a restroom.

Imagine being halfway through a tennis match at whites-mandatory Wimbledon and the issue becomes apparent. If this seems like a problem that players should have been louder about a long time ago, remember that just two generations earlier it was considered shameful to discuss a breast cancer diagnosis because of the word "breast." Approaching a tournament director about anything that spotlighted a challenge of putting women in a space once reserved for men might ricochet. It is easy to think they'd have been told not to play during their periods rather than to have made accommodations.

Back at Gotham, Betos addressed the change to dark shorts for travel uniforms, then added that the team's trainers were experimenting with different combinations of vitamin supplements, depending on where individual players were in their menstrual cycles.

"We're at the beginning stages of it," Betos said. "You've seen a lot of women having injuries, and our medical staff doesn't take anything for granted with us. We have a certain supplement protocol that comes around our periods. I think, honestly, there's not been enough research. They're doing the work with every tool they have they're providing for us, but there's just so much more to be known."

Just four months earlier, the *International Journal of Environmental Research and Public Health* had published a paper titled "Menstrual Cycle and Sport Injuries: A Systematic Review," by a group of Spanish researchers led by Núria Martínez Fortuny.[5] It sought a connection between injuries and hormone levels in female athletes.

"They're going to start figuring it out during this generation and again, hopefully, the next generation, everything solved and you're not seeing the injury rates," Betos said. "It is something we're aware of and working on, but we just need to know more."

The paper found that the ovulatory phase of the cycle is associated with more injury, although no causal relationship was established. Medicine, like society at large, has a lot of catching up to do in reckoning with the capabilities of bodies that weren't traditionally part of the sports landscape.

"I think one of the girls said [that] if this was a men's problem, this would have been solved already," Betos said. "So unfortunately, we're probably going to be the guinea pigs."

Interrogating the Binary

As I was reporting this book, I was often asked about transgender women competing in the women's category of different sporting events. This was always asked in the context of women, not men, even though there are instances of transgender men playing and competing against men. For example, Chris Mosier made the Team USA Sprint duathlon team to compete in the 2016 World Championships after transitioning.

Politically, this has been a potent issue. Republican lawmakers have proposed and passed laws to inhibit the ability of people to both present in the way they feel matches their identity and live in concert with that identity, whether it is in choosing a restroom or competing in sports.

This has often been framed as "protecting women" or "protecting women's sports." As of April 2023, according to the ESPN report "Transgender Athlete Laws by State: Legislation, Science, More," by Katie Barnes, twenty-three states had proposed or enacted legislation to inhibit transgender women's ability to compete in school sports in the category that matched their gender identity. Barnes gives more expansive treatment to many of these issues in the acclaimed book *Fair Play: How Sports Shape the Gender Debates*.[6]

"There's so many of these politicians who say, 'We've got to protect women's sports,'" Cooky said. "Where were you when we were talking about lack of funding in terms of college sports or high school sports? Where are you when we're talking about lack of media coverage? Where are you when we're talking about sexual harassment and sexual assault?"

Is it women's sports they want to protect or the model of femininity that women's sports has struggled to overcome? There are strong opinions on both sides of the issue, including among women such as the tennis icon Martina Navratilova and the three-time Olympian Nancy Hogshead-Makar, who are concerned that the spaces to compete remain open for traditional athletes in women's sports. For these women, the gains of Title IX are not theoretical, and changing categories to be more inclusive means girls might lose out in the medal count.

"Once you go through puberty, you have an advantage that's inherent, that you cannot do away with, so it's not fair," Navratilova said in an interview for my podcast. "Those high school boys that now compete as girls, they've already gone through puberty. . . . I'm all for inclusion, but I'm also for protection of women and girls, and most of all, I'm for fairness."

Lia Thomas swam for the University of Pennsylvania and won the NCAA title in the 500 freestyle in 2022. The NCAA has had an inclusive transgender athlete policy since 2010, but Thomas's inclusion was controversial. She became a talking point on Fox News shows as different people within the sport and beyond protested and defended Thomas's right to compete.

Navratilova was coached for a time by Renee Richards, a transgender player who played in the 1970s on the WTA Tour.

"It's a tricky situation," Navratilova said. "We want to include everybody, but at what cost?"

Billie Jean King tells the story of including Richards over initial opposition. "We'll let her play for two weeks," King said, "and if other players still object, she goes." But by the end of the period, King said, she heard that Richards was a welcome addition. Richards stayed.

"The reason that we love sports so much is because of the community, because of the relationship we get to have with our bodies and our minds, because we play sports, because of our teammates, because of our coaches," said E. R. Fightmaster as they hosted a panel at the 2023 espnW Women + Sports Summit in Ojai, California. "So excluding people from that feels like a kind of particular act of cruelty. And I don't know that we think about it in those terms."

The WNBA's Layshia Clarendon, who identifies as nonbinary, was on the panel and discussed the way sports was a neutral space for them as a kid. The sweats, the jerseys, the designation "athlete" were more primary than a pronoun.

"I think sports become such a safe haven," Clarendon said, "especially for queer kids that can't see themselves yet. Because you are wearing this clothing that you don't have to assign gender to."

Clarendon's idol in sports was Seimone Augustus, an eight-time WNBA All-Star.

"Think of her career," Clarendon said. "She retired in 2020, but before that, when she won four championships with the Minnesota Lynx, like, she should have been heralded. She should have been marketed in a way that we still owe her because she's a Black woman, because she is masculine. She was not given those same opportunities and deemed beautiful and sexy and gorgeous because we still, I think, don't quite market those Black women in the correct way and give them as much space."

And the WNBA has been more inclusive than most leagues, certainly in the past decade.

The size of the controversy dwarfs the actual number of transgender athletes competing in the United States. Some anti-inclusion laws have been passed in states where just one or two athletes would be prevented from playing.

"I do feel so much safer in woman-designated spaces because those spaces are deeply rooted in inclusion," said the transgender mid-distance runner and six-time NCAA Division I All-American Nikki Hiltz during the summit panel.

This is meant not to be an exhaustive look at the issue but to examine one aspect: how our ideas about who can be called women and what assumptions are made about their bodies intersect with sports and athleticism. Right now, there is increased scrutiny of womanhood from a standpoint of genetics and identity.

"Sports are really becoming a safe place for queer people to celebrate themselves and each other, which is always why, I think, . . . people come out of the woodwork to try to take that away," Fightmaster said from the sunny stage at the summit.

"I think that sports is as much a reflection of society as a driving force," Davis said. "I think using bodies as highly visible sites of soft politics is big. And I think that trans athletes have become that in and of itself. I think the discourse around protecting women's sports is absolutely hollow because it's never from the same people who have given any hoots or hollers about investment or actual protection in terms of abuse, harm in a number of ways, whatever.

"I think that the scrutiny on the body is harmful for everybody. But the thing about the way oppression works—it drafts other people into upholding it; it invites other women to buy into the idea that their spots are being taken or their games are under threat. But I think you can only glance at some of these viral campaigns that have gone on against athletes who are perceived to be trans [but] are not, . . . who people have decided lay outside the bounds of womanhood [because] their shoulders are too broad or they're too tall or, like, 'Oh, we can totally tell.' And I think that that just continues to underscore that box and how relevant it remains, because if . . . everybody is open for scrutiny and policing in that way, you see how many people are in the crosshairs."

When the categories are rigidly policed, then accusations are made against competitors regardless of identity.

The tennis player Martina Hingis, who is five foot seven, once slighted her muscular opponent Amelie Mauresmo by calling her "half a man"; that was in the early 2000s, when being gay was still somewhat taboo. In 2023, after winning a bronze in the women's heptathlon at the Asian Games, Nandini Agasara was accused by a competitor of being transgender in a quickly deleted social media post.

The conversation around these issues can get very harmful. The proposed remedies, such as invasive physical examinations of girls or tracking teen periods, are humiliating and Orwellian. And there are likely more ways, at the youth and recreational levels, where inclusive play should be welcome, but these policies filter from the top level of competition to the feeder systems. A determination of what is fair at an Olympic level could be inappropriate if applied to a youth league.

"I can't help but wonder how much of the conversations around trans inclusion in sport—and, specifically, the powerful anti-trans movements in and the concerns about fairness in women's sports and protecting women's sports—[are] in response to the growing popularity of women's sports," Cooky said. "The explicit recognition of the value of women's sports; the kind of potential business opportunities, growth opportunities in women's sports; the growing fan base; or, at least, the growing recognition of the fan base for women's sports. Like, how much of that is perceived to be a threat in some ways? Is this anti-trans 'protect women's sports' movement a response to that? These two things are happening at roughly the same historical moment. I don't think that's by accident."

A lot of energy is being directed at what the limits of the category "women's sports" are at the moment—so much that I hear the echoes of what Davis said earlier: "What bodies should be playing, what bodies are worthy, what bodies are marketable, what bodies are consumable, and what bodies are disposable."

In short, issues that affect the politics of women's bodies, whether around reproduction, consent, identity, value, or desire, affect women's sports. The rigidity of categorization reinforces the gender binary and, for athletes who choose to play in the women's category, competing is a historically rebellious act.

Looking Forward

A few months after winning the 2023 Women's World Cup, Spain's Jenni Hermoso spoke at the International Football Hall of Fame ceremony. She spoke up for herself and her team and for a cause, as the 2019 U.S. team had done on the subject of pay equity. The center of this story wasn't just the reform of an abusive system or administrative misogyny. It was what sports always is: to allow the players to have power over their own bodies—both current players and the generations to come.

"We became world champions because it was the only way we had left to be heard, respected, and valued," Hermoso said, as reported by ESPN. "My national team changed the way many people see women's soccer. I am sure that millions of girls around the world have felt identified and protected by a group of brave, committed, and honest players, who in every step they have taken have always thought about their future."

4

KNOW YOUR AUDIENCE

Like it or not, people like it!

It's a cool early summer afternoon in Brooklyn, and the New York Liberty are warming up before hosting the Chicago Sky. The Barclays Center hasn't opened to fans yet, but Michael Giammanco, in a white oxford shirt with a sparkling gold collar, sunglasses, high-cuff jeans, and heavy patent leather boots walks in and spots Liberty's center, Brianna Stewart.

"Brianna!" Giammanco yells over the noise of the pregame shootaround. The league's most valuable player (MVP), new to the Liberty this 2023 season, sees him, smiles, and moves her six-foot-four-inch frame over to say hello and catch up.

Every team needs the fixture fans. The celebrities. The locals in the community. The retired players. The face painters. The Spike Lees. They need the retirees who go to every local college lacrosse game because their thing is college lacrosse. The band. The fans who become part of the institutional legacy, who can recite rosters and histories by heart.

Giammanco is one of those fans. He's a decade-long Sky courtside season ticket holder who, when the point guard Courtney Vandersloot moved from the Sky to the Liberty for the 2023 season, bought courtside season tickets for the Liberty, as well.

He has a presence—one that makes the game feel like an *event*. He's loved the league as it struggled and as it soared and is on a first-name basis with players, coaches, and the front office.

"It's a real honor and a privilege to see these women play and grow," he said.

In the mid-2000s, Giammanco was freshly sober after a career in the music industry as a creative consultant to Elton John. His story is definitely worth an entire book, but for our purposes, money that used to go to substances found an outlet in a different form of entertainment.

"I wasn't spending money on alcohol and drugs, and I started watching college women's NCAA games and that translated into the WNBA," Giammanco said. "I just started loving it."

And now he's seeing the league take off. Between Commissioner Cathy Englebert and new ownership and leadership at the Sky—the Chicago native and former NBA player Dwyane Wade just announced he was investing, and the technology executive Nadia Rawlinson came on as operating chairman the winter of '23—the competition for those prime season tickets was increasing.

"There were some super fans at the game on Friday," Rawlinson said. "There's three guys. They were college guys—like, total, like, bro guys—and they're screaming harder than anyone else in the arena."

From conventional to nontraditional sports fans, the Sky welcomes them. The 2023 season brought the team the highest ratings and highest league attendance in a decade, and Giammanco could feel the momentum in both New York and Chicago.

"The activity is tenfold, and I just see it getting better," Giammanco said from the vantage of his literal front-row seats.

Advantages of a New Market

As female athletes work and advocate to be paid more and given the same respect as male athletes, they make the case that, if leagues, sponsors, and media invested more in them, they would be able to grow their audience of fans and reward that investment, as female athletes have in tennis, Olympic sports, and the U.S. Women's National Soccer Team.

So who are the fans of women's sports? Are they fans of men's sports who view women's sports in much the same way? Or is the fact that it's women playing—the "femininity" of women's sports and the social meaning of that work—an important part of the appeal? And if so, in what version of femininity are potential fans most interested? That's actually a trickier question to answer than you might think. For a long time, the data just weren't compiled or readily available.

That is changing, and one of the groups at the forefront is Sports Innovation Lab, started by the ice hockey player, four-time Olympian, and former president of the Women's Sports Foundation Angela Ruggiero. She is quickly becoming a legend in marketing women's sports. Ruggiero is sought after for panels and comments on the emerging opportunities in sports. And Sports Innovation Lab is creating opportunities of its own. One of the data analysts there is Molly Tissenbaum, a researcher who played ice hockey for Harvard and graduated in 2017.

Tissenbaum noted a lack of prior data in the women's sports space.

"The fact that there's such a lack of data is a data point in and of itself," Tissenbaum said.

Research is now being done to identify those fan constituencies, meet their interests, and home in on how they want to be connected to their favorite teams and players. In an era of big data, there has been a revolution in the way teams, and sponsors, are thinking about the fan.

It used to be that what mattered was attendance and ratings. They still matter but are no longer the only factor determining potential market.

The rating measures how many people are tuning in to watch games on television. As we've seen in the case of tennis and Olympic coverage, the platform women's sports is given in its broadcasts to viewers matters for viewer interest. But beyond the issue of the importance media outlets grant to women's sports, is the raw rating of the number of people who tune in to a given event the only, and best, way to think about the audience for women's sports?

That's not the only way advertisers think about audience. Composition and the potential for growth matter, too. The pure number of viewers is not the only way to compare the overall value of women's sports with men's. That's because viewers of women's sports are not simply a subset of viewers of men's sports. For many years, as I discuss in a later chapter, league strategies were to try to convert men's sports fans by playing up personal attractiveness and not speaking up about obvious inequities. As the decades have gone on, research shows, people who watch women's sports don't need a sanitized version of who these athletes are and what they care about.

Sports Innovation Lab, which came out with a revolutionary look at how fans of women's sports behaved, spent, and cheered in its 2020 report "The Fluid Fan Is Here," has followed up with other ways to measure the fans of women's sports.[1] It's a crucial moment for this research. Both the NWSL and WNBA are looking to expand the number of teams in their leagues, and they need data not just to convince future ownership to take the plunge, but also to assess and assign interest levels to potential WNBA and NWSL cities. A new team has to be supported by the local community. With television deals and sponsorships on the horizon, information is power.

"The fact that you've got a young, engaged, digitally savvy, heavily loyal group, if that's not your message when you're pitching media and sponsors and partners, we're all missing the mark," Tissenbaum said. "Again, [it's] the numbers, the straight-up numbers from a fan count and attendance perspective. Yes, we still have a long way to go to be Super Bowl Sunday. Nobody's going to lie and say that we're there. But when you look at the growth and the number of new fans coming into what we call the fans of women sports community, the growth trajectory over the last five years, the shape of the lines just looks different."

Has this always been there, and it just took something like the democratizing force of social media to make it obvious? There is no denying the soccer player Megan Rapinoe's influence when she has two million Instagram followers.

The key asset for women's sports, say the people who measure, is the potential for growth.[2] That's how you can have Nebraska's Volleyball Day sell 92,003 seats. The growth in appetite for Nebraska volleyball meant an interest that once had been met by the eight thousand-seat Bob Devaney Sports Center ballooned to fuel a record-breaking event. Leagues and conferences respond to demand to search for right-size stadiums and schedules in men's sports. Women's sports need the opportunity to do the same.

Emma Schilling is a consultant with the Sportsology Group, where she advises and helps sports industry clients recruit and build teams. A lot of her work now happens around women's sports, leagues, teams, and investors—where everyone is looking for numbers.

"We've never gotten a true number of the actual TAM, the total addressable market," Schilling said.

The TAM tells you where the market has been met, and where it hasn't. So let's take the 92,003 fans for Nebraska volleyball. That team might not be able to fill Memorial Stadium for a full season, as it managed to do on that record-setting day, but there is a much larger possible market for the team than attendees in Devaney. How about for jerseys? The broadcast rights? What's happening to the 84,003 fans who went to Memorial Stadium but won't be able to get tickets this season? What about Nebraskans who never watched volleyball but now want to support this team?

You aren't just converting Nebraska football fans; you're creating new volleyball fans with an event like that. How are you making space for them in the current infrastructure? Or do you need to, as Haley Rosen says, build a new house?

"I think about the way conversations are now being had around women's sports, and I think what is really, really, really recent is that people are focused more so on who is our customer, not who is a sports fan," Schilling said. "Who is a women's basketball fan, who is a women's soccer fan. And what do they want to see? What do they care about?

"That's why you're seeing way more inclusion nights," Schilling said. "At [NWSL] Gotham games, they don't just have Pride. They have multiple inclusion nights coming up. They know they're looking at their market and they're saying, 'How do we address it?' That is going to be key to unlock because you're not going to convert an NFL fan to become a WNBA fan overnight. What you can convert is the person who's not watching sports because there was never somebody who looked like them playing to get them to turn on their TV and watch it."

According to polling data by Marist College, more people who watch women's sports are female, of color, and young compared with those who watch men's sports.[3] The people who watch women's sports are a growing demographic. A Marist poll in October 2021, timed to coincide with the fiftieth anniversary of Title IX (full disclosure: I helped formulate the questions and analyze the data with the incredible group who works there, led by Lee Miringoff and Barbara Carvalho), found that 66 percent of sports fans are watching women's sports. Keep in mind that no sport, not even football, captures more than, say, 70 percent of self-described sports fans. About the same percentage of respondents said they were watching the WNBA as said they watch National Association for Stock Car Auto Racing (NASCAR). As confirmation of that early indication, see how the WNBA has grown in the years since.

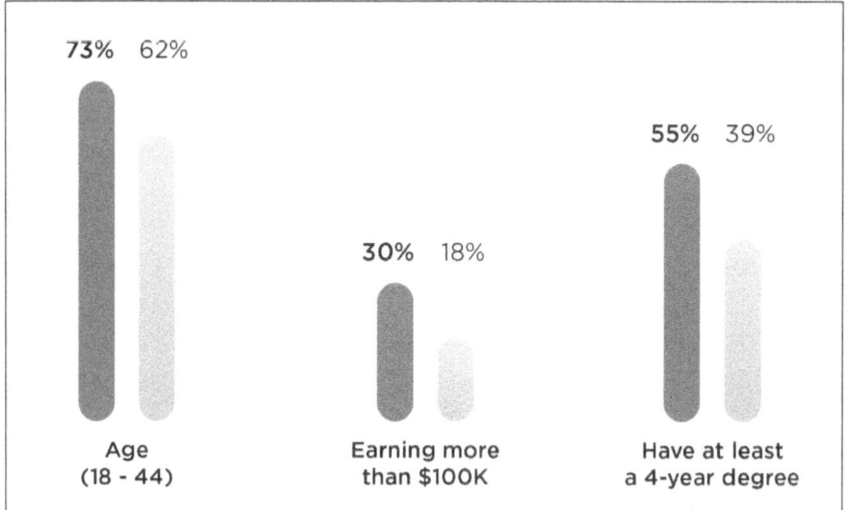

Figure 4.1 While the audience for women's sporting events may not have the same volume as the audience for men's, advertisers appreciate its advantageous demographic features. (The Collective)

The takeaway is that the audience may be different but is still quite valuable in the traditional sense for advertisers.

From the data synopsis: "Cultural divisions are present as well, with sports fans who are Black (79%) more likely to say they follow women's sports at least a little. Sports fans who are Black (56%), Latino (52%), under 30 (55%), and women (50%) are more likely than white sports fans (34%) and sports fans as a whole (41%) to say that there are not enough women in sports as broadcasters or reporters."

In a report titled *The Growth of the Women's Sports Community*, Sports Innovation Lab puts the growth score for the women's sports market just below the new U.S. sports betting market. That's a measure of economic potential, and there is no shortage of enthusiastic investment in the U.S. sports-betting space.

Sue Anstiss, the author of *Game On: The Unstoppable Rise of Women's Sport*, notes that while fans' expectations for games in Britain are completely different from those in the United States, even in Britain attendance at women's events is breaking records. More than forty-seven thousand attendees watched a Women's Super League (WSL) soccer match in Emirates Stadium in London in September 2022 when Arsenal beat Tottenham by a score of 4–0. In April 2023, 58,498 fans watched England beat France 38–33 in a Six Nations rugby match. A friendly match between the Lionesses and the U.S. Women's National team brought 76,893 fans to Wembley Arena in October 2022.

"The real success is going in and finding a whole new audience," Anstiss said. "And the audience that was at the Amazing Six Nations at Twickenham—oh my God, families, friends, groups of girls, older women. You know, it's just fabulous. But they're never going to ever go maybe to Twickenham for A and B game, and they'd certainly never go to a Premier League football match. Come on, it's the last place you take your family."

Anstiss is wary of labeling women's sports "family-friendly," as though it implies the competition is "less than," but American fans may not understand that violence is a regular occurrence at European soccer matches, and drunken fans sometimes chant homophobic and racist slurs. This became so pervasive that in 2013, FIFA and Union of European Football Associations (UEFA) decided to impose penalties on teams for their fans' racist conduct.

So to be able to present an event with an atmosphere free of that would genuinely bring a new audience to games. Again, women's sports are drawing a new fan to the sports marketplace.

"I slightly worry that we've spent a long time thinking, 'Oh, we need to go and get those male football fans and bring them over to the women's game,'" Anstiss said. "And we're seeing actually last year for the women's Euros, 1.6 million or something . . . didn't even watch the men's World Cup. So we've got this huge audience that loves women's sport for all it is but has no interest in men's sport."

Research by the Women's Sport Trust in the United Kingdom, which fills a space similar to that filled by the Women's Sports Foundation in the United States, found that 11.5 million of the 29.9 million people who watched the 2023 Women's World Cup had not watched the 2022 men's World Cup in Qatar. The research, published and available on the Women's Sport Trust website in September 2023, came with the headline: "Data Shows Highest Viewing Time on Record for Women's Sport as FIFA Women's World Cup Attracts a Younger, More Female Demographic."[4]

England's Lionesses reached the World Cup final in 2023 before losing to Spain. There is a professional women's soccer league tied to some of the Premier League teams, as well. In some ways, the English market for fans mirrors that in the United States, given cultural similarities, even if fan culture at men's events isn't entirely comparable.

"One of the things that we know to be true through research and data," Tissenbaum said, "is fans who are younger, millennials, Gen Z, etc., are much more likely to cheer with and support with their wallets brands and teams that align with their values."

Fans of women's sports—FoWS, for short—are also more likely to make charitable contributions on giving platforms. By extension, they are more likely to care about how teams and brands position themselves when it comes to causes and issues with which they align.

One of the key metrics for espnW is that fans who are familiar with the brand's site for women's sports register thirteen points higher in positive feelings for ESPN itself, according to espnW's own research. That metric goes up more among espnW's more loyal consumers.

The affinity site launched in 2010 with a raft of data on female sports consumers. (Another disclosure: I was one of espnW's original five columnists.) Founder Laura Gentile came from a marketing background, so this kind of research was part of her DNA. She used it to successfully pitch a women's sports site to ESPN, and the group continues to measure the audience to show its value to the network.

Regardless of what espnW publishes, creates, and produces, its very existence has a halo effect for the overall ESPN brand. There are also data showing that female consumers were responsible for driving the growth of the ESPN app and grew to become 29 percent of ESPN's total linear audience in 2022. It's the data on streaming consumers that might be more useful to ESPN and its sponsors, as the cable audience shrinks. Young fans are consuming media on their phones, so when espnW can show that women are driving that streaming growth, it is a valuable piece of data to show stakeholders.

New Audience, New Ways of Engaging

Victoria Jackson, a sports historian and clinical associate professor of history in the School of Historical, Philosophical, and Religious Studies at Arizona State University, can draw on her own experiences to put the evolution of sports fandom into the digital space—and its expanded possibilities for female fans in context.

She grew up in an atmosphere dominated by men's sports in the 1980s around Chicago. The Bulls, White Sox, Cubs, Bears: Chicago was an area with no shortage of storied teams to root for.

"My dad got us season tickets to Northwestern women's basketball when I was in middle school, and I would have never thought to do that," Jackson said. "It was his idea. I was watching. It was the Chicago suburbs in the 1990s—so, the Chicago Bulls. And then I was a huge fan. I was a huge Michigan fan. It was my dad who got me watching women's sports by getting these season tickets. And if not for that, I wouldn't have been watching women's basketball.

"It was amazing. I got to watch Big Ten women's basketball as a kid, which was really kind of horizon-expanding for me."

Where would Jackson have seen these games if she hadn't been in the stands? Women's sports were not on television in the same way they are now. The girls who wanted to watch sports mainly had the option of watching men's sports, so they become generational fans of men's sports. The NFL's fan base is a case in point: according to the league, 47 percent of its fans are women.

"Those of us who grew up with traditional cable and didn't have all of the streaming possibilities that we now enjoy today, like, we were just shut off access," Jackson said. "So . . . if you wanted to watch sports, you had to watch men's. And the few times that women's were on, that was awesome. But inevitably your more consistent fan affinities were men's sports because you got to see them more frequently."

Her father's decision to get those Northwestern tickets has cascading effects.

Once Jackson started following women's college basketball, she became aware, as an adult, of how challenging it was to track down the sports and athletes she wanted to see. She saw how easy it was to follow the men's teams she had rooted for as a kid and how much work was required to find and follow the teams and events she wanted to see.

Her experience illustrates a recurring data point around FoWS.

"The percentage of fans of women's sports who put their credit cards down and say, 'I'm going to pay for all five of these streaming platforms because I have to in order to get the content I want—the W[NBA] and the NWSL and the European Soccer League,' it's significantly higher on the women's side than it is on the men's side," Tissenbaum said.

It isn't that "nobody cares about women's sports," Tissenbaum continued. Rather, the economic and awareness demands on fans of women's sports has been higher than for fans of men's sports looking to follow their players and teams. "We're forcing these people to pay more for the same things that you get [in men's sports] again just by turning your TV on," she said.

Sports Innovation Lab data chart how fans watch women's sports, such as the UEFA Women's Champion League final on the British streaming platform DAZN with 12.3 million unique viewers and the way those fans follow athletes on social media. Sports Innovation Lab uses the gymnast Simone Biles and posts about her partnership with the fitness-wear brand Athleta to show the endorsement's value.

The arrival of streaming technologies has been a boon for fans of women's sports. Even if the price of entry is higher, at least there is access.

It has been hard to find women's sports on TV, in newspapers, and elsewhere. In fact, Google posted an article to its blog before the 2023 Women's World Cup to announce that it was going to make it easier to find women's sports results through searching. That's because the default result for searches has been men's sports—even during major women's events.

Google's blog says: "As we continue to roll out more improvements and similar experiences for more leagues and competitions globally, we recognize there will still be times when our systems don't get it right—especially given the disparity in content related to men's and women's sports that is present on the web. Nevertheless, we remain committed to creating an equitable experience for sports on Search."[5]

It wasn't exactly a mea culpa. Google has been intentionally advertising around women's sports, so while it would be easy to lament the decades of contributing to the problem, the company did own up to the inherent bias in its search algorithm and committed to fix it.

Different parts of a company don't always speak to one another, but given the profile Kate Johnson, Google's director of global sports, media, and entertainment marketing, has had, and the tremendous advocacy she's done, for Google's own search results to underplay the sports they are using to advertise undercuts Google's ability to maximize that investment.

Rita Ferro, advertising sales president at Disney, got her start at ESPN and said ESPN's parent company saw overall advertising revenue in women's sports grow 23 percent from 2021 to 2022. A big chunk of that came from the NCAA women's basketball tournament, where ratings surged. The women's Final Four ad sales in 2023 were up 53 percent over 2022.

"I would say five years ago, we started the conversation, and I would say in the last twenty-four months, it's become a real important piece . . . not only [of] strategy with major brands, but also the importance of the audiences that they want to make sure they're representing, speak to, and are very deliberate in their intentionality around how they engage with those customers, how they support women's sports, and how the elevated presence of that across their entire media campaign and partnership is really important," Ferro said. "And I'm talking major brands. We have a long way to go with the full marketplace, but I'm talking major brands who are really stepping in."

She named Google, Ally, T-Mobile, and Target as brands that are particularly astute.

And advertising cares about the breakdown of male-to-female in the audience demographics. Sports traditionally have been a way to reach men, but the demographics of television viewers are more balanced for women's sports than for men's. Advertisers that want to reach more men or women can put their ad dollars into men's or women's sports. However, even in an age of on-demand streaming, where sports make up a significant proportion of live television programming, many advertisers still do not think of sports, based on its historical associations, as an avenue to reach female viewers. It will not surprise you, dear reader, if you have made it this far into this book, that advertisers continue to want to reach men through sports.

Advertisers' comfort in using sports to reach male audiences has obscured the value of women to broadcasters, and to sports markets more generally, until quite recently. One of the cases made for prioritizing women's viewership came from looking at who makes purchasing decisions in a household.

"Women make a lot of the business purchase decisions in the home," Ferro said, "And so as a brand, if you're not talking to them directly with programming and messaging in the content they choose to watch, it's really a missed opportunity. And yes, women watch the NFL; women also watch women's sports. And by the way, so do men. So it's an important strategy for us as a brand and a platform to make sure that we're elevating those stories in the platforms and in the windows on those platforms where you can have the broadest impact of audience."

And here's another interesting nugget from Tissenbaum, who is continually finding that taking a closer look at fan behavior disproves the criticisms and misinformation she's become accustomed to hearing in the women's sports investment space. The consumption of women's sports content between women and men may be different depending on the medium.

"When we did that very first fan project report that came out in 2021, the split was, I think, closer to 55 [female] to 45 [male]," Tissenbaum said. "We asked sports fans to download their social media archive and give it to us. Then we analyzed all of the different ways that they engage on social media. What pages do they follow? Where do they authenticate? What do they buy on [Facebook] Marketplace? All that kind of stuff. And we had a 45 percent male [to] 55 percent female split in terms of our audience. And that was actually one of the really interesting and, I think, powerful data points, because . . . when you talk about women's sports, the first thing that the skeptics say after they give you that 'nobody cares' is, 'Oh, well, it's only women.' It's actually not only women. And even if it was—which it's not what we know to be true about spending power in this country and in North America in particular—women are the ones that are in control of household finances. So if you're a brand or if you're a team and you're trying to build an audience, even if the split is, call it sixty over forty women to men, why aren't we paying attention to the people who are holding on to the purse strings?"

So, just like men, women can be sports fans, and fans of women's sports. We will get into gendered advertising more in a later chapter, but assumptions about who is a fan of women's sports and whether or not they are a valuable market has been a drag on investments in women's sports for decades.

See and Be Seen

How has the experience of being a fan changed in the past two decades? I checked in with my former espnW colleague Sarah Spain. She bought into the Chicago NWSL franchise, the Red Stars, to do more than just root for the success of women's team sports. Another Chicago-area native, she had been a regular at NFL and NBA games but wanted to use her cultural capital to support local Chicago women's teams.

She's seen the game-day experience evolve.

"You go to a [Chicago] Sky game now, and it's a blast, but back in the day it was small. There's not a lot of people," Spain said. "They don't have a lot of entertainment other than the game itself. So you're trying to get your friends out there, and it's not the same as going to, like, a Bulls game. Whereas now I can get my friends out to Red Star games all the time."

Just as consumers are mindful that their brand choices reflect their social values, celebrities with social capital are thinking conscientiously about where they spend it. The idea of using your platform to lift women's sports has become more important to sports professionals such as Spain and the genre's celebrities. Where are you putting your focus? If you only watch and talk about men's sports, you are supporting the status quo, even while you are empowered as part of sports culture. This is why having NBA players talk about the WNBA has brought crossover respect. Women's sports can't be invisible culturally and succeed.

Spain, Kate Fagan, and I hosted *The Trifecta* on ESPN Radio on Saturday mornings for three years starting in 2014. In that time, we contributed to a lot of shows, including *First Take*, *Outside the Lines*, *His and Hers*, and *Sports Reporters*, where we would pitch ideas for the show's rundown. Those shows set the agenda for discussion, and we were constantly angling to get in conversations around the WNBA, women's soccer, and tennis. We knew that there's a circularity to what sports consumers are casually aware of or interested in. A show discusses what producers think fans are already aware of, but fans' casual interests in sports topics follow what they see in the culture.

"Think about how many people probably don't even really care about going to a Cubs game or an NFL game, but that's what everyone has watch parties for, and that's what everyone spends their Saturday doing," Spain said. "Then they go get their beer at the bar beforehand and then spend the game, like in *When Harry Met Sally*, talking about their divorce and doing the wave instead of watching the baseball. But no one's judged for that. You're a part of the community, and there hasn't been, until more recently, that community around women's sports."

Beyond die-hard enthusiasts, men's sports have had the privilege of engaging a portion of their audience just by being a normal part of the background, a cultural mainstay. There's no reason women's sports can't have the same function for casual fans, with people attending because sports are part of the culture. Things have evolved not so much because traditional media has evolved, but because people are watching and showing up for women's sports; attendance records were broken in 2023 for the NWSL, Women's World Cup, and NCAA women's tournament. Spain thinks the change is due to a number of things, such as demonstrated fan interest on social media. But there's also cultural currency. Some sports columnists—notably, Bill Simmons—would routinely use women's sports as some sort of punch line. There was a 2010 post on Alex Belth's *Bronx*

Banter blog that strung together examples of Simmons's sports misogyny, including the assertion that WNBA scores should be banned from the ESPN score ticker.[6] Those kinds of keep-the-girls-out-of-the-clubhouse asides were once unremarkable in sports media.

"[There's a] cool factor around it, because of social media, because of the removal of gatekeepers deciding what has value," Spain said. "Because of the athletes themselves, because of our deciding that they're multidimensional and don't have to be infantilized and only be role models, there's a million other reasons why [women's sports surged]—because of fashion, because of crossovers with music, like, all those things that give it more of a cool factor—it's easier to get people to go. It used to kind of be a joke; like, it's not the butt of a joke anymore, unless you're a total incel. You might not care, but you would just not hear, for instance, a major ESPN person now say, 'It was about as quiet as a WNBA game,' whereas that [once] was extremely common."

Spain said she heard Sue Bird describe the phenomenon of people who pretend to be apathetic when it comes to women's sports but loudly communicate their disapproval.

"You don't have to like it, but stop poisoning the well," she said.

But now, typical sports fans who might have thought women's sports were beneath their notice are showing up for Sky games and cheering loudly enough to attract the notice of the team's operating chairman, Nadia Rawlinson.

"There's a great competitive aspect to it, and they love the players," Rawlinson said. "When you're looking at the fans that are coming up that are identifying with the teams that represent them, they don't think there should be a difference between men's and women's sports. They just think they're just great sports, period, and great ball."

Women's teams and leagues don't need to win over every Pittsburgh Steelers fan (although I did go to a women's tackle football league championship facilitated by Franco Harris on Heinz Field; Harris, a Steelers Hall of Famer, was a huge ally). No one needs to win over the haters when women's sports are minting new fans. Generations of them. Fans who've now grown up cheering for the Sky and the Bulls.

Those fans are being recognized as the market they are.

"Something that's happening right now that's very cool is, with teams like Angel City, for example, like they're selling out week over week, and there's young girls and there's young boys and there's teenage girls and boys and, like, there's just this diversity of fandom," the entrepreneur Haley Rosen said. "But it's a lot of young people, and it . . . feels like the beginning of something that is important.

"My feeling has been we're going to keep having, like, little wins, and we have to keep stacking those wins, but we'll feel the big wins in five years, eight years, ten years. I think that's just important to keep in mind."

5

BROADCASTING GATEKEEPERS

It really is a boy's club, because it's built that way. But now the sports networks that have sidelined women's sports are belatedly developing a fear of missing out.

Erica Vanstone was convinced that if the grassroots resurgence of roller derby was going to break through to the next level, the sport needed to be on ESPN. The coed sport, full contact and on roller skates, was popular in the 1960s and '70s in a campier version, where the banked-track action was choreographed but still drew crowds to arenas such as Madison Square Garden. It was even televised, and Raquel Welch starred in the movie *Kansas City Bomber* at the height of the craze.

In the early 2000s, roller derby reemerged in Texas. This time, however, many of the women who strapped into their quad skates and pads had grown up playing organized sports and following rules. They were the daughters of Title IX, and whether new to skating or sports, they came in on the ground floor of a sport that was being reinvented as it was being played.

By the mid-2010s tens of thousands of women were playing this full-contact sport under the banner of the Women's Flat Track Derby Association, where skaters picked pseudonyms but the rest of what fans saw was 100 percent genuine. Crowds were growing, and the Gotham Girls in New York City could sell out the college venues they were using to play.

And why wouldn't roller derby grow with more coverage? Derby was genuinely fun and visually arresting. Teams often had theme nights, such as Killers versus Prom Queens; the aesthetic was part cheeky pinup and part horror show. Local leagues had personalities and fan bases and team names such as Yonkers's Suburban Brawl and Queens of Pain representing New York City and Denver's Mile High Club.

(If you find this amusing, there is a rabbit hole of fun to tumble down looking at derby's team and individual names. I played for Suburbia for seven years as Lesley E. Visserate, a.k.a. Viss, an homage to the pioneering sports broadcaster Lesley Visser.)

The skill level was dramatically improving in this first WFTDA decade. One player, Atomatrix, had been a nationally competitive speed skater and was devastating opponents with her speed and steadiness: she was difficult to bring down, despite a solid hit. As the rules changed, teams were finding ways to exploit loopholes to stop players like her, and the game was evolving.

The profile was growing, as well. Drew Barrymore made *Whip It*, a derby movie starring Elliot Page. Suzy Hotrod, a dynamic player for Gotham's aforementioned Queens of Pain home team, was featured in *ESPN Magazine*'s "The Body Issue" in skates and all her inked glory.

The best teams and skaters were regularly reaching the WFTDA championship tournament, which became an annual trek for the people who played and loved the sport. There were vendors and afterparties where, instead of a coat, you had to check your pants at the door.

Vanstone, a.k.a. Double H, a Philadelphia roller derby skater and the executive director of the WFTDA wanted to take this sport to the next level. She'd led the league as it developed its own digital platform and created a boot camp for announcers. Many teams had their own trackside announcing pairs to call games, and the best were plucked to develop for the bouts that aired for broadcast. Some bouts had been streamed on ESPN's digital platforms, which WFTDA paid to produce at about $20,000 each, but in 2017 ESPN called with an offer that could change everything.

It wanted to broadcast the championship final on ESPN2.

Vanstone was ecstatic. This could take derby to the next level. To be fair, there were plenty of logistical hurdles. ESPN was not offering to pay production costs, and the network broadcast required more bells and whistles than the streaming version, so it would cost about $40,000. The WFT-

DA agreed to cover the additional costs, by far the biggest investment the league was making.

But the championship would be on ESPN2. Think of the new fans the league and the sport would reach. Surely the potential growth was worth the investment.

Vanstone was excited to take the all-hands conference call to start the planning process with the network. She was about to meet her producer, and they both arrived on the call early and made introductions and small talk.

"So," she recalled him saying as they waited for other people to join the call, "is roller derby real?"

Vanstone's heart sank. He was referencing the 1970's version; he hadn't even done basic homework about the sport.

A Mixed Record

It's important to lay out how the momentum to cover women's sports in broadcast media has been stifled: by misunderstanding the opportunity and the audience; by failing to support the intended audience; by choosing not to grow a new audience for fear of losing an existing audience; and by treating women's sports as peripheral to the sports culture. Plenty of the stories and data around women's sports broadcasts in this chapter involve ESPN, and the network helpfully cooperated with my many requests for interviews and data. As the preeminent American sports channel, ESPN has owned rights to broadcast the WNBA, the NCAA women's championships from basketball to softball. It has aired women's tennis and the Grand Slams, niche sports and one-offs. Women's sports highlights have made *SportsCenter* and debate shows.

The network has also hired women, not only for traditional sideline coverage roles, but as beat writers, columnists, producers, interns, vice presidents, a chief financial officer (Christine Driessen), and radio hosts and as football analysts for the flagship National Football League (NFL) shows. On one level, it recognizes the importance of growing its audience.

The same could be said of its record in diversity. In fact, in the 2000s, ESPN was briefly the only local or national media outlet with a Black woman writing sports columns: Jemele Hill. The network created *His and Hers* to showcase Hill and Michael Smith. It moved them to the 6 P.M. *SportsCenter* in 2017. The show lasted a year and a month and ultimately became a flashpoint in the culture wars when, after the Unite the Right Rally in Charlottesville, Virginia, in August 2017, Hill posted on Twitter that President Donald Trump was a white supremacist.

The network didn't want to drive off fans, some of whom said they turned to sports to avoid politics. But Trump was politicizing sports himself. Unlike his predecessors, Trump didn't invite women's championship teams to the White House unless, like Baylor University's Coach Kim Mulkey, they praised him publicly. And Vice President Mike Pence went to an NFL game, only to leave theatrically when players kneeled during the National Anthem. Analysts at ESPN routinely take umbrage, loudly, over the smallest details in a game or player's comments, but Hill's assessment of this national story was not treated the same.

By 2020, both Hill and Smith had been severed from the network. The episode is another case study in how ESPN embraced cultural diversity but then didn't know how to support the people in those roles or manage a backlash to the elevation of nontraditional anchors.

Still, not many sports networks have made a fraction of the effort ESPN did to air and elevate women's sports. The network launched espnW in 2010 to focus on stories about women's sports and develop nontraditional voices at the network. It created a meaningful series on women's sports around the fortieth anniversary of Title IX that featured stories about women in sports. It has hired and promoted women in production and on-air roles for those games.

Why haven't these efforts been sufficient? The drive to represent new and different voices and speak to new and different audiences, including audiences interested in women's sports, is only one of the measures of effecting change. Because the ESPN portfolio is so vast, you will find examples of the best stewardship and platforming of women's programming and the most disappointing; of careers both wrecked and elevated due to identity issues. You will find examples of people supportive of women's programming; some who are quietly opposed; and some who are indifferent. As of the writing of this book, there has never been an ongoing program to talk about women's sports at the network the way *Inside the NFL* regularly talks about one football league. Meanwhile, the United Kingdom's BBC had a weekly women's sports show all the way back in 2017.

Talk and Highlight Shows

There is a stat for that apathy, and it's the 4–5 percent of traditional sports coverage that goes to women.

That's the amount of time an average sports-highlights broadcast devotes to women's sports, according to research conducted by Cheryl Cooky, professor of interdisciplinary studies at Perdue University, and Michael Messner, professor of sociology and gender studies at the University of Southern California.[1] The measurement has been taken since 1989, and the amount of coverage has stayed about the same through the 2019 report.

"The challenge with that particular stat is [that] the data point . . . took on a life of its own," Cooky said. "We were studying a very specific type of media, looking at sports news media specifically and televised news and highlight shows. So in some way that particular data point is specific to that particular form of media. However, even though we're looking at sport news media highlight shows in particular markets and particular time frames, what we see across the data, and what we see across the research—hundreds of studies that have been done when we're looking at the quantity or the amount of coverage between men's and women's sports—women's sports content rarely exceeds double digits."

In the past thirty years, a great deal has changed even as that number remains stubbornly low. Cooky said it is possible that a more optimistic number could be produced by a wider sampling or by adding streaming platforms and women's-sports-heavy sites such as *The Gist* and *Just Women's Sports*, or even *Teen Vogue* and *The Atlantic* when those outlets tackle women's sports. But finding that measure and duplicating it as the platforms evolve would be challenging.

"I do think it's complicated," Cooky said.

Given the variety of sports, and different times of year, the kinds of sports in a highlight show change. The Olympic Games bring more focus to women's events, and the USWNT has won the Women's World Cup four times. Yet these and other content fluctuations have never lifted the overall numbers. The inclusion of women's sports, or lack of them, could not have been more consistent if the networks had let them languish intentionally.

As you'll see, ESPN historically has owned the broadcast rights to a number of women's properties—most notably, NCAA women's games and the WNBA. Yet even during March Madness, when CBS holds the rights to the men's basketball tournament, ESPN hasn't consistently activated its own coverage during *SportsCenter* highlights or included content in sports debate shows.

"ESPN has had the rights fees for the women's tournament since, I think, like, 2002 or something like that," Cooky said. "But when you look at the coverage at ESPN *SportsCenter* in terms of the samples that we look at in our data points, [it] spends over three hours talking about the men's tournament, which is broadcast on their competitor networks, and spends, like, two minutes talking about the women's tournament."

Cooky said that this shows that decisions at the network aren't being made from a point of maximizing the value of its own properties. She points to ESPN's traditional emphasis on the men's NCAA tournament when it also has the rights to the NCAA women's tournament.

"[It] isn't purely economic decision making, because I can't understand why you would do that," Cooky said, "or why you would use your talking head programs or your highlight shows to build audiences for the content on your sister networks. It just doesn't make sense to me."

Bob Ley was one of ESPN's earliest anchors, joining the new regional sports cable network in 1979. He was already a legend when I arrived in 2009, having been a *SportsCenter* anchor and then moving to the prestige journalism program *Outside the Lines* in 1990. Although known later in his career for having a deft hand with the issues around sports, he spent a great deal of time calling games, as well, particularly in soccer. He was the founder of the Center for Sports Media at Seton Hall University, where I was the inaugural executive director.

Ley was a regular on the international soccer beat, covering World Cups and Euros for the men and women. He headlined coverage for the Women's World Cup in 2011 and called games during the '99 Women's World Cup. With a front-row seat, he saw the way those teams inspired fans but fought for sustained coverage.

"In terms of coverage," Ley said, "if you want to get into validation through *SportsCenter* coverage, that's always a tough menu and a tough rotation to break into—and not just for women's sports, but speaking as a guy from soccer, I mean, for years. You fight to get important news and/or developments into the mix because you had your meat and potatoes, roast beef and gravy: major sports and headlines. So it took something nationally; it had to be formed around the flag. You can't go wrong with that, clearly. And waving the flag, which in '99, that took it all to the next level."

It's a fair point. Think of the kind of coverage that bolstered that surge in the late 1990s. The American Basketball League (ABL) and WNBA were formulated around the success of the 1996 Atlanta Games, where American women won gold medals in soccer, basketball, softball, and gymnastics. Then came the Women's World Cup, which came to the United States because of the Olympics success of the USWNT. Those events, those victories, generate headlines, but it doesn't sustain them. To generate familiarity and day-to-day interest, fans can't check in only every couple of years.

"The calendar restricts it, makes it episodic," Ley said. "There's no flow to that. The start of the Olympics, it's every two years. You're not cheering for a women's team. You're cheering for the national anthem inevitably on the medal stand. So for it to get down into the nitty-gritty of a WNBA season, as we are now, and to see the level of commitment on the part of networks and corporations, it is interesting.

"But again, it all comes back. It all faces the reality. And we see this proven more and more every flippin' day of the economics of it," Ley said. "It's got to work in the brave new world here of this revolution in sports media that we're talking about. There's no room for loss leaders."

espnW

Given the pressures, the cord cutting, the regularity of layoffs starting in the mid-2010s, and new generations less interested in watching live sports, there is an aversion among media executives to the risk that scaling up coverage of women's sports would take. I saw that aversion during my time at ESPN.

There have always been people pushing ESPN internally to air more women's sports. The headquarters were founded in Bristol, Connecticut, a stone's throw from where the UConn women play basketball. Plenty of UConn fans and players have worked for the network over the years. Employees might have season tickets. There has been an archetype for a successful women's team in ESPN's backyard going back decades.

One of the few early women with real power and title at ESPN, Laura Gentile, rose as executive assistant to George Bodenheimer to become the company's executive vice president of marketing. Gentile hired me to write for espnW, and I respected her tireless advocacy for more coverage and to recognize women as fans of equal stature.

Gentile had been a lacrosse player at Duke University. In 2008, when she was in her thirties, she started to think about the untapped female sports fan. Ratings for women's sports on ESPN were low, but Gentile also wanted to elevate some of the women who worked at ESPN as writers and producers, on the business side, and in other roles.

The ESPN analyst and host Sarah Spain was one of the original five columnists for espnW, as was I, and Spain recalled the first time we all got together in person. We went around the room and introduced ourselves, talking about what we had played in college, the sports we cared about or covered.

"I remember I wrote a whole story about not being the only person in the room that loved sports that was a woman," Spain said. "We had that first meeting in New York, and everybody's like, 'Well, I was the all-American at Duke' and 'I covered this' and 'My favorite teams are this.' And I'm, like, 'Oh God! Look at all these women that love sports and want to talk about this shit and played them.' You just don't usually have them all in one place."

The espnW brand launched in 2010 with an event that went on to become annual: the invitation-only espnW Women + Sports Summit. It was held at posh hotels such as the St. Regis and the Ritz Carlton, and it featured the top women in Olympic and professional sports. The summit was three days of serious and frivolous conversation among women in the sports industry who were notable through their media and corporate involvement. There were days of panels, meetings, and surfing and golf lessons, capped by dance parties at night where one might catch the 99er and soccer commentator Julie Foudy doing the worm on the dance floor.

"It was a catalyst," Gentile said of the espnW brand in 2023 as she was in the final months of her twenty-year career at ESPN. "It didn't accomplish everything we wanted to accomplish, but we sent up a major flare in the area."

Ratings versus Audience

There was the will inside ESPN to provide more programming, and the network had the rights to broadcast women's college sports and the WNBA. But ratings weren't often high, and that led to a lack of investment in getting those women's games on television and in time slots that traditionally get higher ratings. So what are ratings, and how did they come to be the standard of measurement?

For this discussion, I relied heavily on three experts in the sports business space. Richard Deitsch has covered media for thirty years, first at *Sports Illustrated* and now at *The Athletic*. His *Sports Media* podcast is a must-listen. Jon Lewis is the owner of *Sports Media Watch*, a website that analyzes ratings data. And John Ourand was a reporter at *Sports Business Journal* before moving to Puck in 2023.

Ratings are a measurement of who is watching a television show, or listening to a radio station, at any time of day. In the 1980s and '90s, this involved having families literally writing down their viewing habits back in the days when everyone in a house watched the same shows on a single television set. Those households were a demographically representative snapshot of how many people were watching any given TV show.

Ratings are often broken down into demographics such as age and gender, which advertisers use to target their marketing campaigns. If someone were to say a show had a 1.0 rating, that would mean 1 percent of all televisions were tuned in to the program. If someone referenced men age eighteen to forty-nine, they would be discussing demographics of a segment of the audience. The actual numbers of viewers in a rating can change depending on overall audience, but that is the general idea.

Proponents of showing more women's sports argue that even if there are more people interested in watching coverage of men's sports—an assumption that has not always proved true, as I show when I look at the history of women's sports broadcasts—expanding the sports and leagues covered to include women's sports can bring new audiences and offer new options for different advertisers to reach different viewers. But as our ways of watching have fragmented, the methods of collecting the data have evolved. Now ratings are calibrated to include single-viewer metrics, streaming, and other ways viewers can access a show.

ESPN can look every fifteen minutes and see the audience going up and down. So it can observe how many people turn the channel when a show such as *First Take* moves from one topic to the next.

"If I take a look at the shows on ESPN, it's very NFL- and NBA-driven," Ourand said. "They're looking at a minute-by-minute rating."

This encourages a mindset in which executives aren't just concerned about expanding a debate or a highlight show's programming to reach new audiences; they are also concerned about taking a conservative approach to guard against losing viewers each time the topic changes. But what is really at stake when we compare the male and female viewers of men's and women's sports?

"The majority of the female sports audience, I would say, is male," Lewis said. "But there's a lot of men watching women's sports and a lot of women watching men's sports, because these are big mass audience events."

Lewis picks a recent game and goes through the numbers.[2] The gender breakdown for men shows that more of them are in the viewing audience, but the overall numbers are strong for women, as well.

"The male demographic is watching more sports," Lewis said. "But still, a 1.0 in eighteen- to forty-nine-[year-old] women is a pretty strong number. I mean, you're not going to beat that with anything else on TV."

Since the late 2010s, the NFL is the most watched entity on American television sets. According to *Variety*, the top six shows of 2022 were *Sunday Night Football*, *Yellowstone*, *Monday Night Football*, *NCIS*, *FBI*, and *Thursday Night Football*.[3] The NFL estimates that 47 percent of its game-day audience is women. You can't draw the monster national ratings the NFL does without them. The NFL sits on the top of cultural relevance *because* of women, not as counterprogramming.

And that 47 percent was before the Kansas City Chiefs won Super Bowl 58, which became the most watched game in NFL history, due in no small part to the singer and songwriter Taylor Swift. She was dating the Chiefs' tight end Travis Kelce and introduced an entirely new fan base to the game of football as the season progressed. That Super Bowl had a whopping 123.4 million viewers.

The investment the NFL and its media ecosystem make in building familiarity and respect for the sport—through programming, broadcast talent, scheduling, different media—has helped build an audience regardless of gender.

It has been this way for the better part of a decade, but the indisputable dominance of American football hasn't always been thus. And perhaps that can be instructive for supporting women's sports.

"The NFL's ratings weren't very good in the '90s," Lewis said. "I mean, they were great, but there were all sorts of think pieces about why the NFL's ratings were down during that period of time."

Ourand said he used to believe that the ratings justified a lack of coverage, as well, but recent history has shown there are ways around that cycle of broadcasting inertia. "I was kind of duped," Ourand admits.

"If you were to talk to a CBS exec[utive], for example, they'd say, 'Look at the ratings. We can't pay X,'" Ourand said. "And the old me would have bought that. But look at where they put those [women's] games, and there are no storylines."

So it is possible to build audiences' familiarity with a sport and their viewing habits with investment over time, even in the absence of the immediate ratings to justify it. But the truth is, sports networks haven't really wanted to disturb the status quo.

And here's why.

The Commercials

In 2023, at the espnW summit, Sarah Spain hosted a conversation among four heavy-hitting women on the selling of women's sports. She opened with a question probing the critical intersection of player, sponsor, and fan—one that got to the heart of why coverage of women's sports hasn't been monetized in the way men's sports have.

"When we talk women's sports, sometimes we don't really know what we're talking about," Spain said. "Are we talking about women playing sports? Are we talking about women watching sports? Are we talking about women and men watching women's sports? Why is it important for us to actually see the business as made up of those three distinct things?"

There have been two metrics that have been functional obstacles to broadcasting more women's games: the ratings and ad sales.

Networks sell ads against the programming they plan to show and often guarantee advertisers a certain number of eyeballs on those ads. If there aren't as many viewers as projected, the networks compensate with free future spots, which they then can't sell for more money. So networks need to make their viewership forecasts. And if broadcasting women's sports means fewer viewers, or fewer of the viewers advertisers are trying to reach, that's a problem for broadcasters.

"The caveat is, in my opinion, the people that watch women's sports—and this is proven data—[are] men," Meg Aronowitz, then the senior vice president of programming at ESPN, said. "Women need to fall in love with women's sports. We are 51 percent of the population, and everybody wants to point a finger and say, 'Why doesn't ESPN televise more? Why doesn't CBS televise more?' Because we're [as broadcasters] cannibalizing our audience."

A major, and hidden, impediment to women's sports, according to people inside networks, is the way advertising is sold in sports. Women are about 40 percent of the audience for a broadcast in most sports except the NFL, where women are about half of the audience. That includes women's sports, which may have a larger percentage of women but still most likely will consist of a majority of men. So if a network is selling ads to a potential sponsor who is interested in reaching women, why wouldn't that advertiser advertise in a men's sports broadcast, where there are plenty of female viewers and more total viewers?

Let's say you are a women's brand and you want to break the mold and use women's sports as an advertising platform. You would still find a majority male audience. So if your goal is to reach women, women's sports might not seem to be the right vehicle for that.

This creates a problem, because sponsors who want to advertise on a women's game are often looking for women in the audience.

If a women's game might draw a less valuable—to advertisers—audience in the spot than a men's game would, then it's hard to sell a network on covering more women's sports.

"That was always the biggest challenge because there was always the assumption that you'd be selling to a female fan base, but the numbers didn't bear that out," Rob King, a longtime ESPN senior vice president and later editor at large said. "The audience was 60 percent men, and advertisers were looking for women."

For some strategists, the answer is in how women's sports are sold and the environment that programming creates for the audience.

"The sales model is broken," said Carol Stiff, the president of the Women's Sports Network who for decades led ESPN's effort to air women's basketball. Stiff was given the 2020 John W. Bunn Achievement Award by the Naismith Basketball Hall of Fame and has been inducted into the Women's Basketball Hall of Fame. A longtime vice president at ESPN, Stiff has been in the trenches of women's programming for as long as there have been trenches.

Stiff cites the commission structure as part of the problem. Salespeople knew they could make money selling the NBA and NFL. Stiff wanted to incentivize activity around selling other properties on ESPN, women's sports included. That meant going to companies that might not already be partnered with ESPN.

There are plenty of such companies that have stayed away from the traditional sports broadcast for good reason.

Think about your average sports broadcast: you see ads for beer, for razors, and for other products that men tend to use. Men's sports are a great vehicle for those ads to be sold. There is a side effect of that, however: it sends messages to audiences about who the intended viewers are.

"I think the sales model was and is completely broken," said Emma Schilling, a strategist for Sportsology. "If every ad you watched wasn't targeted to you and no one looked like you, would you feel comfortable in the space?"

The ads and the programming that dominate a typical sports broadcast are designed to make men feel comfortable, assuming that the consumer is pursuing a particular vision of masculinity. That consumer is catered to not only through the ads but also through the roles that women are given to play in front of the camera during the broadcast. Historically, women in sports have been sideline reporters and hosts, where they might direct conversations among men. Often those women are young and conventionally attractive compared with the men they work alongside. They are often excellent in their roles, but experience doesn't necessarily offer longevity in front-facing roles on sports networks. A network could be exposed to lawsuits if it were to say why it wasn't renewing some contracts as opposed to others, but there is incredible turnover for women in front-facing roles. Again, exceptions such as Pam Oliver, Hannah Storm, and Linda Cohn stand out and they often had to maneuver behind the scenes to keep their jobs. Men in the business will say the medium also favors younger and more handsome men, which is certainly true, but expertise is a larger part of the equation for them than looks.

The architecture of a sports broadcast that seeks to comfort male audiences does not seamlessly adapt to serve the women's game. A network thinks through the best way to shoot and showcase sports it puts on the air, from basketball to baseball, but the women's version of a sport was often just the same as the men's version, rather than rethinking a broadcast from the bottom up.

Even the artificially deepened voice of the play-by-play announcer, who rarely sounds as manly when having lunch in the media center before a game, helps create the atmosphere. The storytelling, where words such as "toughness" and "battle" and "beast" get thrown around quite liberally, conveys values without needing to be explicit.

When you try to transfer all that masculine pageantry to a woman's game, it doesn't mesh with the social meanings the game has accrued. The qualities we think of as exemplifying femininity don't apply to this vision of sports. The word "beast" would have an entirely different connotation. In the past, it was easier to overlook that women were in the audience, too.

Thanks to social media, women in sports are everywhere. Think of the viral videos you've seen of Simone Biles launching herself to the moon in the 2021 Olympic Trials or the University of California, Los Angeles, gymnast Katelyn Ohashi setting the crowd on fire with her inspired floor routine at an NCAA competition two years earlier. Think of the soccer star Megan Rapinoe's 2.2 million Instagram followers. Heck, think back to that elementary-school teacher, Kathleen Fitzpatrick (a.k.a. Ms. Fitz), who hit a half-court shot during recess.

Young sports fans are moving to streaming platforms at a clip, which means that the most valuable eyeballs, according to the old standards, are migrating. Those viewers want to feel good about what they're watching. They don't want some fossil to tell Eugenie Bouchard in the post-match interview to "give us a twirl and tell us about your outfit"—which is exactly what the broadcaster Ian Cohen said to Bouchard after she won her third-round match at the Australian Open in 2015.

"If you ask the women, you have to ask the guys to twirl, as well," Billie Jean King tweeted at the time to show how ridiculous the request was. "Let's focus on competition and accomplishments of both genders and not our looks."

Cohen's words were out of place in 2015, if only because he showed too much ankle, to borrow a similarly antiquated analogy. They revealed a disconnection between the appeal of the sport the audience loves and the team sent to cover it coming up short. The power brokers making decisions on marketing and broadcast deals didn't have the pressure of a microphone and a crowd, but many decisions about women's sports were made with the same "give us a twirl" energy.

All this is to say that, while advertisers and broadcast networks may point to similar demographic percentages consuming men's and women's sports, men have been targeted and catered to in the programming, and the products being advertised have been for them. And that opens an opportunity for a sponsor looking to reach a live television audience that isn't served by a broadcast that caters to traditional masculinity.

Radio

In sports talk radio, the challenges and opportunities for reaching women are even more pronounced. Richard Deitsch said that some informal estimates are that the audience is 90 percent male, but the truth is that women aren't officially counted, because the numbers are used to sell advertising to men. Spain, Fagan, and I found this out as we worked on *The Trifecta*. I once asked whether we'd drawn more women to the radio during our time slot and was told ESPN didn't count women in the audience.

"They don't track them," Spain said. "I was at one of those town halls, and they were going through statistics on the big-picture year for the whole company. Every time, they said—same thing with virtual town halls for radio—they would say 'We went up in every meaningful category, men eighteen to forty-nine.' As if no one else existed."

Once I understood that the network wasn't counting women, I realized that even if we drew an entirely new audience to sports talk radio each Saturday for our show—one that offered a different audience profile to potential advertisers but lost five male listeners in the process—it would be counted as a net loss. The success of the show would be evaluated through the ratings and not through the profile of the audience we brought, how engaged they were, or which new sponsors might be interested in reaching them.

"I do know that ESPN Radio really programmed for [ages] eighteen to thirty-four, for young men," said John Ourand. "That's who the advertisers were looking for."

There is still power in the audio medium. Sports talk radio could dictate a day's sports coverage in the 1990s and before. The medium has the luxury of time to really get into issues, and the hosts become familiar to the community because of the intimacy of the airwaves. Regular callers reached a level of fame, as well, such as WFAN's Ira from Staten Island and Doris from Rego Park. But often the misogyny was apparent—for instance, when the only women discussed were players' girlfriends.

As for sports talk radio, Deitsch notes that the medium is losing audience and radio ratings "are known for not being accurate."

"It's very much in decline," he said, "although it might not feel like that in New York. Sports talk radio continues to decline year over year. Most major cities may have a station, but some don't have any. Podcasting has changed the game on that."

Might terrestrial radio's insistence on targeting one demographic to the exclusion of others have left it more vulnerable to changing times? For those who drive a lot, Sirius/XM provides satellite radio, but the sports offerings reflect the gender diversity of terrestrial radio. There may be a few female hosts—such as Michelle Beadle of Mad Dog Radio, Maggie Gray of WFAN, and Anita Marks at ESPN Radio—but they are exceptions that prove the rule. In such a conservative medium, one that's never counted female listeners, there is plenty of space still for growing a different audience profile. Podcasts are beginning to crop up to meet that goal.

Weighing the Factors

That's talk shows. What about ESPN's experience selling the pregame and postgame shows? We've all seen how the respect and prestige that the NFL maintained through investment in talent, scheduling, and making sure fans knew the storylines during its less successful years paid off. Could that work for women's sports? The issue with programming around televised women's games on the network is not only that it had to be conceived and executed, but it also had to be paid for.

That's because the history of women's sports ratings, which have been lower, meant those ads would be seen by fewer people. There was little room for growing pains.

"It is hard to attract advertisers when you are not necessarily getting the ratings draw," said Meg Aronowitz. "If they have $100,000 to spend, and they can spend it over here and guarantee that they're going to get three million eyeballs, or they can spend it over here to 'Do the right thing to help grow' and only get three hundred thousand eyeballs, if I'm a chief financial officer or chief executive, I'm saying to myself, 'We're in the for-profit business. I've got to spend my money here.' And I think that's why you see a lot of advertisers challenged to get in this space, because we can't guarantee the big bonanza of ratings yet."

This was a tough problem to get around. ESPN isn't in the money-losing business, and without changing the way ads are sold or looking at metrics other than ratings—which always worked well for men's sports—that accounts for some of the perpetual reluctance around broadcasting women's events.

"To a large extent, I think the media groups and the brands are still assuming that you'll end up with the same demographic that you've always had," Molly Tissenbaum of Sports Innovation Lab said. That initial assumption leads to more assumptions, even for brands that know they have to think differently: "Major League Baseball is a perfect example. They're doing things differently because they know something about their demographic is changing. They're not necessarily paying attention to gender in the same way they're paying attention to age, because the most important thing for them right now is the aging fan. But we haven't seen that kind of interest or research or even data that goes along with why we're still buying and selling ads the same way."

How do international broadcasters justify the investment? While the BBC, a public broadcaster that has the public good as part of its mission, can put on a weekly women's sports program, any ESPN offering, under the current calculus, is going to need to make the same amount of money in advertising as any other show.

As of 2023, ESPN still had never had a branded show to discuss and highlight women's sports. There have been several attempts—and I know, because I was part of one effort in 2015 along with Fagan and Spain. We had three test shows, but ultimately the network decided not to pursue the project. There is no memorial in Bristol for all the shows that didn't make it from concept to time slot, but our show met the same fate as every other one meant to focus on women's leagues.

That lack of coverage sends a message, whether inadvertent or not. The issue of respect and prestige is cyclical. As networks invest airtime on the leagues they've already created an ecosystem of highlight shows, radio shows, ads, personalities, and storylines to sustain, anything that thrives outside that ecosystem is going to seem peripheral at first.

"And so the historical, the cultural problem that you alluded to earlier, which is if there's not a culture to value it, the marketplace isn't going to value it," Economics Professor Andrew Zimbalist of Smith College said. "That's been abundantly clear in all these other sports where the women aren't getting the attention; they're not getting the advertising; they're not getting the promotion. If you want to watch women's golf, you can't turn on the U.S. Open and see the men and the women on the same golf course. So the cultural prejudice is highlighted for these other sports where the women are not getting promoted and the men are getting promoted."

A History Lesson

But are women's sports fated always to be a less popular product? Women's sports have actually drawn big television audiences, Jon Lewis said. The best-rated WNBA games likely come from the first year of the league, 1997, when the finals between Houston and New York were on ABC. And that's not the only example.

"I think it's a period of time that people have memory-holed [when] women's sports really got very big," Lewis said. "That Women's World Cup final in 1999, I believe, had more viewers than any game of the [1999] NBA finals. Now, you know, that was Knicks-Spurs. It wasn't a great year for the NBA, but that previous year Michael Jordan was playing, and no one would have expected a year later for the Women's World Cup final to outdraw any NBA finals game."

Women's tennis might also outrate men's.[4] It really depends on who is playing. The USTA made the decision to move the women's final to Saturday night on CBS when Venus and Serena Williams were young. It had been the undercard to the men's event prior to the USTA's move, but this decision gave it a showcase. Serena won her first U.S. Open title in 1999, and by 2001 the final between the sisters was in that coveted spot.

"When we talk about women's sports and TV, that is a big part of it," Lewis said. "I mean, as big, I would say as the Women's World Cup in '99, and all of that was going on, as you said, in a very short amount of time. Between the launch of the WNBA, the Women's World Cup, Venus and Serena, even [the Swedish tennis player] Annika Sörenstam kind of broke through in a way that women's golfers have not since, and the ratings for those Annika Sörenstam U.S. Opens were surprisingly strong and have not been matched."

That television interest in women's sports was not capitalized on. As Ourand noted: Where were the games positioned? What was the storytelling around them? How did they fit into the sports media ecosystem that had been fine-tuned to support a different product?

Carol Stiff remembered that ESPN took some of the prime WNBA spots in 2003 and put other sports there. Ratings predictably dipped. The declaration that no one watched women's sports was again a self-fulfilling prophecy.

Ourand said that what's been notable about the most recent years of conversation around women's sports is that investors and sponsors aren't just asking about tennis, the Olympics, and the Women's World Cup.

"They're talking about the leagues," Ourand said.

There is a lot of good news in this area, and if you can just hold on until the next chapter, you're going to see how the fragmentation of the marketplace, a pandemic, and new ways of gaining insight into how women consume sports is absolutely upending this stagnation.

Of Two Minds

In the end, those 2017 WFTDA championships didn't run live on ESPN2 after all. The deal fell apart after the network decided to put the event on its gimmicky day broadcasting as *The Ocho*, a reference to a running joke in the movie *Dodgeball*. The WFTDA is an organization made up of the women who play, and many didn't want their premiere showcase of skill and strategy to be a punch line. Erica Vanstone could sense that enthusiasm was waning. At least when the WFTDA did its own broadcasts, it could use home-grown derby announcers and be as funny and profane as it wanted.

The final straw was when the network asked a player to change her name for the broadcast. That name: Biceptual.

ESPN had standards and practices, to be sure. That name might be cheeky, but it didn't make sense to ban it even under ESPN's own guidelines, which had an LGBTQ employee resource group to support and go to at these very moments.

Vanstone sought out the player to ask her to change the name: "I went to her, and she looked at me, like, 'Really?'"

Roller derby was a place that endeavors to welcome skaters of all varieties. Early on, the sport even had a policy to include transgender skaters, and many players identified along the gender and sexual spectrum. How could Vanstone face them if she caved to a weirdly prudish edict?

Vanstone knew she couldn't start compromising core values over a name that was objectively innocuous.

The word "biceptual," according to Webster's dictionary, means "having two heads."

6

BROADCASTING

The Road Forward

A determined hunt for solutions.

Pat Lowry has been working around women's basketball for as long as that's been a paying job. She had been at ESPN for twenty years, most recently as a vice president in programming.

You could say she grew up around the game. Her mom, Rubye Jean Parham, played for the May Hosiery Mill travel team in Nashville. She worked in the Accounting Department and would get an hourly supplemental wage to play basketball in the late 1940s.

"She was an accountant, but this was her way to get to continue to play," Lowry said. "And they played teams like the famous Nashville Business College and exhibitions and things like that."

So here comes Pat. She grows up loving the women's game, watching it with her mom, and the WNBA launches in 1997 and she's working on the broadcasts.

You have to understand that producing women's basketball, even the NCAA Women's Final Four, wasn't a sought after assignment when she started. Producing women's basketball often meant having expertise that wasn't in demand.

She recounted how an average getting-to-know-you conversation might go.

"Oh, you work for ESPN. What do you do?"

"Women's basketball," Lowry would say.

"Yeah, whatever."

But that apathy didn't keep her from trying to differentiate the women's broadcast in a way that showcased its strengths. After experimenting with ways to shoot the game, Lowry placed cameras in a spot near the rim where a viewer could really see the physicality of the players during a replay.

"I don't think people really understood how physical the women's game is," Lowry said. "Then you start seeing replays from that angle, and you're like, 'Oh, right.'"

When Sedona Prince, then of the Oregon Ducks women's basketball team, called out the NCAA on TikTok for its failure to give the women who played in the 2021 NCAA tournament the same resources as the men, Lowry knew that her own broadcast team had fewer robotic cameras than it wanted because the equipment had been rationed. The inequity, during a conversation about equity, wasn't lost on her, and she just hoped viewers didn't call out ESPN's broadcast as they were calling out the NCAA.

But at the start of the 2022–2023 season, Lowry could tell that the conversation around equity that Prince amplified had taken root in visible ways. The storytelling around the women's game—players such as Louisiana State University's Angel Reese, South Carolina's Aliyah Boston, and Iowa's Caitlin Clark; coaches such as South Carolina's Dawn Staley and Louisiana State University's Kim Mulkey—was *the* NCAA basketball conversation, even as the regular season was starting.

That prominence kept going during the regular season. Then came the tournament, and Lowry was in charge of the production for ESPN. First off, the tournament sold out of commercial spots.

"So as I'm starting to see the ratings throughout the early rounds and everything, the buzz was so weirdly different," she said. "Like, my sons and men were talking to me about the women's game—more so than I was hearing about the men's tournament, which, by the way, I didn't have a second to watch because I was watching the women's tournament."

"And it was just, I was like, 'Is it really happening?'" Lowry said. "It was kind of like, pinch yourself. Is it really happening?"

Turns out, it was really happening. Louisiana State University's win over the University of Iowa, the matchup of Angel Reese against Caitlin Clark in the 2023 NCAA Women's Championship game, averaged 9.9 million viewers on ABC. It was, as Jonathan Lewis's *Sports Media Watch* pointed out, a record-breaking audience, more than double that of the previous year.

For Lowry and the many other women who have labored to get women's sports on television, it was a jaw-dropping number.

"I've got the ratings," Lowry said. "I'm sitting there going, '9.9 million, baby—I got the ratings!'"

That number was a wake-up call for many in sports more generally. It was proof of concept: if you build it, they will come. Put women's events on broadcast networks, do the storytelling around these events to make them compelling, and fans will want to follow the games.

The first game of the 2023 World Series between the Texas Rangers and the Arizona Diamondbacks later that year earned a 9.1 rating, so fewer overall viewers than the women's final.

"That was an enormous, very rare kind of year-over-year growth that you don't usually see," Lewis said. "I don't think anybody, even the most ardent advocate of women's basketball and women's sports, would have thought 9.9 million was possible [in 2023]. Maybe three, four years down the line. . . . We knew what the ceiling was for the women's tournament. It was, like, maybe 5 million. If that game had had 5.7 million viewers, that would have been a huge success."

Nine point nine. That's a tidal wave, a paradigm-shifting rating in women's sports. It opened up a world of possibilities.

Access and Discoverability

While it has been hard for women's sports broadcasts to find fans, it's often just as hard for fans of women's sports to find their teams.

Here's one relatively historical example, even though it's just a few years old.

On opening night of the 2021 WNBA season, a night when casual viewers might have been most interested to get hooked into a new season, the league was in a good place. It had pulled off a successful pandemic bubble season, one of the first sports to carefully return as the world remained gripped by the coronavirus. Ratings for the WNBA had been way up in the summer of 2020, making the league one of the few professional sports to see viewership increase in the brave new world. The league's players had proved that their teamwork extended off the court after many campaigned for Reverend Raphael Warnock in his run against Kelly Loeffler, owner of the WNBA's Atlanta Dream, in the Georgia Senate race.

Kate Fagan, a longtime sports journalist at ESPN and former NCAA Division 1 basketball player, was looking to watch one of the first four games of the season. She went to ESPN, the lead WNBA broadcaster, and was surprised to see no game was being broadcast. Same with ESPN2. "What?!" So the hunt to find a WNBA game began. A Google search found some streaming options, but the only nationally televised game on opening day was on the NBA.tv website. Fagan didn't have the app on her phone, so she had to download it and sign up for a free trial, putting in her credit card information, to watch a WNBA game on opening night. The experience left her imagining it being so difficult to find a major event in the men's league.

"You're telling me that the NBA season opener is going to be that inaccessible to people?" Fagan asked. "And I don't need it to be one to one. I don't need 180 [WNBA] games on TV. But the fact that the league opener wasn't on the main broadcast partner? That, to me, is unacceptable."

When the popularity of these difficult-to-find broadcasts of milestone events are then compared with the ratings of comparable events in men's sports ratings, no one will be surprised when they fall short. It just gets used as more evidence against women's leagues and the players—evidence that no one, so the trope goes, wants to watch women's sports.

"Women's sports fans, men or women, are very loyal to women's sports because it takes a lot to opt into women's sports," said Thayer Lavielle of The Collective. "You have to opt out of being a men's sports fan. You can't miss it. It's everywhere."

Fagan's experience hints of de facto market suppression, but this may be fading. Since that game, WNBA ratings have been up; games have moved to ABC; and Ion has become the league's new Friday night broadcast partner. But this comes after decades of advocacy for putting games in watchable windows, giving these sports shoulder coverage like pregame shows and highlights on *SportsCenter*.

Change won't come because the sports industry and men's leagues finally feel like ceding more territory. It will come because women who play and their fans are demanding it. As the soccer great Abby Wambach put it to Haley Rosen, a young woman who is raising seed funding for a women's sports media start-up: "I have no interest in breaking the glass ceiling, I want to build a new house."

So here's the good news. It's happening.

Since so many fans of women's sports have been used to the chase, it may make them a more desirable market once they can be matched with coverage.

Measuring Rising Tides

There is a lot of good news on the sports ratings front for women and women's leagues. Not only was the NCAA basketball tournament a ratings winner, but other women's sports were up, as well.

The U.S. Open women's final, with Coco Gauff winning her first Grand Slam title against Aryna Sabalenka, again outrated the men's. On ESPN, 3.42 million viewers tuned in to watch, according to *Sports Media Watch*. The men's final a day later, between Novak Djokovic and Daniil Medvedev, brought in 2.32 million viewers. When ESPN released the data for the 2023 WNBA All-Star game, viewership was nearly one million, making it the most watched in sixteen years.[1]

Ratings for the WNBA finals in 2023, when the Aces defeated the Liberty in the fourth of a five-game series, were up 36 percent year over year, averaging 728,000 viewers a game.[2] It was the most viewed series since the 2003 season. The WNBA regular season had fifteen games that averaged 600,000 or more viewers, about twice as many as the year before, as reported by *Sports Media Watch*. The WNBA's best days were still in the first three years of the league, and these ratings aren't necessarily strong on their own, but with increased attendance, they are trending in the right direction.

These trends began before the pandemic started, but in that moment of upheaval, with people home and consuming media, ratings were up for women's sports and down for men's.

The NWSL was the first American league to return after the pandemic shutdown. In the summer of 2020, a sequestered tournament drew ratings that were 500 percent higher than before the shutdown.[3] Part of the success is that the games were *actually shown*. There had been so many years when women's games just weren't broadcast, and putting them on in prime spots yielded results.

In 2021, ESPN announced ratings that were up for NCAA women's basketball and softball tournaments, as well as for the WNBA. Meanwhile, in 2019 the USWNT World Cup Final was up 22 percent in the United States from the men's World Cup final the year before, according to CNBC. In international competition, the U.S. women's matches consistently outrate the men's.

As in men's sports, the entire idea of fandom and consumption is being upended right now. Young fans don't have to be fans of one team to be interested in a sport and its players—particularly for the level of popularity reached by athletes who play women's sports, even among casual fans. For example, social media allows players direct access to a fan base. You don't have to follow Olympic rugby to follow Ilona Maher, whose TikTok videos during the 2020 Olympics went viral.

"I think female athletes are much more famous among people who don't necessarily watch," said Lewis.

He pointed to Naomi Osaka in women's tennis. Osaka is a household name but hadn't played for a year at the time of our interview. So people who considered themselves die-hard fans might not be watching tennis much at all and consuming sports in a different way. For those fans, content might not even include live sports.

Some of the media delivery systems are changing. New streaming services are democratizing access to delivery platforms. A women's sport doesn't have to beg a bunch of men in suits at major networks to get a Saturday afternoon broadcast anymore. It can go around them to streaming platforms to reach viewers hungry for content. Leagues can produce shows with their own analysts to talk soccer or profile players. One day in the not-too-distant future, fans won't have to track down a season-opening WNBA game across mediums; the game will come to her or be a link on a platform specially designed for women's sports broadcasts.

Athletes can take their powerful stories to independent outlets such as *Players' Tribune*, which will work with them to write and edit stories that can send shock waves across the sports landscape. Think of Sue Bird's brilliant "So the President F*cking Hates My Girlfriend."

The *New York Times* would have never run that copy—even back when it had a sports section.

But the traditional broadcast framework is still how leagues make money, and for them, ratings and sponsorships are still the coin of the realm.

Pat Lowry was just one of the people inside ESPN working on women's college sports. Two more, Carol Stiff and Meg Aronowitz, were also in meetings advocating for resources and better broadcast windows. Stiff is a basketball Hall of Famer and the president of Women's Sports Network. Aronowitz was charged with producing NCAA championships.

Aronowitz's area, college sports, has seen increases in softball and volleyball, although now she is responsible for more of ESPN's content, having been promoted to senior vice president of production in the summer of 2023.

"I've seen the support. I've seen my budget grow to support that and comparison to the male counterparts for those different sports," Aronowitz said. "And I think you're seeing the return on investment now. They're actively trying to find us ABC windows for women's sports. You saw gymnastics on ABC. You saw the Women's Final Four obviously have a very successful tournament with their ABC championship final. And obviously we had our two ABC games at the Women's College World Series that, you know, [rated] 1.4 and a 1.3 on a Saturday and a Sunday afternoon, during a time where people are out at the beach or on vacations. That's a commitment. So I feel like we are in a very good space and place at ESPN for the growth and opportunity for women's sports."

But the reality is that ESPN has made championships available to viewers but hasn't always found traction with audiences. It had to take a chance. As the veteran broadcaster Bob Ley said earlier, ESPN is in the bottom-line business. It is challenging to sell ad spots if coverage hasn't been proved to connect with a fan base, although there are branding reasons in favor of giving new ideas a college try.

"There's ninety NCAA championships," Aronowitz said. "Five of them actually make a profit. Not to say that everything is about the for-profit business. If you're the home of the NCAA championships, you want to make it about champions. You want to make it about the student athlete and the student athlete experience. But the truth of the matter is that we are spending significant production dollars to produce some of these NCAA championships that are just simply not moving the meter, and it's hard to sell against that. So, while we're committing to the Women's College World Series and the women's tournament, and the return on investment is there, people need to realize that we're also producing thirty other championships that we're not selling and that aren't necessarily a ratings bonanza for us."

Aronowitz said that equity does factor into how college championships are produced by ESPN and broadcast, often on the brand's college property, ESPNU. After the pandemic, her team members evaluated what they could do differently. The calculus is starting to shift a bit to recognize what investment might mean and that payoff might come down the line.

"After the pandemic, we looked at equity and we said, 'Wait a second. We're producing the men's Frozen Four [ice hockey tournament] at this level; the women's Frozen Four should be produced at that level, as well,'" Aronowitz said. "And we did. ESPN made the commitment in dollars to produce it. The women's championship got a 0.03 on ESPNU. The men's championship got almost a million viewers. We're spending the same amount of money. So I do think that there is a fairness there that should be known that ESPN does commit to women's sports and to the production of women's sports, even if the return on investment has yet to be proven for some of those sports.

"I think it will be," Aronowitz said. "I think over time you will see return on investment on those sports because people will start to fall in love with them. They will start to watch."

Aronowitz has advocated for changes that she thinks will make for better ratings. She's asked those in charge to change the days and times games are played so the schedule is better for television, even if it disrupts tradition. Those asks aren't just to those holding the purse strings; they are also to those shaping the content.

"I have made it a point to befriend the coaches in the sport of softball and be honest with them about what is necessary for opportunity and growth," Aronowitz said. "They have all reciprocated because they understand that exposure begets opportunity. It begets facilities, it gets them salary raises. [University of Oklahoma Coach] Patty Gasso is making $1.6 million this year, which is a pretty impressive sum for a softball coach. And she'll be the first to tell you that without television, that's probably not something that's going to happen for a sport like softball."

The question in the current media environment, however, is: Are ratings as relevant to the long-term profitability of a sport?

Take that World Series 9.1 for example. It's true that baseball has struggled to find younger fans. Polling consistently finds that the average baseball fan is older than fans of other sports. And given that broadcast deals can last for a decade, the projection of today's fan and future fans is a factor.

But the World Series matchup was between two small-market teams, and overall ratings picked up in 2023 as Major League Baseball (MLB) changed some rules to make the games run at a quicker, more entertaining clip. We need not take one year's rating as the last word on whether the MLB's changes helped. The same is true for women's sports: we should look at other measures to see whether there is growth.

Fans are consuming sports in many different ways: streaming, traditional cable and network coverage, digital commentary in written or audio form, highlights on social media, social media posts from athletes.[4] In the next decade there will be more ways to engage with sports. Sitting and watching an entire game or reading the game story in a newspaper might seem as quaint as a telegram.

"[Do] Nielsen ratings matter as much as TikTok followers?" Lewis asked. "When I've talked to students about this kind of thing, they would basically say, 'I follow this person on TikTok,' but they're not necessarily watching the game. Now, of course, you can't monetize TikTok followers the way you can someone watching a thirty-second ad, so ultimately ads or Nielsen ratings are still the currency."

As a counter to that, TikTok business did run a spot leading up to Paris '24 on the power of the platform featuring—you guessed it—rugby's Ilona Maher. In it, Maher draws a direct line between social media influence and brands.

As Aronowitz alluded, as long as ads and ratings are the way we measure success, they are also the best way for leagues and teams to guarantee revenue. Those broadcast contracts have changed men's sports from hobbies to industries.

Package Deals and Broadcast Rights

Women's sports have often been package deals; the WNBA with the NBA, the USWNT with MLS, and NCAA women's games with men's non-revenue sports. This model attempts to incentivize broadcasters to invest in the one league if they want a piece of the other league, for the good and growth of the sport. In the case of soccer, women were actually the bigger ratings draw. In each case, the deal obscured the value of the women's property.

The next rights deal is always being formulated.

Some of those deals have been renegotiated as this book was being written. In November 2023, the NWSL announced it sold its rights for $240 million for four years to a suite of media entities that include CBS, ESPN, and Amazon. According to the NWSL, the deal was worth 40 percent more than the one it replaced.

"Given that we are in hypergrowth mode, we feel like it's really important to make sure that we have discoverability but also put ourselves in a position to maximize the fact that our fans are digitally savvy," NWSL

Commissioner Jessica Berman said. "That is a unique byproduct of women's sports in that most women sports fans, they're trained to have to work really hard to find their content. And so all of that practice, I think, helps us from a data perspective because we know our fans are very digitally savvy, and they're very comfortable navigating to find what they need. But we also know that the future fan is not today's fan, so we have to do both."

While discoverability through other avenues is still key for growth, building its own broadcasts can help a league highlight the storylines and create the audience experience other broadcasters don't. It also gives the league leverage in broadcast negotiations.

While that deal was announced, WNBA Commissioner Cathy Englebert was not far behind, working to create her own package.

"That's my number one focus: media rights, media rights, media rights," Englebert said in the summer of 2023.

At the moment she said it, a bunch of sports were negotiating in this competitive environment. The NCAA's women's championships were up, as were the NWSL and NBA championships. Balancing that is the fact that having rights to a league brings fresh content and gives fans a reason to choose one sports outlet over another.

"They [broadcasters] need women's sports properties, too," Englebert said. "They can't only be men's sports properties. So we'll benefit no matter what happens. We're going to benefit because of the strength of our league [and] the strength of these players—the players on the court, the generational players, the building of household names. So I feel very confident that no matter what happens in that disruption that's going on in the media landscape, we're going to come out a winner here."

The risk-averse broadcasters are sometimes led by their sponsors to be more equitable toward women's sports. In 2023, Ally Bank announced it was going to make its sports sponsorships more equitable and would be moving toward an even split. Stephanie Marciano, head of sports and entertainment marketing at Ally, told the audience at the espnW Women + Sports Summit in October 2023 that the company looked at its portfolio and saw it was 90–10 invested in men's sports.

"It's pretty embarrassing, but honestly, it's probably where most brands, their splits, are," Marciano said. "So that's where we started. By the end of this year, we'll be better than 60–40, and as we look to next year, we'll already be to 50–50. So it's been work."

The pledge itself has been an actual news story, and Ally has probably seen a fair return on a lot of those dollars in free media.

"There has been a lot of storytelling, but this is absolutely not a [public relations] headline," Marciano said. "This is a sophisticated investment strategy. Every dollar we spend is intentionally spent, and every dollar we spend is measurable."

Ally was able to leverage its spend with Viacom to have the NWSL championship game upgraded to prime time on CBS in 2022.

When Marciano says that Ally upgraded a game, it means that a broadcaster didn't need to give up the advertising money that might have been missed if the game didn't draw a rating that was high enough. It's an innovative strategy. When companies such as Google and Ally say they want to spend their ad dollars on women's sports, it makes it more difficult for broadcasters to say no.

Another panelist at the summit, Sara Gotfredson, founder of the Trailblazing Sports Group, actually spoke up after Marciano finished to emphasize how meaningful that strategy was and how it gave broadcasters the confidence to invest prime TV spots and coverage into women's sports events.

"It had never been done before, and it was the highest-rated NWSL championship game," she said.

The Portland Thorns and Kansas City Current averaged 915,000 viewers on CBS. In 2023, the championship game was again broadcast on CBS. Gotham beat OL Reign in front of a championship-record 25,011 fans at the neutral San Diego Snapdragon Stadium, and averaged 817,000 TV viewers.

"I really do believe that we are nowhere near the pinnacle of what women's sports and women's sports viewership will be," Aronowitz said. "My personal belief is that there will be more pro leagues that evolve for some of these sports that will become solvent and will become profitable. And as they become profitable and sponsorable, you're going to see more and more of that content out there. I think women's sports are going to evolve as the broadcast industry is going to evolve. . . . What I mean by that is it's no secret that all of us are ultimately going to go direct to consumer. The idea that a 7:00 prime-time window is what you have to have at some point is going to become obsolete because it's just going to be 'I want to watch the NWSL' and, poof, here come all the games that are available to you in a curated content space that's going to allow you to do that."

There are other people trying to skate, not to the puck, but to where the puck will be. One of them is Rita Ferro, the president of advertising sales for Disney. Ferro got her start at ESPN and is still engaged there as a part of Disney's advertising strategy across the company.

One of the things that keeps Ferro busy is trying to determine what viewership will look like in its next iteration.

"It's why I spend so much time with my teams talking about measurement, because where people watch—on what device and screen they watch—and what the conversation is around what they're watching all are incremental to the total delivery of that opportunity," Ferro said. "We have to be really good and smart about that. When I say where they're watching, we know about 20–25 percent of our viewership happens out of the home. . . . And a lot of that happens in clips and highlights and social conversation around what happened because that shot was so good I have to watch it again and I have to talk about it.

"So there's just this opportunity to create much more fully dimensionalized partnership experiences around live [events]," she said. "Sports is the biggest power in terms of 'live' [programming], so it created this opportunity to do more, and you have this momentum around women and sports, so it's a culmination of many things aligning and being great around measurement and around people understanding it makes good business sense."

Polling shows that women and young people are more flexible in their viewing habits than prior generations. Where their Gen X parents may still be paying for a cable subscription, younger viewers such as Fagan who want to watch women's sports are downloading apps and putting their credit card information down.

Once that fan has been identified as someone willing to pay for content or sports experiences, they may be more valuable as a viewer. You'll read more on how research is helping to position fans of women's sports as more valuable customers. So even if women's sports are delivering more women in an audience (and remember from our last chapter that a gender-balanced audience is not what sports networks have traditionally sold to advertisers), there are new ways to monetize that.

"A lot of clients want volume of opportunity," Ferro said. "When I look across 2022, for example, we had over 33,000 hours of women's sports across our ESPN platforms. When I say, 'ESPN platforms,' I'm talking broadcasts on ABC, all the ESPN networks, and all our streaming platforms. That's volume of hours that, if someone really wants to deliver female audiences as part of a guarantee of a buy—because we did 33,000 hours, I think it's, like, 18,000 events—we're able to deliver. So the other piece is we've actually built enough scale and investment and commitment around that to be able to do that at scale so clients understand when you park your money here, we're going to be able to deliver that for you."

All through 2023, this conversation was taking place on stages from New York to Cannes, where women's sports investment was a topic for panels filled with powerful women. Ideas that were just a seed in one month were bearing fruit by the end of the year.

It was a summer of the Barbie movie and major concert tours by Taylor Swift and Beyoncé that seemed to add heft to the narrative that women move markets. Growing ratings and attendance from the World Cup to the WNBA and NWSL meant women's sports were a participant in these cultural trends—again, perhaps, but at last.

"It's been the joy of my career to be able to help take some of these sports and really elevate them and push them toward the promised land," Aronowitz said. "And again, I don't think we're done. I think there will be those that come up after me that are going to carry the torch and keep fighting the good fight. But at the end of the day, sports is sports, and all it takes is a good product. Then people will get over their opinions and watch because they're entertained."

7

THE FUTURE OF SPORTS COMMERCE

Women are at the forefront of NIL gains in the NCAA and stand to benefit from streaming services, sports betting, and other innovations.

In 1995, the Air Swoopes hit the market.

The women's basketball sneaker, named for the iconic player Sheryl Swoopes just in time for the 1996 Olympic Games in Atlanta, was a giant leap for women's sports apparel. Swoopes won a gold medal there, and the WNBA debuted a year later.

As a basketball player in New York City in that era, I bought a pair with the money I earned from my first adult job.

Air Swoopes were the first sneakers I'd seen made specifically for women back then. It was the dawn of the sneakerhead era, but I just wanted a pair I could play in when I went to the Prospect Park YMCA to play pickup games. You had to up your game in a flashy shoe like that, because everyone noticed.

The Air Swoopes were a branding sensation, furthering Swoopes's comparison to Michael Jordan as the WNBA launched. Women and girls should have been a huge market for apparel companies, but the cost of the premiere shoes was steep, and girls were usually just sent to the boys' basketball shoe section for a mid-range option. Having something made to fit a woman's anatomy, and there are differences, was a revelation.

When I agreed to do a Q&A with Swoopes for the spring 2022 TEDx-Boston event at the 'Quin House, I went into my closet to pull out my later-edition Air Swoopes, an iridescent dark-blue version from the late 1990s, and took them with me to meet the basketball legend.

Because I played, I paid a little more attention to issues around basketball. I was the target market for those sneakers, and when I first became a sportswriter, my own surprise at the lack of sneaker options for women inspired an enterprise piece for the *Journal News* that ended up named in the Associated Press Sports Editors writing contest.

On that May day in Boston, my well-worn Air Swoopes were frayed and the plastic was a bit yellow with age, but Sheryl laughed when she saw them and signed them with a black Sharpie.

My nostalgia was soon punctured by Natalie White.

If you aren't familiar with the TEDx format, events are a series of elevator style pitches. Some are innovations; some are products or even just ideas. At that TEDx in Boston focused on women in sports, more than a dozen people squeezed their life stories or best ideas into a fifteen-minute kernel of spoken word performance.

The event was held in a dark hotel event space with low ceilings, and White had the energy of a kid who had grown up playing pickup in New York City. Which she did. Younger than most of the speakers, she was coiled and smart and seemed as if she could easily pick your pockets but then laugh as she gave you back your wallet before you knew it was even gone.

White explained that she started her own company, Moolah Kicks, to manufacture basketball sneakers designed for a woman's foot because there were so few options for women in the marketplace.

"I realized I was playing in boys' shoes, and so was every other female hooper," White said. "What does that message say?"

White, who graduated from Boston College in 2020, had encountered *the same problem in the same place* where I had played twenty-five years earlier. The truth is that Nike didn't make the Air Swoopes for very long and only sporadically contracted for other signature shoes from women's players until recently.

The fact that White and Swoopes took the same stage at that TEDx event was a reminder that new solutions don't ensure that problems remain solved.[1] At a time when an estimated four million girls regularly play basketball, according to a 2022 state of the industry report by the Sports and Fitness Industry Association and Sports Marketing Surveys

USA, in thirty-five years no company had found a way to sustain momentum in the shoe marketplace.[2] Girls are still settling for men's shoes; there's a disconnect between market need and product. This is an example of untapped revenue around the women's game. *Sports Business Journal* analyzed the report's findings and wrote that the number of girls playing hoops was up 13 percent in the year before the study was published.[3] That's about a third the number of boys who are defined as "core" players. But it's a larger market than boys who play tackle football or ice hockey, and there is no shortage of apparel and equipment in those sports.

We like our stories to function in a linear manner—beginning, middle, and end. Problem identified, problem addressed, problem solved. But the story of women's sports is more like a game of Chutes and Ladders.

White, by starting her own company in the early 2020s to make these sneakers, pointed out a key difference in Nike's approach to the sneaker market and her own. While Nike was building a lifestyle brand with some sneaker lines, White just wants girls and women to wear sneakers that fit on the court.

There is no stigma if a girl wears a boy's shoe, but I never saw a man on a court wearing Air Swoopes. And basketball hasn't been the only sport where this is an issue.

"I went to this presentation from Allyson Felix about the lack of research innovation and data around women's footwear," NWSL Commissioner Jessica Berman said just before the 2023 World Cup. "For example, cleats, and the fact that even sitting here right here today, female athletes are playing with footwear that are built for men. Like, they're just [men's shoes but] smaller. And my favorite quote that she said is: 'Women are not just small men.' It's, like, the best thing I've ever heard anybody say. Like, we are not just small men. Our bodies are different. The way we move is different. Our hips are different; our biomechanics are different; our hormones are different. Like, everything is different. So I think the world is getting smarter to that."

White doesn't need girls to wear her shoes to school; she needs them to wear her shoes on the court. This is about a long-term performance tool, not a high-status casual brand.

White partnered with the former Dallas Mavericks owner Mark Cuban, and her sneakers were sold in more than 140 Dicks Sporting Goods stores by 2023. Moolah Kicks has signed WNBA players to sponsorship contracts, and women's college players in name, image, and likeness (NIL) deals.

There are again major sneaker brands creating shoes for WNBA players such as Brianna Stewart, Sabrina Ionescu, and Elena Delle Donne. If you noticed something in that list—that in a league dominated by Black women the only three current players with a signature shoe are white—you wouldn't be alone. In its first high-profile sponsorship, Moolah Kicks signed the Sky's Courtney Williams in another sign that White's company will do things differently. Even in an age when other companies are catching on to the women's market, White is focused on her brand's mission.

"It's awesome that brands have decided to make one shoe for women's basketball, but what we're doing is much bigger than that," she said. "This isn't dipping a toe in and out. What Moolah is is the answer to the future of the women's market. We're creating something. It's not under another umbrella."

She's building a new house.

The size of the market for women's performance basketball shoes might not be as large as the one for men's and boys', so having similar expectations of sales and revenue would be foolish. But that doesn't mean it still isn't a significant market. When a brand such as Moolah Kicks is looking only at that market, however, rather than seeing it as an offshoot of another business, it can create opportunity.

"What I can say is the lifestyle market is the biggest category, and a lot of brands used sports to get to the lifestyle market, and we're focused on performance," White said.

The renewed interest in women's sports as a market has spurred a wave of investment and creative thinking. For some companies, that means returning to market problems that weren't completely solved, and for others, that means reimagining the way brands partner with players to reach the fans of women's sports.

It all boils down to this: if, instead of adapting an existing brand to a new market, you could remake a marketplace for fans and players in women's sports, how would that look? What would be done differently or better? This is the time.

Deirdre Maddock, Disney's vice president of sports brands solutions, had a succinct way of discussing the difference in how the marketing world has traditionally approached men's and women's sports.

"I have never in the history of my career had somebody come in to me and say, 'Hey, I'd like to get involved in *men's* sports,'" Maddock said at the espnW Women + Sports Summit in 2023. "They are coming in with specificity. They are coming in and saying, 'I want to activate in this way, with this sport, at this time of year.' But for the most part, although we've been seeing a huge influx of requests for women's sports, a lot of what we're seeing is, 'Hey, I'd like to be involved in women's sports.'"

It's time to apply that same specificity and creativity to women's games.

Rising Demand, Same Old Supply

Fans are beginning to expect to be treated like a visible, and valuable, market. When the WNBA's Los Angeles Sparks tweeted on Christmas Day in 2023 for fans to show off their gear, the responses centered on a lack of affordable merchandise for WNBA teams more generally. As @BruceTopher79 said on the social media site formerly known as Twitter, "You have people wanting to pay for merch to promote your brand yet continue to overprice and underproduce stock."

Nike made a similar miscalculation for the 2023 World Cup. England's goalkeeper Mary Earps was one of the breakout stars of the tournament, and Nike hadn't been producing or selling her kit, despite fan demand. According to *Sky News*, once it was finally made, the merchandise sold out in five minutes.[4]

"On this topic, they know they got this one wrong, and that's why they've done this correction," Earps told *Sky News*. "A big company like Nike—they wouldn't do that if they didn't know it wasn't right and that there was an injustice there."

Nike didn't forgo producing enough of a hit product out of spite or to make a social statement. Rather, it was a victim of its own low expectations—ironic for a company named after the goddess of victory. Unfortunately, this is a recurring theme. In 2019, Caitlin Murray reported that Nike had only made one thousand USWNT jerseys in the first batch.[5] The jerseys quickly sold out, and despite an attempt to meet demand, fans of the team couldn't find the merch.

"The athletic shoe and apparel companies like getting hit in the face with this, like, obvious body of evidence that if they listen to women consumers, they'd be making bank," said Professor Victoria Jackson of Arizona State University, "and they fight it and they fight it and they fight it."

And this is why a young woman like Natalie White could walk into a shoe store in 2018 and wonder where all the women's basketball shoes were.

In the past, demand could simply be ignored. Not anymore. Now, White is part of that movement to build a new house.

"The flywheel is broken at every spoke, if you will," said Thayer Lavielle, executive vice president of Wasserman's The Collective. "What an athlete makes is a piece of it. How they're supported on the court or field of play is a piece of it. How fans are able to access that is a piece of it. How they're able to visualize and express their fandom through merchandise is a piece of it. How they're able to buy a ticket and get there and be excited is . . . a piece of it. So for us, we try to do as much as we can because of the talent side of our business to educate, inform, and support our agents and our talent across music and sports to understand their own value."

Partnerships

In 2021, Victoria's Secret announced a partnership with the soccer star Megan Rapinoe. This was a brand in crisis and transition. Just a month earlier, the lingerie company had agreed to pay $90 million to address claims of a bullying and misogynistic workplace culture.

Rapinoe could see how her image might be seen as the company apologizing for those misdeeds. She is an LGBTQ icon who has not dressed for the male gaze or sought approval for her choices. However, *Forbes* estimated in 2023 that Rapinoe had made less than $1 million directly from her fifteen-year career on the soccer field.

Forbes estimated that Rapinoe had earned $7 million in her career in total, the great majority of that from endorsements. That fits with Wasserman's data point that athletes in women's sports earn 82 percent of their total income in endorsements.

During that time, Rapinoe won two World Cup gold medals, an Olympic gold medal, and the 2019 Ballon d'Or. She was a household name while taking on a whole system of low wages and sparking chants of "Equal Pay" from Broadway to the Bastille. Using *Forbes*'s estimates, Rapinoe earned roughly what an average U.S. worker made over that same period of time, which, in 2023, estimated annual wages at $59,428.

The best woman playing soccer in the world earned a salary on par with an average U.S. wage earner. Even if the numbers are inexact, that there is even an argument for comparison is astounding.

To compare, in 2023 the lowest-paid soccer players in the English Premier League (EPL) made about £10,000 per week, and, according to

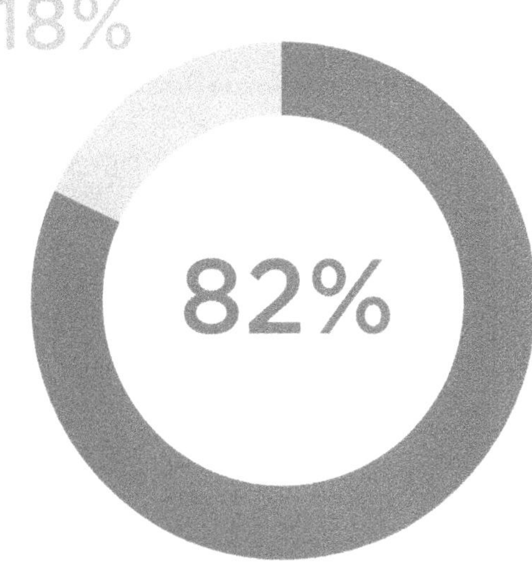

Figure 7.1: Athletes competing in women's sports rely on endorsements and partnerships for the larger portion of their income. (The Collective)

Spotrac.com, a mid-tier EPL player earned roughly $2.5 million a year that year.

These are the stakes. An athlete who is the very best in the world at her sport needs supplemental wages to be able to afford to play in many professional sports.

Thus, it is crucial for athlete representatives to find brand partnerships for their clients.

"How do you get brands into the funnel to actually care?" Lavielle said. "And then how do you help them decide what to do with that? And then how do you continue to educate them with measurement tools and stuff like that? Some brands are like, 'We're in. What should we be doing?' Others are like, 'So this whole woman thing, I don't know what to do with it. Help me.'"

In the case of Victoria's Secret, Rapinoe made no excuses for the company as she did press interviews and was frank that she felt like a misfit when it came to these kinds of partnerships.

"This world isn't made for me, this marketing machine isn't made for me," Rapinoe told me for *The Ladies Room*, my podcast with Julie DiCaro.

What Rapinoe was clear about was how much traditional brands were botching the messaging to an emerging generation that reads gender differently from their grandparents.

Rapinoe didn't bear any resemblance to a painted waif who stomped the runway in lace and underwire, so what emerged from the collaboration was different. When "The Megan Rapinoe Edit" emerged on the website, Rapinoe was wearing a cozy cotton set, with abdominal muscles front and center. This was a design meant to be wearable and comfortable.

"Listen, I'm not a fortune teller, but it's, like, I'm living in the future and I just want to tell you, 'It's OK. Everything's going to be OK. But give me the keys, and we'll take it from here,'" Rapinoe said.

"I hesitate to say that to a lot of people because I don't want to [imply], 'Oh, I know everything,' which I clearly don't. But I do know a path forward because I'm living it. I'm actually living it. I understand how you change the narrative or you flip branding on its head."

"Part of what 2020 brought us in terms of the social movement, whether companies actually believe this shit or not, they know they have to do something, they have to be better," Rapinoe told me in July 2020, before the Tokyo Olympics began. "If you don't do it in a really authentic way, the kids are coming for you, the internet is coming for you, everyone is coming for you. You can't just slap a Black Lives Matter sticker on your window and call it good. I think we really are past that, and so brands and companies and broadcasters and streaming services are trying to find a way to authentically reach people—certainly this next generation, which literally doesn't take any bullshit from anyone. So I do think [women's sports are] in a place where it is very relevant."

Maybe Rapinoe really thought she could modernize a brand such as Victoria's Secret, but she is also compelled to seek out sponsorships because the work to play women's soccer was not properly compensated during her career.

The brands that get it really get it. Given the numbers on how fans of women's sports of all genders are aware of engaged brands, and the purchasing power that women have in households, partnering with athletes in women's sports is potentially a low-cost, high-reward strategy.

The soccer player Ashlyn Harris addressed her own partnerships in the lead-up to the 2023 World Cup. It was June 7, Gotham's Pride game at Red Bull Arena, and Harris had designed her own outfit for the celebration. At the time, she was freshly retired and married to the Gotham star Ali Krieger. Harris had played her last season for Gotham the year prior. In 2017, Harris was the first female brand ambassador for the British sports equipment manufacturer Umbro, so she had seen the evolution of those partnerships and how brands have learned to treat the investment.

"For so long it was about checking a box, and the blueprint didn't work," Harris said. "It wasn't successful, so we have to pivot; we have to be transformative, not transactional."

Harris said the marketing liaison at Gotham "sat down with every single player and asked what brands they like, what they want to be a part of, what values do they stand for. Because when you bring partnerships into the equation, they want access to the players. If they believe in what we're doing, they'll want to activate so it's not so transactional. It's really paving the way for change."

That night for Pride, several brands had been at the arena to meet with players and families.

"We had our sponsors here, from Johnnie Walker and [the alcohol company] Diagio," Harris said. "The conversation is: How can we help you? What can we do better? How can we show up more for the players?"

Harris detailed that this doesn't have to be business as usual, or performative, or "give us a twirl." It can be both necessary and intentional. What goes beyond a logo on a stadium or naming rights to a facility? What draws fans and players together over shared interests and values? Women's sports and athletes are no longer in the position of having to partner with a cigarette company because it is the only one that wants their audience.

"We want to blow things out of the water because women's sports are the moment. This is the moment," Harris said. "But we have to do it right. We have to do it right by the players in that locker room."

That can go as far as stipulating who else might benefit from a sponsorship agreement.

"What I think differentiates women's sports from men's is that they're very focused on the community," Lavielle said.

Lavielle pointed to a Wasserman client, Simone Manuel, an Olympic gold medalist and eleven-time world champion in swimming. She was the first Black woman to win an individual gold in swimming for the United States. Given the history of discrimination in access to public pools, Manuel's victory acknowledged the burden of that history.

"She's able to say, 'Well, I want to make sure that my hair and makeup person understands my skin tone and my hair, and that that's something that is a non-negotiable for me,'" Lavielle said. "We have inclusion riders to make sure that there [is] a well-rounded representation of underrepresented people on set, whether those are camera people or caterers or whatever that is. And it doesn't take that much to ask. Most people are like, 'Oh, we didn't even think about that.' Of course."

There is power that comes with those contracts. Even the Victoria's Secret deal, for Rapinoe, was about the visibility of LGBTQ athletes; about expanding the idea of who gets to be in a space that was very heteronormative. Thinking beyond the immediate transaction can empower people beyond the dotted line.

"And that's really the benefit of that, this kind of lifting up of a community of women, particularly women around them, that would never have had that opportunity," Lavielle said.

Companies see the value of signing women. And in one case, the perceived "halo effect" of partnering with a female athlete came at an opportune moment.

Name, Image, and Likeness

UConn's Paige Bueckers was the first freshman to win the AP Player of the Year award and the John Wooden Award in her first year in the NCAA. The five-foot-eleven point guard averaged twenty points, 5.8 assists, and 4.9 rebounds a game as a freshman, and UConn reached the Final Four. Bueckers looked to be a generational talent on a powerhouse team.

So as she was heading into her sophomore year, Bueckers became the first college athlete Gatorade signed in the era of name, image, and likeness (NIL). It's a deal that could be worth as much as $1 million, according to the *Wall Street Journal*.

How did this come to be?

In 2021, the NCAA was desperate to keep some kind of control over college sports after several states had created laws allowing students to profit from their own NIL. A governing body that once penalized college players and teams for giving away cream cheese with a bagel was forced to reckon with a marketing system that had become a leviathan. If college football coaches could make $9 million a year, a player should be able to sign an autograph.

But fairness to athletes was not why the NCAA changed its rule at the eleventh hour in July, as those states' laws were about to take effect. No, it was because states such as California and Nebraska might then have a recruiting advantage over states without NIL laws. The NCAA wasn't recognizing what made sense in the world of big-time college sports. It was responding to internal grousing from schools that didn't want to miss out on recruits.

Some schools argued against reforming the rules of amateurism because it would upset the balance of Title IX; that men would access more resources than women. As if to defray that argument, Gatorade showed that it wouldn't just be about signing men.

NIL deals are allowing some college athletes to earn while playing, but what was meant to open cash flows to students without disrupting revenue flows to teams and conferences is upending the barely balanced NCAA system. It is likely the NCAA will create additional rules, but given the amount of money now in the system, it would be difficult to cut players completely out of the equation again.

New Business Opportunities

There is opportunity in these disrupted systems. For women's sports, that means creative new business.

Portland's Sports Bra, a bar that showcases and broadcasts women's games in a friendly market, is one of these. After being the only sports bar in the country that primarily showed women's sports, the company announced in April 2024 that it planned to franchise the popular concept.

Ellen Hyslop is a cofounder of another new media business: *The Gist*. She noted how much things had changed since she and her two cofounders started their media enterprise in 2017. For Hyslop, the content is only part of the change. The delivery hardware throughout the category is also evolving. When rethinking the structures that would better fit the women's games, she also wants to think about emerging technology.

"It is night and day," Hyslop said. "I'm really proud that, hopefully, *The Gist* is part of that change and is a part of, hopefully, changing some people's minds with respect to women's sports. I really think that there still is a very long way to go, but I'm really encouraged and energized and excited about the current changes with women's sports. I think what is going to be very interesting for the sports industry on the whole is how technology is going to impact sports and how different audiences react and relate to sports."

This is all part of the new house. It took men's professional sports decades to find an audience, but their modern success is used as a yardstick pulled out again and again to declare that just-formed women's teams are coming up short. But that's not a judgment that women's teams and leagues have to accept. As Dawn Staley communicated on her T-shirt in December 2023 as she coached South Carolina, "Everyone Watches Women's Sports."

Being on board with that as a company sends a message to consumers and helps to support a growth industry. In the summer of 2023, the *Barbie* movie and blockbuster concert tours by Beyoncé and Taylor Swift showed that women and girls are an economic force.

There are those who have seen this coming. When Rapinoe was telling companies she could see the future, she really wasn't far off.

"Now, that certainly doesn't mean that everything changes overnight," Rapinoe said. "There is still funding that needs to happen and resources that need to be allotted and structures and systems that need to be built to allow women's sports to grow at the rate they really should be growing. We've had cinderblocks tied to our feet for all these years."

Cinderblocks tied to our feet.

"We've been ready," Rapinoe insisted.

8

INVESTING IN WOMEN

The Set-Up for League Success

They'll know you by your cathedrals.

The office of NWSL Commissioner Jessica Berman is a work in progress during a July morning in 2023. The space has start-up vibes, from the concrete floors and exposed brick and spare interiors to the stone façade views outside the retro arched New York City windows. Alexis Ohanian, the founder of Reddit and an investor in the league, had been at the Midtown East space earlier in the day to see the fresh quotes painted on the white walls, including one by his wife, the tennis icon Serena Williams. Ohanian repeatedly used the word "bullish" when he met with the crew at the NWSL's headquarters, which would be a good tagline for the league's current moment.

"Bullish" was the right term, referring to a market trend that is on the rise. Ohanian imparted a message that stuck with Berman and her staff.

"If you as an American close your eyes and say, like, 'When I think of greatness in the sport of soccer,' what comes to mind? You will think of women," Berman recounted. "It's one of the only sports where that is true. And you will think of American women. It is etched into the minds of multiple generations in our country, which presents such a unique opportunity to be able to convert that into fandom and a real thriving business because women are actually thought of as the equivalent of great."

The NWSL is in ultra-growth mode, looking to expand from twelve teams to sixteen by the time the men's World Cup hits American soil in 2026.

Berman came to women's soccer after a career spent mostly in men's professional leagues, such as the NHL and the National Lacrosse League. When she first arrived, there was a new book waiting for her at her desk by Suzanne Wrack: *A Woman's Game*.

The book details the overwhelming popularity of women's soccer during World War I in the United Kingdom. Men were at war, and women were stepping into nontraditional roles, working in factories and playing sports.[1]

"It was the story following World War I where women's soccer, women's football was deemed illegal, literally, by the country," Berman said. "And that policy was exported into other European countries, all out of fear that [the enthusiasm for female athletes] would potentially surpass the success of the men. When the men were coming back from fighting in World War I, because the women were starting to draw forty thousand or fifty thousand a game, . . . the legislation actually says, which she cites in the book, that the reason was that women's bodies are too fragile and they can't get hurt because they have to be childbearing."

The ban in England wasn't lifted until 1971. The work of women's sports leagues today has to undo the work of generations against it in laws, in language—even the word to describe the optimism in the space, "bullish," has connotations tied to men's success—in economics, and in culture.

Or, as Megan Rapinoe put it, *cinderblocks tied to our feet*.

This is a kind of history that Berman wouldn't have encountered in her work with men's hockey or lacrosse. Men in sports simply don't face this kind of opposition. Men's leagues may (and do) fail; there may be unpopular people or economic constraints on men's sports. But there is no cultural opposition to the idea of men playing sports for money. And there is certainly no official prohibition.

"It's the first book someone gave me when I got this job," Berman said, "and it blew my mind. It has stuck with me from the perspective of, we have to be careful because history could very easily repeat itself. And some of the systemic barriers and challenges in culture, like, are all around."

Berman's task is to make sure history doesn't repeat itself—not just legal history, but the history of U.S. women's soccer leagues.

Soccer has been an outlier in the United States. Although it is the most popular sport in Europe and many parts of the rest of the globe, the sport languished in the United States, with inconsistent popularity on the professional men's side at the same time the NBA and the NFL started to gain traction in the 1970s and '80s.

The Women's World Cup launched in 1991, and American women have won four of those titles. The highest American soccer ratings have come from women's games. The players are household names. This is the excellence that Berman and Ohanian were discussing earlier in the day.

But a professional domestic league has not captured the lightning of that event and bottled it.

After the USWNT won the Women's World Cup in 1999, two professional American soccer leagues were founded and folded.

Those failed leagues are a reminder that it isn't enough to have enthusiasm, or investors who contribute in the spirit of charitable donation. Economics Professor Andrew Zimbalist of Smith College describes the short-term mindset after 1999, arguing that a league's success requires a prolonged engagement and sustainable infrastructure.

"The women won the World Cup, and Brandi Chastain pulled her shirt off, and all these men thought, 'Wow, this is good stuff. People are going to really dig this,'" Zimbalist said. "So they invested in this women's soccer league, and then they realized that it wasn't that simple. Then the league collapsed, and they weren't willing to put any more money into it. So if you can make the argument to male investors that this is simple and all we need to do is put a little seed money to this and you're going to get rich, then you get enough jerks who go along with it. But then they realize that it wasn't true. You have to put a lot of resources into this if you're going to start a new league."

Meanwhile, MLS, the American men's soccer league founded in 1996, has enjoyed sustained investment, despite similar challenges attracting fans and coverage. Keep in mind that the men's league lacks the success of the women on the international stage, but MLS capital was there for the long game.

Only now is the NWSL achieving the same.

"If we calibrated women's sports success on the basis of how much has been invested and the number of years, you might actually be like, 'Oh, wow! It's incredible how far it's come,'" Berman said. "And now that investment's actually happening at the right levels, you're finally seeing the impact of that."

So Berman's challenge is one of investment. Given the history of attempts and failures that seem to support the trope of apathy around women's sports, the success of the NWSL would provide much-needed proof of concept that an American women's league can take its rightful place among the most watched leagues in the sports landscape, not just every four years at the World Cup.

But that goal became so important that those same players were tacitly asked to endure abusive coaching environments at some of the teams in the NWSL.

For players, this created a dilemma: do you complain about treatment publicly when you know it could mean that another soccer league fails? Or do you endure a workplace that is unacceptable, that undermines the very values and goals that it purports to represent, in hope for the success of those values?

"For years, to remain part of a team, women had to put up with this stuff," said Karen Weaver, an adjunct assistant professor at the University of Pennsylvania and an expert on sports and leadership. She pointed to the coaches who would be forced off of one team, only to find purchase at another. "And then those men keep getting hired because they have experience."

Players spoke out, and an investigation into allegations was done. In 2022, the NWSL and NWSL Players Association released a damning report: about half of the teams in the league were not providing a work environment these players deserved.[2]

Specifically, the report stated: "The Joint Investigative Team found that the underlying culture of the NWSL created fertile ground for misconduct to go unreported. Players were frequently reminded of the fragility and financial instability of the League. From the early days of the League, they were told to be grateful, loyal, and acquiescent, even as they were not afforded the resources or respect due to professional athletes. Players told the Joint Investigative Team that this environment dissuaded them from reporting misconduct. Compounding this effect, the League lacked trainings, policies, and other resources on harassment, abuse, and other forms of misconduct. Players and staff members alike were often unsure of whether behavior rose to the level of misconduct and, even if they were able to identify behavior as misconduct, where to report it."

As if it wasn't hard enough to get a women's league off the ground, this toxicity might have been the final chapter.

Berman was hired with a mandate to transform this tarnished brand, with all its potential investment and hope and the tangle of broken promises, into the professional women's soccer league that America has deserved for decades.

She arrived to greet a player population homed in the fight for equal pay with U.S. Soccer and frustrated by abusive locker room conditions in a league that should have been home. Would anyone be able to right this ship? Could she?

Investment Culture

Berman is dealing with the very real concerns of her players and today's investment momentum. But she is also mindful of the history of failure and investor reluctance. As we've discussed, investors assess the promise of success based on the cultural assumptions about who has value in the sports space.

The comment by Molly Tissenbaum, research analyst at Sports Innovation Lab, about the lack of data around the women's sports market being a data point in itself still echoes.

Economics Professor Dave Berri of Southern Utah State University says the decisions about whether or not to invest come with this historical baggage.

"It is not the case [in] women's sports that the outcomes are driven solely by supply and demand and an impersonal marketplace," Berri said. "That is definitely not true. There is a history that makes a big difference. There's a history of discrimination. When it comes to private investment, it's very clear men are biased toward men. Men are doing most of the investing because they have most of the money, and they are mostly choosing men's sports.

"They don't invest in women's sports at the same intensity. You can see that with the investment in Major League Soccer or the investment in minor league football. The fact that minor league sports get hundreds of millions of dollars in investment when there's no money in it tells you that men are not choosing this based on market fundamentals."

And the inherent failure of one men's league doesn't have a negative effect on other leagues in a similar category—much less on the entire category of men's sports.

"When somebody goes and invests $10 million in the [Xtreme Football League (XFL)], nobody bats an eyelash and says, 'Nobody cares about the XFL,'" Tissenbaum said. "Even though that's kind of true. Nobody really cares about spring football. That's not when we as a society have deemed it important."

The XFL relaunched in the spring of 2023, underwritten by Disney and RedBird Capital Partners and fronted by Dwayne "The Rock" Johnson and his business partner Dany Garcia. A *Forbes* article by Jabari Young written after the May 13, 2023, championship game cited $60 million in losses that season, according to industry sources. ESPN is paying the league $20 million a year to broadcast XFL games.[3]

The WNBA's deal with ESPN that year was worth $12 million a year, according to *Sports Media Watch*.

"There's an emotion gap between men and women," Berri said about sports league investment. "Men make investments in men's sports based on emotion. It's not based on profit-and-loss statements. But when it comes to women's sports, they invest as if they're investing in a cardboard factory. That's the way I put it. They look at it like it's a Taco Bell. It's like, 'I'm buying a business, and I'm hoping it'll generate a profit. And if it doesn't, then I'll get upset and leave.' The amount of time they give women's sports to generate a profit is far too small for it ever to have a profit. You would not have a profit in a professional sports league in the first twenty, thirty years. It just doesn't happen."

Where men's sports might have an inherent emotional appeal to investors, women's sports are appealing to reason. They've had to develop the data and measure the fan engagement and the marketplace. Leaders such as Berman can then make the pitch.

League Valuation

One of the arguments that has sway when it comes to women's sports is the idea of potential. The great jump in the value of an NFL team happened in the 2000s as the league maximized its broadcast contracts. The NFL's Dallas Cowboys jumped 20 percent in one year to a market valuation of $9.2 billion, according to a *Sportico* look at NFL franchise values.[4] In 2020, the Cowboys were worth $6.43 billion, according to the same equation.

That's a great return on investment and one that isn't tied to the stock market. With just thirty-two NFL teams, those billionaire owners aren't giving up their assets with any frequency. There are only so many NFL teams, NHL teams, and so on.

A women's team franchise won't have the same ceiling, but in terms of the potential investment and the future valuations, an investor might do very well. With expansion and a broadcast deal on the horizon, valuations could quickly rise.

Kelsey Trainor is a lawyer, a longtime women's sports advocate, and chief strategy officer for the Wrexham Association Football Club (AFC) owner Rob McElhenney's new investment venture.

"Everyone and their mother is trying to get in right now," Trainor said. "I think it's because people are finally waking up to the low buy-in compared to the men and the potential return on investment. Women's sports are just on the ground floor in a skyscraper, and the elevator is going up. I think that's good and bad, to be honest. Women's sports need to have viable and sustainable growth."

Zimbalist discussed the balance between short- and long-term views in terms of the WNBA.

"They have to be deep, deep, patient pockets," Zimbalist said. "If you really want to develop something, you have to deal with the culture; you have to deal with promotion and advertising. So it shouldn't be just the reflection of today's marketplace. It should be the reflection of what the marketplace could be."

"[Sports have] typically been non-correlated to the market," said Nadia Rawlinson, chair and co-owner of the Chicago Sky. "If you think it is a hedge in your portfolio against other investments you may be making, it's great. And it's had greater returns than the market over the last decade or so. So getting in would be great if you can. That's still one of those places where you still can make a pretty hefty return over time."

At the moment of our meeting in her New York office, Berman was looking to expand the league, seeking out new team owners and new markets, and to negotiate a new broadcast deal—or a series of deals, given the fragmented market—all of which would allow her to invest back into her players. The U.S. women's professional league wasn't the only one trying to make a go of it. There were professional leagues in Brazil, Colombia, France, Germany, Italy, Japan, Mexico, Nigeria, and the United Kingdom, to name a few countries.

There may have been a time where a U.S. league could have drawn worldwide talent to the United States, but not by the time of our meeting. Britain's

EPL, Germany's Bundesliga, and Italy's Serie A were all vying for top talent. Thanks to Title IX, the United States may have had a head start when the Women's World Cup debuted in 1991, but the world had caught up.

The NWSL needed to go big and do it fast.

Once the NWSL assessed the case of its own value, it raised the demand for future owners. In January 2023, the *Wall Street Journal* broke the news that the NWSL's franchise fee had jumped from $2 million to $50 million for new franchises in the Bay Area and Boston.[5] Women's leagues traditionally have found momentum in large international events, and with North America hosting the men's World Cup in 2026, a clock was ticking. Expand, negotiate, and play.

It wasn't a coincidence that the NWSL and the WNBA were both talking about expanding the number of teams in the league as they were in the process of negotiating their broadcast deals. That's when life-changing money can arrive. Think about the NCAA men's basketball tournament in 1991. The $1 billion, seven-year deal with CBS ushered in the modern college sports era.[6] Love it or not, a broadcast deal can solidify a league and make invested parties rich.

For Emma Schilling, a consultant at Sportsology Group who delves into the data around the investment space in women's sports, expansion in anticipation of a broadcast deal is a matter of simple math.

"If you add more teams, you add more games to your season," Schilling said. "[That's] more of a lever when you're negotiating your broadcasting deal."

Finding the Right Investor

The audiences are growing, and the ratings are going up, but women's sports still pull a smaller audience than men's sports. The success of men's leagues has been enormous, with the value of NFL teams and NFL broadcast deals skyrocketing year after year. That's a tough set of expectations to hold any new league to, and that anchor point has proved detrimental to selling new owners on joining the WNBA or the NWSL.

"That's what everyone thinks about when they think about success in sports. Like, it is the golden medal," Schilling said. "It's the icon. What we think about when we think about American sports is American football. It's not going to be the case for other leagues regardless."

Women's leagues may not approach the NFL (and neither do American men's leagues), but if women's leagues could position themselves for a more lucrative contract for broadcast rights, with invested and committed ownership groups, it would change the game. Although the WNBA has had the advantage of the NBA's backing, there has not been stability for women's leagues in soccer, hockey, and elsewhere.

The NWSL is growing, expanding, and Berman is mindful that the most sustainable investment comes not only from the highest bid for the team. Leagues are curating ownership now; they've learned the lessons from past eras. It's not just about investing but about a continued commitment and one that is mindful of the sensibilities of players who fought for equal pay in the national context, for humane coaching, and for environments free of abuse.

"So you get a billionaire who wants a women's team because of low buy-in and the prestige factor, but then how is the team run?" Trainor asks. "What is the environment like for those players?"

Berman has been thinking about that. Players need to have locker rooms and training facilities that don't feel cut-rate.

"When we think about expansion and when we think about having the opportunity to write our future script, that is a very key priority for us," Berman said. "While we have leverage in a negotiation and we're inviting you to the table, we're going to require that you have a plan and it's an appropriate plan for the future so that these athletes can train and play at a place that will allow them to thrive."

So it's often not about trying to find the traditional billionaire owners of men's teams and convincing them to add a women's team to the portfolio and compare its numbers to theirs. It's about attracting a new owner altogether who cares about women's sports and understands the different kind of commitment required.

Or better yet, it's about reinventing ownership altogether. The NWSL's Angel City franchise, with Julie Foudy, Brandy Chastain, Mia Hamm, Natalie Portman, and Serena Williams, is a model that other ownership groups are following. Julie Uhrman is the team's president and, fortunately, is looking to give away the roadmap for Angel City's success.

Kara Nortman, an Angel City cofounder, and Jasmine Robinson developed the first investment fund for women's sports in 2023 and named it the Monarch Collective. Nortman, the brains behind constructing the Angel City investment group, was a venture capitalist who was beginning to think about what a legacy might mean.

The idea for Monarch came when Nortman was taking her first family trip abroad after the COVID-19 pandemic ended, she told the women at the 2023 espnW Women + Sports Summit, which was livestreamed to listeners remotely. Nortman's family was taking a guided tour, and she was looking at massive gothic churches, a thousand years old, that had required several generations to build.

But there the stones and buttresses still stood, all this time later.

Seeing that sort of creative legacy led Nortman to quit her job as a managing partner and start Monarch with Robinson. The fund had raised $140 million to invest in leagues and teams.

"They're probably not going to know our name," Nortman said, "but they're going to see what cathedral we build."

Remember what Foudy said about the attitude of that Angel City ownership group in the Introduction: "Let's kick some ass, let's go."

That was at the start.

"We got in at, what, $3 million?" Foudy said. "That's how much it's changed in two years. And you have to think, like, that model played a huge role. What's so cool is that the group always wants to— Like, Julie Uhrman will sit with anyone to share the story and how they did it and, like, 'Hey, let's create a roadmap for others.' Natalie [Portman says] the same thing. I mean, like, they're so giving. It's not like, 'Oh, this is our thing.' It's like, 'No. We want this to propagate and procreate.'"

Foudy, who conducted that interview with Nortman and Robinson in Ojai, California, in October 2023 feels the energy around women's sport in a more deliberate way.

"That's, like, $140 million they've raised that's going to go solely to women's sports," Foudy said. "I was on a call with them the other day, and they said we couldn't have done that two years ago. I asked, 'Why couldn't you have done it?' [They answered,] 'Well, the world hadn't woken up to, like, where we are in women's sports and that it's actually a really good investment for not a lot of money."

The area is ripe for disruption, and Schilling points to a change in the mindset around investments more generally. It's patient capital around women's sports, but with the expectation of a return because the ceiling is so much higher than in men's sports.

"The professionalism of the ownership groups in sports in general has changed immensely," Schilling said. "You look at how many people are in multi-asset groups now or they're deciding it's a good idea to purchase a

European football team. People are really, really thinking strategically about investment, not just holding on to this asset forever and being a family-owned business."

Schilling continued: "If you're a professional investor, you're going to want a return on the investment. But they also know that you don't just invest in it expecting that the universe around you is going to provide that return. They're going to continue to invest. It's not just the upfront dollar amount and an expansion fee that you're paying for that team. You're going to continue to invest in it. You're going to build out an entire marketing team for this asset. And that's what feeds the profit."

The NWSL is actively balancing the need to find the right partners with the urgency to grow.

"I come from a very traditional training on professional sports leagues from like the days of [former NBA Commissioner] David Stern and [NHL Commissioner] Gary Bettman," Berman said. "And sixteen teams is a milestone; . . . in the history of sports, [it has always been] described as a milestone. So it's a very important milestone for us to get to and to do it in concert with this very incredible moment in time when the world is going to be paying attention to the United States and the sport in particular. And I do believe that because of the cultural relevance of women and girls right now more broadly, even outside of sports, the World Cup being here will be about more than just boys and men. It's going to cast a halo effect on the sport here. And we believe that there's a lot we can do to invite those tailwinds into our league intentionally."

This was where Berman related the potential of the NWSL, with the World Cup coming to the United States, to the imperative of cleaning up the toxicity in its own ranks.

"It's part of the reason that the board made the decision a year ago to double down and invest in the league when the history of the league presented real obstacles and challenges to the league growth," Berman said. "I wasn't in the room, but I believe I could imagine that there was a crossroads to say, 'OK, we have a big problem to solve, and we know it's worth it. How are we going to get there?' And, you know, the board made the decision to hire me, to empower me to hire."

"To the credit of Jessica Berman and [USWNT Executive Director] Becca Roux, there's a tide that has shifted a bit, and that's the players' knowing their value and worth," said Kelsey Trainor, who has paid skeptical attention to how the NWSL has responded to the challenge. "That has existed on the men's side because of their contracts and money, and it's easy to afford a lawyer. Women have always been told any bad thing they say about the league . . . will [cause it to] go under.

"We're going to have to be cognizant not to let toxic ecosystems grow in the women's sports space," Trainor said.

That the NWSL managed an internal fight for survival and values while positioning the league for historic levels of external investment is impressive.

Finding owners ready to face the reality of issues, whether historical missteps or structural inequities, is happening in other spaces, too. The WNBA is hardly a start-up, but what is new about that legacy women's league is the attitude of the newly invested owners and leaders.

The Sky's Nadia Rawlinson says that financial independence isn't just important in a business sense; it is crucial to truly empower women's leagues and athletes.

"I'm a capitalist and I'm a businesswoman and I do recognize that to get credibility in the broader business world, being able to stand on your own two feet is important," Rawlinson said, "and, I think, specifically for women. I see this in the world of business. When you think about pay equity gaps and women, equal work for equal pay—like, those types of things just in the private sector or public sector—you have some of those broader issues.

". . . I've been the lonely only in almost every room I've been in in my entire life. So this is not new. But this is one of the things that sort of shuts down the conversation when you can say, 'We're financially viable. We can stand on our own two feet. We can fund our own operations from our day-to-day revenue that we're bringing in.'"

Angel City is what everyone wants to talk about as the model for a modern ownership group. Laura Ricketts, whose family owns the Chicago Cubs and has a stake in the WNBA Sky, has brought a group of women to the NWSL by buying the tarnished Red Stars franchise in Chicago and buying out everyone, including the sportswriter and broadcaster Sarah Spain.

"There are just more women who are in a position where they can invest in major sports properties," Molly Tissenbaum said. "The ability and the availability of that kind of disposable income for women is obviously going to be a few decades behind men for a whole host of societal reasons that would require four or five other books to be written."

And many of the women investing are athletes. WNBA players, NWSL players, and tennis players are supporting one another through investment strategies. It's a way of showing support from the next generation of players.

"When you look back at the history of women's sports leagues, people's hearts were in the right place, but they shouldn't be owning a business. They treated it like a charity or a hobby," Trainor said. "Now we have people who are the full package. They have the right motivation and the money."

Many athletes began to invest without the expectation of massive profit, but this money is part of a movement. So, not a charity, but working capital. Capital that communicates value.

"For somebody like Naomi Osaka or Serena Williams or whoever . . . [to] say, 'I'm going to take some of my hard-earned dollars and invest in women's sports,' to me that is the same sort of validation as what you get ultimately from male athletes," Tissenbaum said. "But I think there's something to be said for just the number of women who are able to make those kinds of investments and own the business of women's sports. That to me, again, as somebody who grew up— I can distinctly remember the first time I saw the Team Canada hockey team play in person. And I can remember the first time I heard about a woman who was working in the front office in professional sports. And same thing goes for investing. The reason Angel City is such a lightning rod is it's so unlike anything we've seen, where there's a group of women who said, 'We're going to do this. And if you guys want to jump in on this, come along for the ride.'"

Sponsorships

League valuations are part of the picture. The other driver in financial success is sponsorship, essentially an investment made by a company to gain access to the fans of an athlete, team, or sport.

So let's look at that part of the investment space through the eyes of Thayer Lavielle. In 2019 she launched The Collective at the Wasserman agency to focus on athletes in women's sports. Wasserman had strong clients in the space through longtime agents such as Dan Levy and Lindsay Kagawa Colas and others and could leverage a host of relationships and assets in service of the women they worked with. Focusing on women could be *the* business.

"When we launched The Collective, it was like, 'Well, if we're going to go and be the experts on women, we better be the experts on women,'" Lavielle said. "Other than being a woman, what else do I need to know? And so it was really about how do we start to dive into that research. And the research came about looking at who is she as a consumer—as a fan, as a mom, as a spender, as a media target, as a fan of music versus football versus basketball versus whatever—and trying to understand this nuance that are women."

It's particularly important because athletes who compete in women's sports earn 82 percent of their total income through endorsements, a much larger percentage than for men. The Collective makes matches between those athletes who rely on that income stream and the many audiences their corporate clients are looking to reach. Representing a host of clients in professional leagues and Olympic sports and across national boundaries, The Collective's ability to deliver depends on what's available on the menu.

"Integrate women into your marketing campaigns," read one digital billboard on Lavielle's LinkedIn page. The next item shared a recent statistic reported by the Space Between Agency, finding that only 35 percent of fans of men's sports recall the brands they've seen during games, compared with 65 percent of fans of women's sports—or nearly twice as many.[7]

Before the 2023 Women's World Cup, a poll conducted by Seton Hall University asked sports fans whether they followed the branding in women's sports.[8] The higher the level of self-described fandom, the more they cared. Fifty-six percent of avid fans said their opinion about brands increased when those brands advertised around women's soccer.

"People rarely admit to being impacted by advertising or sponsorship, but the underlying sales figures tend to differ," said Seton Hall's Marketing Professor Daniel Ladik, the author of the poll. "The interest in soccer and the growth in women's sports has clearly attracted the eyes of advertisers. Garnering the stated approval of 38 percent of the sports fans in the United States is no small thing."

These findings allow Lavielle to show why today's female athlete is more valuable to corporations—and particularly to certain corporations looking for certain audiences.

"The way that traditional sports look at the ecosystem is in the Four Horsemen: viewership, sponsorship, merch, and attendance," Lavielle said. "That is the healthy ecosystem of a sports world. But when you're the underdog or you're the new guy and you're trying to establish an entirely new economy like women's sports— And by the way, in a very different time. Fandom has shifted. Fans now are not watching three-hour football games. They are younger; they are less tethered to their televisions. They are more tethered to their SnapChat *SportsCenter* highlights. It's just a totally different world. The athletes are the superstars, not the teams and not the leagues. So I think women have really tapped into what that is."

Again, The Collective is making the rational case to potential partners and trying to excite them about the unique possibilities of female athletes through a sales pitch that values business equity beyond gender equity.

"You see [at] every single game there is a large attendance; the NWSL is posting it, and the WNBA is posting it," Emma Schilling of Sportsology Group said. "Everyone wants to tell every sponsor everything. . . . At the end of the day, [treating women's sports like charity is] not going to be enough. These sponsors are investing in this because the numbers are going up because there's proof. Whether you're an Instagram content creator or you're a professional sports organization, you have to show sponsors the numbers for them to ultimately invest and advertise through you. So what's really going on is they are increasing their attendance numbers, they're increasing the visibility."

"The whole ecosystem is evolving," Lavielle said. "And women's sports, we truly believe, is the new economy. Like, get in early because it's only going to go up. So get in early on your sponsorships; get in early on your relationships with these individual athletes, these groupings of athletes, these special clubs. A whole new hockey system is being established. Get in there because it might be a longer game, but it will win. It just will win. People are completely running up and supporting it now."

Put more succinctly, Lavielle is building a new house.

If Wasserman's athletes need more sponsorship dollars to get paid, they will build that market. While the ratings and attendance numbers rise, Lavielle and others are evangelizing the coming marketplace.

There are trickier questions to be addressed. How does the right to profit from NIL change the marketplace for women in college sports? Are those opportunities equitable to men's?

And should there be a category of product that is off-limits?

Sue Anstiss, who is watching the marketplace develop in the United Kingdom, would like to see some things done differently. As money from Saudi Arabia makes a play for athletes and leagues, she'd like to see standards, even if it means delaying the payoff for all of this investment. Saudi Arabia, which has a track record of human rights abuses and discrimination against women and LGBTQ people, is angling to buy the PGA Tour and bidding to host the WTA Finals in 2023.

"Where do you draw your line on what's appropriate in sports sponsorship?" Anstiss said.

Building a Cathedral

Berman had her staff pick some of the quotes for the walls of their new office space. The exercise is a way to communicate value for their contributions, but it is also a way to invest in a space that is impressive and well designed. It's not grand; it's more like hungry and intentional. You can't operate the league they are quickly aiming to be out of a closet. In a post-pandemic world, it's important to have a place to collaborate and host players and clients.

"We've now tripled the size of the league office in one year," Berman said, "which is a beautiful—granted, very start-up feel—office here in New York on Madison Avenue. [We're] showing up in the world like the professional league we believe we are. And I think setting those foundational pieces, [such as] investing in our own brand and our marketing and our communications [and] thinking about the things behind the curtain that make our league the best in the world, . . . [is] ensuring that the players have a safe and positive and professional environment to play and train. And ensuring that our owners, legacy owners, and new owners understand the expectations of them when they're investing in women's sports. They need to be set up for success."

And here's where the lessons of her first year on the job coalesced into the point of it all.

Three months after that meeting, on the weekend of the NWSL Championship game, Berman's name splashed into the headlines as the league announced its new broadcast deal.

The NWSL partnered with CBS, ESPN, Scripps, and Amazon, with the league getting a historic $240 million for the four-year deal. The multi-prong package included traditional, streaming, and nontraditional partners, at once solid and innovative.

But most important, that revenue is money to grow.

That's a shorter deal than most in the space. But Berman is betting on the value of her league going up during a stretch when the United States will be at the center of the global soccer universe. It's risky. It's bold. But what would be the point of playing it safe when the wave could be just about to crest?

9

FINDING ALLIES

You're a Warhol. . . .

Nadia Rawlinson was hunting for investors in early 2023. As the newly named operating chairman of the Chicago Sky, coming into the WNBA from leadership roles in Silicon Valley, Rawlinson was trying to match the team with investors of a certain sensibility.

The Sky were the reigning WNBA champions, and in New York the league was in the middle of a $75 million capital raise. Investors were starting to understand the value of investing in the WNBA, so there was not only opportunity but also the challenge of finding partnerships that made sense.

The face of the average investor was changing. Instead of legacy investors in men's sports, women's sports teams were attracting new people.

Rawlinson said there are three main types of potential investors she's encountered in women's sports. There is the person for whom this is an ego play—and I'll add that you see this frequently in men's sports. There are others who come into the space because they have a daughter who plays sports or look at women's sports as a charitable part of the portfolio.

And then there are the new investors, who see women's sports as a patient investment and who like the sport and the athletes who play.

People such as Rawlinson.

One of the challenges with the business of women's sports was that the people who most believed in them didn't have the money to buy and maintain professional sports teams. Most of the billionaires in the United States have been men. The WNBA's original ownership strategy in 1997 was to assign WNBA teams to a portion of its NBA owners. Some wanted and invested in both their men's and women's basketball teams. Others lost interest in the women's team, if it was ever truly there. Not only is the business of owning a woman's sports team different from that of owning a men's team, the appeal of ownership—the dream of owning a sports franchise and what it meant to those with access to it—was different. And for many men who want to own a sports team, the appeal is the association they maintain between sports and masculinity.

But that may be changing.

At forty-three, Rawlinson was looking for a new opportunity after a career at Slack, Live Nation, and Google Ventures, helping Silicon Valley companies develop workplace cultures. With a degree from Stanford and then an MBA from Harvard Business School, Rawlinson was sought after for her acumen on corporate and nonprofit boards. She was used to being the Black woman in a room.

When the time came to choose her next area of focus, after Salesforce bought Slack for $27 billion, Rawlinson had a moment to consider.

"I was in a position to make different decisions about where my time was best spent," she said. "And I had a couple of first principles that guided this next chapter of my life, which were [that] I wanted to build and shape institutions for what I thought the future should be. And I think sports is an institution. It's one of the few things in the world that defines and shapes culture and crosses class lines, race lines, nationalities. It's a visceral, emotional experience that connects people. But outside of shaping institutions, I care a lot about women and seeing women win.

"I care a lot about social justice and equity," Rawlinson continued. "And in a women's league that is primarily minority, African American, and a high percentage of people that identify as LGBTQIA, I thought the very existence of the WNBA was predicated on this notion of equality and authenticity. So, if there's a way that I can do my work and bring my experience to bear on something that can be impactful and influential, the WNBA—and specifically the Chicago Sky—was a place I could do it. That's how I was attracted to the opportunity."

So screening investors is for her a process of shaping an institution for the future. As she considers investors, she must ask herself, is all money created equally? She started to sort potential investors into buckets—passion, ego, philanthropy—but she still felt as if something was missing.

At a crucial moment in the process of assessing her new landscape, she had a conversation on Zoom with Marc Lasry, a co-owner of the Milwaukee Bucks and a private equity manager. Both of them were at pivotal moments with their franchises: Lasry was selling, and Rawlinson was looking for investors.

She recalled their conversation:

"Nadia, I'm going to change your investment thesis."

"OK, so what is this?"

"You need to value yourself like a piece of art."

That's when Lasry moved his laptop so she could see the Warhol hanging in his house and continued.

"You have to look at the franchise as people's willingness to pay. People will pay for this Warhol. You think of yourself as a Warhol."

Lasry was right. It completely changed Rawlinson's strategy. She went from appealing to investors' egos, hobbies, and philanthropy to seeking out those who saw the value she did.

"So that's where I really segmented my investors into those three buckets and then focused on the buckets where people thought that we were the Warhol," Rawlinson said. "And that's where we won."

Scaling the Idea

Like so many who work in women's sports, Rawlinson is looking for allies. They might be people who can be convinced to lend space, cash, prestige, and advice. And many of those allies in the sports space will be men. For the most part, men still control resources. They are the billionaires that Ilana Kloss mentioned earlier who have the money and can be brought to the table.

But as Rawlinson proved, some are already sitting there and happy to help.

There are plenty of genuine allies in sports—people who use their clout to open new doors to new rooms where people might otherwise have looked at you skeptically. Look at Mark Cuban's enthusiasm about Moolah Kicks. Or Scott Pioli's work around the NFL and team front offices. Jon

Patricof and Jonathan Soros of Athletes Unlimited and the NBA players Kevin Durant and Stephen Curry. All have been helpful in keeping space for women at the tables of sports industry.

"It's never the male athletes who are the ones saying nobody cares about women sports," Sports Innovation Lab's Molly Tissenbaum said. "They're the ones buying the orange hoodie and showing up and sitting courtside and touting how impressive these athletes are. It's the people who have no concept of women's sports as a whole that are saying nobody cares about women's sports."

But those people might be persuaded to follow the lead of influential players such as Durant and Tom Brady, the former NFL quarterback who has invested in the WNBA's Las Vegas Aces, owned by the Raiders' owner Mark Davis.

"The nice thing is we're seeing more of those ownership groups that are getting involved for the right reasons," Tissenbaum said. "Something like Tom Brady investing in the Aces, to me that's incredibly meaningful because you've got millions and millions of NFL fans who have followed his entire career who now have a reason to think about the WNBA and they never did before, . . . [It may be] their first entry point to thinking about, 'If the GOAT [Greatest of All Time] thinks that this is real sports and it's an investment, perhaps it's an investment.'"

Billie Jean King and Kloss have talked about the traditional access point for men: the determination to provide opportunities to their own daughters. It's a good entry point. But that isn't enough to find sustained investment at the scale currently envisioned.

"This isn't a cause," Rawlinson said. "This is a business. And that's the way that I've approached how we look at the types of investors we want to be aligned with."

The WNBA has what most other American women's leagues don't have, and that's stability. The stalwart, sometimes stodgy NBA has been the benefactor and bane of women's basketball, but there wouldn't be a Warhol if it hadn't been for David Stern.

Origin Stories

When Val Ackerman was growing up in New Jersey in the 1960s, she wanted to be a lawyer. She'd seen one on TV arguing in front of the Supreme Court. Her father and grandfather had been athletic directors in high school, and she played basketball in college, so by the time she got to law school in the early 1980s, her career goal had been amended to being a lawyer in sports.

There was just no career guide for Ackerman, who is now the first woman to hold the title of Big East Commissioner. Title IX was instituted in 1972, and it was initially meant to open colleges and graduate schools to women. By the time she graduated from the University of California, Los Angeles (UCLA), School of Law, women were entering the legal field, but few were in leadership roles at those law schools and firms. She was hired by the NBA to work on men's basketball at a time when the league had roughly one hundred people, and Commissioner David Stern, even then, was looking to diversify the staff.

"The senior management team was all men. People I worked for were guys. They had wives that didn't work," Ackerman said. "I was literally the first woman at the NBA who worked on men's basketball."

With only four attorneys, it was a close-knit group that saw every part of the league business: the collective bargaining agreement with the union, the players' contracts, event contracts, draft issues, the competition committee. It was like a class in Professional Sports League 101. Ackerman learned what the framework for a successful league was, how it actually ran, what the metrics of success were.

Ackerman was forging relationships across departments and leagues. She had colleagues such as Russ Granik, the deputy commissioner of the NBA, and Gary Bettman, the NBA general counsel who later went on to a long tenure as the commissioner of the NHL. Ackerman represented the league across the sports industry. As a woman, she was easy to spot as a potential partner to groups that hadn't always had a seat at the table. So it wasn't surprising when Betty Jaynes of the Women's Basketball Coaches Association came to Ackerman when her organization needed money for a party at the women's Final Four in 1990.

Party planning wasn't a class at UCLA's law school, but Ackerman got out a pen. What kind of party is this? How many people? Ackerman asked. Jaynes said it was mostly a pretzel and beer party for about eight hundred people. So Ackerman took the request of funding up the chain.

"We'll take it out of the fine money," she was told.

Back then, players' fines went into a pool that was shared by the league and union for charity. That's how some well-aimed NBA elbow or the like paid for the coaches' party at the Final Four of the NCAA Women's Basketball tournament, and how Ackerman came to hand out free NBA water bottles to guests at the door.

As the NBA started to become more involved in women's basketball, Ackerman became the point person. When the U.S. women's national basketball team was formed in 1995, Ackerman was there. When that involvement evolved into the idea of a pro league, as the rival ABL began to form, Ackerman was the natural candidate to be the league's first commissioner.

"I'd been at the league for eight years," Ackerman said. "I knew the place inside and out. I knew how the place ran. I was the women's basketball person."

The WNBA was trying to outcompete the other women's start-up league, the ABL. The way it was going to do that was through efficiencies: uniforms, ticket sales, infrastructure—the WNBA had a head start.

"We knew how to run a basketball league," Ackerman said. "I could go to Rod Thorn, who was running NBA basketball operations, if we had an officiating issue. We had to write a game management manual. We knew how to do this. That could be easily transferred over to the WNBA. It was easily transferred over to the D-League, which now is the G League, which started around the same time. David was very ambitious."

Stern was always looking to grow the audience for basketball. With the resources and tools and expertise already built for the NBA in-house, the WNBA had a decided advantage over the ABL. The WNBA's inaugural game averaged 5.1 million viewers on NBC, according to Jonathan Lewis of *Sports Media Watch*. It was a huge rating then and it's a huge rating now.

The ABL paid better than the WNBA, and it played in the regular fall and winter window, when American fans were expecting to watch basketball. The WNBA played in the summer, but crucially, according to Ackerman, it didn't make players sign a noncompete agreement, so they could make money playing overseas. Meanwhile, the ABL players had to agree to be exclusive to that league.

"The ABL made them choose, and they offered lofty salaries that they couldn't support in the end," Ackerman said. "Why? Because they didn't have a very good business model and didn't have the expertise and they went out of business after two years."

The WNBA paid players as a league, and not a lot in those early days. Later, the salaries would be the responsibility of the individual teams, which is the general model in professional sports. A renegotiated collective bargaining agreement in 2019 substantially raised salary minimums, and players are now paid between $62,000 and $250,000, with that latter going to the rare few.

Ackerman saw short runways doom other women's leagues across that timeline. The start-up costs are very high, and the networking and business relationships are difficult to gather and maintain. When leagues failed, it was assumed that the reason was general apathy for women's sports, when Ackerman saw that the problems could be attributed to other areas.

"I'm an operations person," Ackerman said. "I have a lot of that in me. And so the whole notion of how is this getting run, how is it getting funded? Who's got the expertise here? Running a sports league is really hard."

The WNBA has had a number of commissioners since Ackerman, but in many ways the current one, Cathy Englebert, is picking up the thread. Her background at Deloitte gives her the operational perspective the WNBA needs at the current moment.

"It was important, in this moment of time around women's sports, to hire a business leader who had built businesses, who had grown businesses, who had managed large businesses and large accounts like I did at Deloitte," Englebert said. "So I think from that perspective, you know, over my tenure at Deloitte, when I was CEO we grew revenue by 30 percent. I think [current NBA Commissioner] Adam [Silver] and the owners were like, 'OK, we have this moment now as an ownership group. We're all going to be investing. We've been investing a long time, but we're really going to double down now. And we need to hire a business leader who's going to transform the business.'"

The WNBA's first few years were so successful, but years of frustration followed. With women's sports surging again now, particularly NCAA women's basketball, capitalizing on interest while competing for broadcast rights and investment dollars is key.

"We're really preparing ourselves for a great next round of what the economic boom here could be because we've spent all this time raising capital," Engelbert said. "Raising $75 million in February 2022 was really key because if you don't have financial capital, you can't hire human capital. If you can't hire human capital, you can't grow. I mean, it's just the ABCs of growing a business."

The NBA may not have been the perfect partner, or even a good one at times. There have been decisions about structure and personnel over the past twenty-five years that didn't help advance the WNBA. But both Stern and Silver, who succeeded Stern as commissioner in 2014, were committed to the women's basketball league as an idea.

And it's through allies who understood the business investment women's sports represented that the WNBA and USWNT unions both found a way to further monetize their popularity.

In 2019, when the USWNT was in the World Cup and pushing for equal pay, Nike ran out of official team jerseys. Somebody drastically underestimated how popular the most popular women's team would be, and, according to *Yahoo News*, the first order was for just one thousand shirts. What was essentially a small order that would have covered USWNT friends and family was supposed to satisfy nationwide interest over the month of the World Cup. It's laughable, but it's also serious. U.S. Soccer turned potential revenue away, and in negotiations a mistake like that means the women lose a metric to prove their popularity and value.

"There is definitely opportunity being lost," Steven Scebelo, president of the sports licensing and consulting firm REP Worldwide, told *Yahoo News* at the time. "More jerseys could be sold for the USWNT, there's no doubt."

But the USWNT had already suspected that U.S. Soccer hadn't been maximizing revenue, so in 2017 the USWNT actually negotiated the rights to sell its own player merchandise, separate from Nike's deal with the team.

The issue was: How do you do that?

Meanwhile in 2017, DeMaurice Smith was the executive director of the NFL Players Association. Smith and his second, George Atallah, liked the idea of using their power for what they perceived as good causes, and helping an undervalued group of athletes reach markets was one of those.

Smith called the USWNT's head at the time, Becca Roux, and volunteered his assets and networks. So Roux, and later the WNBA Players Association (WNBPA), partnered with the NFL Players Association's REP Worldwide to make their own jerseys available to fans.

When the official Nike gear sold out in 2019, the USWNT still was able to sell T-shirts with the faux campaign slogan "Rapinoe-Bird 2020."

Players Helping Players

There is the structural support from the NBA front office, but there is also fraternal support from players. It can be as simple as a social media post that shows an influential NBA player watching the WNBA Finals. Or sometimes it can be a comment that shows awareness of the women's side of the game.

Kobe Bryant was one of the most visible fans of women's basketball, and his daughter Gigi was considered an early prospect as a girls' basketball player. Their loss was mourned by WNBA players and the league itself when they died in a helicopter crash in 2020.

"No NBA player supported the WNBA or women's college basketball more than Kobe," the ESPN analyst and former player Rebecca Lobo tweeted at the time. "He attended games, watched on TV, coached the next generation. We pray for his family."

Englebert herself posted about Bryant's loss on social media and included a photo of him in an orange WNBA hoodie watching a game with Gigi.

There are similar allies across sports.

In 2017, the tennis player Andy Murray had lost his Wimbledon match and was dutifully seated in the front of the smaller arena of reporters. This is often a tricky moment for player and press, when a favorite has to address pointed questions before an exit. Murray, a top player—part of the Big Four of that era with Roger Federer, Rafael Nadal, and Novak Djokovic—was battling a significant hip injury and had a disappointing finish.

For Murray, a Scotsman, Wimbledon was his home slam. His mother, Judy, was a venerable figure in tennis circles. She was the more visible tennis parent as he grew up and coached Andy and his brother Jamie to the ATP Tour. Murray later defied convention when he hired Amelie Mauresmo as his coach from 2014 to 2016. When he hired Mauresmo, a French player with a great looping backhand, Murray received the sort of response that he said made him a feminist, and he certainly meets the definition, particularly when judged against many of his peers.

"I've been involved in sport my whole life, and the level of sexism is unreal," Murray once said.

As much as Billie Jean King had changed the sport for women, there were plenty of men along the way who couldn't be bothered. King's opponent Bobby Riggs was hardly the last of the great sexist pigs. The French tennis player Gilles Simon said women don't deserve equal pay in 2012, and Djokovic publicly echoed that skepticism four years later. In 2016, the tournament director Raymond Moore was fired by Indian Wells—one of the few tournaments that, like the Grand Slams, held men's and women's draws at the same time—for saying that women should "get down on their knees" and thank the men's tour for its success, since the women "ride the coattails" of the ATP.

And these are just some of the remarks that went public.

At any rate, although women in tennis have attracted the same kind of ratings, respect, and endorsements as men for decades, there are those in the sport who still consider the men's draw the premiere event and the women's matches the undercard. This is sometimes reflected in the language around titles—for example, when Federer might be referred to as the U.S. Open champion and Serena Williams as the women's champion. You see the same in NCAA basketball and in soccer, where only the women's side gets the gendered adjective.

The women on tour are aware of these subtleties, and so was the only Grand Slam–winning man on tour who had hired a woman to coach him. So it was in this context that Murray sat down at his Wimbledon postmatch press conference, where he was asked about the man who defeated him that day, the American player Sam Querrey.

Reporter: Sam is the first U.S. player to reach a major semifinal since 2009. How would you describe—
Murray: First male player.
Reporter: I beg your pardon?
Murray: Male player, right?
Reporter: Yes, first male player, that's for sure.

Murray's gentle prod that the media consider the men's game and women's game alongside each other and not as the "real thing" and an imitation gave prominent voice to a complaint many women had raised for years. But surely it struck the reporter differently coming from Murray, and Murray realized that. King has spent the past fifty years looking for allies like Murray. There was Joe Cullman at Phillip Morris to start, and many more along the way on the field and in boardrooms, as King asked for meeting after meeting.

There is no point in trying to win over the Raymond Moores of the world. But if you find the Murrays, the Bryants, they can change minds.

Sky's the Limit

Rawlinson's vision in Chicago didn't take long to materialize.

In the summer of 2023, the WNBA's Sky made news when it announced that the thirteen-time NBA All-Star Dwyane Wade was joining the ownership group. Wade was a homegrown celebrity, whose childhood on the South Side was chaotic, yet he had grown to become a deeply respected philanthropist and entrepreneur along with wife, Gabrielle Union. He had an ownership stake in the Utah Jazz and now was adding the Sky to his portfolio.

The reporter Emily Caron wrote the story for *Sportico*, reporting that Wade bought in at the $85 million valuation at which other high-profile investors, including the Chicago Cubs' co-owner Laura Ricketts, Foot Locker's Chief Executive Mary Dillon, Smartly.io's Chief Executive Laura Desmond, and the Chicago Museum of Contemporary Art's Chair Cari Sacks, came in.

Appropriately, $85 million was the price paid for the second-most-expensive Warhol ever sold at auction, *White Disaster [White Car Crash 19 Times]*.

The WNBA was evolving from a beer and pretzel party to a portfolio of Warhols in a little over twenty-five years.

10

NEGOTIATING VALUE

The WNBA players advocate for a CBA that fits them.

Sheryl Swoopes thought she might be pregnant, and the possibility had her twisted up in knots.

It was 1996, the WNBA was about to launch, and she, Lisa Leslie, and Rebecca Lobo were the faces of the new professional women's basketball league. After decades in which college basketball could only ever be followed by playing overseas, women in the United States were going to have a league backed by the financial might of the NBA, able to play in arenas such as Madison Square Garden in New York City.

Swoopes, a Texas native, had won the national title at Texas Tech in 1993 and was named the Naismith College Player of the Year, in addition to numerous other accolades. She was iconic: she wore puffy leather jackets and had her hair styled like the rap duo Salt-N-Pepa, who were all over the airwaves in that era. Even her name sounded like a verb you'd use to describe the way she played.

Swoopes

Back then, athletes in Swoopes's position had a binary choice: you were either a professional athlete or you were a mother. There weren't many exceptions. Women didn't come back from pregnancy to continue their professional careers. There weren't enough roster spots to hold one open, and going through a pregnancy was assumed to leave a softness that was incompatible with the tightly honed frame required to be truly competitive.

Swoopes was married and wanted a family, so that wasn't the issue. It was the timing that made everything messy. Swoopes was unquestionably one of the best women to play the game in the history of the sport already, and now there was a question mark.

"I was like, 'What is going to happen?'" Swoopes said on a chilly May day in Boston as I interviewed her on stage for a TEDxBoston event in 2022.[1]

Swoopes recalled she took three pregnancy tests, one after the other, because she didn't really believe what was happening. All the tests came back positive. She still didn't believe it.

"I was like, 'No. Can't be.' So I remember I called my doctor and said, 'I think I might be pregnant.'

"She said, 'Well, did you do a home pregnancy test?'

"I said, 'Yeah, I did three.'

"She was like, 'Well, Sheryl, you could have stopped after the first, right?'"

The line landed with the small crowd of women's sports enthusiasts packed into the TEDx event room, who burst into laughter.

Swoopes pinpointed the reason she had so much trepidation about an unplanned, but not unwanted, pregnancy.

"Honestly, it wasn't a matter of, 'Am I going to have the baby or not?' It was more about, 'What's going to happen?'" Swoopes explained. "I was the first player signed. I felt like I was letting down a lot of people. The WNBA was just getting ready to start. Nike had come out with a shoe, so I was like, 'What's going to happen?' Because to your point, it had never been done before."

You'd think having the top player in the league get pregnant before the WNBA's official launch would have been taken as a sign of a coming issue for the new league to work out with its players. Women are at the height of their reproductive fitness when they are at the height of their careers, so that confluence might mean that this scenario was likely to replay again and again.

And yet.

Negotiation as Branding

A lot has happened since 1997, but for basketball players facing the dilemma Swoopes did, it has been slow and incremental progress. When the WNBA and players renegotiated their collective bargaining agreement (CBA) in 2020, they finally addressed some of the issues that Swoopes originally encountered about how a player could simultaneously be a professional athlete and a parent within a WNBA career.

"We were really kind of starting from the ground up," said Nneka Ogwumike, president of the WNBPA. "We know the composition of our league, and we understand the resources that we need. We're athletes, and we identify in so many different ways, but mostly as women and mostly as people with ovaries. So it was almost— It felt innovative. But it also felt like we were talking about something that should have been established."

That's been the experience of so many players in women's professional leagues. Why haven't these issues already been thought through? What may be a helpful benefit for a men's league, such as day-of-game childcare at a stadium, is crucial in a league with athletes who may be primary parents or nursing parents. But so many CBAs were written in the 1900s for players who weren't having babies or who were assumed to have stay-at-home wives rather than for traveling, playing parents.

Ogwumike and other players who are active in their players' associations may stumble upon these vestigial digits as they read through the fine print in these and other documents. They did well, then, to set a new agenda for a new era. To build a new house. And to take advantage of a new ally to help them.

Starting a Fast Break

Terri Jackson had the perfect job at the NCAA. Or so she thought. The Georgetown Law graduate is married to the former NBA player Jaren Jackson, and their son, Jaren Jr., was drafted by the Memphis Grizzlies in 2018. Terri Jackson knows basketball, and she knows value.

She was minding her own business when the WNBPA executive director's job description landed in her inbox. Now that's a job I could do, she thought. First, and most important, she understands the players she represents. She wants to support them, connect them, fuse them to community and business leaders so their influence and possibility extend beyond the court.

Jackson is a listener, a negotiator—she builds consensus where before there were factions.

When Jackson got the job in 2018, she fought for the players to be able to message their support for social justice causes on their apparel. There was a lot to address, including the fact that players made an average of about $35,000 for the season and needed to play abroad in the offseason if they wanted to make a living playing ball. So fresh on the job, Jackson moved to open the league's CBA a year early.

"Girls and young women growing up in sports are sometimes made to feel grateful to play—at any level," Jackson told me for a column in the *New York Daily News*. "While boys and young men have expectations in sports, their sisters have a very different narrative. Yet as a testament to them, they have turned this notion of gratefulness into something productive and powerful. For them, there is no sense of expectation or entitlement. Instead, they are protective of the opportunity and see themselves as caretakers of a legacy."

The WNBA began in part because another women's league got started first. The ABL was the first to capitalize on the success of the 1996 Atlanta Olympics, where American women won so much gold.

The NBA didn't want to get smoked at its own sport by an upstart league, so it set up the WNBA. With deeper pockets and arena space, the WNBA prevailed and then spent twenty years trying to figure out how much to invest in women's basketball.

For too long, the WNBA's CBA had been a cheap pink version of the men's. What would a built-from-scratch CBA for women even look like? Jackson listened to the players. How about childcare on-site? An extra bedroom for mothers of small kids? A concussion protocol that took into account the very different response women often have to the injury? Definitely better pay.

They accomplished this and more. The union and the WNBA crafted a CBA that upped player salaries 53 percent and started a revenue-sharing agreement between the league and players that brought those players respect. The union worked to build in a benefit for veteran players that would allow them to freeze their eggs or undergo fertility treatments. For a league with players who identify as LGBTQIA+, the flexibility to plan their families is key.

"We were able to forge forward and, of course, give guaranteed maternity leave pay," Ogwumike said. "There's still so much more that we have to move forward on because the fact that [if you are pregnant] you're regarded as injured and you come off the cap. That just . . . doesn't make sense in a league full of mostly people who are probably going to be the ones carrying their kids. And we want to be able to create a league that people want to be a part of, not just because of the basketball that we see, but because of also the lives that we support in the WNBA."

The WNBA's CBA doesn't just allow for parents to play in the league if they happen to get pregnant; it actively assists in a player's family planning. Lindsay Kagawa Colas, an agent at Wasserman, said some of her early discussions with clients now involve family planning, given her experiences with in vitro fertilization when starting her own family.

"This is something that is not talked about enough: fertility, family planning, women's health generally," Kagawa Colas said during the panel at the 2023 espnW Women + Sports Summit. "I think talking about it and normalizing it takes so much stress off us as people, and athletes are people, and these things are happening in the background and in our minds as we're competing and as we're preparing, and this is life. And so I feel like it's a really critical part of my role to make sure that my lived experience becomes part of how I represent my clients—or, at least, how I advise them on thinking about the things that matter most."

Ogwumike, one of her clients, was on the stage next to Kagawa Colas and said she planned to freeze her eggs later that year since the benefit was included in ESPN's health plan, where Ogwumike serves as a commentator on basketball. The conversation that day included a frank discussion of fibroids, polycystic ovary syndrome, infertility, and other topics that are often kept private. Athletes may feel betrayed by their finely honed bodies when facing these reproduction-related challenges, so having built-in health care and support is important.

"I'm in year twelve now going into year thirteen, and we have moms that are planning to have kids while they're playing," Ogwumike said. "I think for me, it really just helped dispel this age-old, I guess, haunting or stigma of you can't have kids until you're done playing—like, you can't do it until you're done. And . . . it just really bothers me that that's kind of what we grow up thinking."

Ultimately, the new WNBA Commissioner Cathy Englebert and Jackson agreed that the league would be stronger if the athletes who played in the WNBA were valued more, and convinced owners that this was the moment to invest in the league to grow revenue.

"We've seen a lot of headlines when it comes to mothers in the WNBA, both positive and both challenging," Ogwumike said. "We want to make sure that the resources are not only available, but also that it's not a second thought. It's not an afterthought. It's something that should be foundational. It's something that should be standardized."

Think of how different Swoopes's experience might have been if leagues then had acknowledged that women play sports during their childbearing years rather than pretending the two were mutually exclusive.

Institutional Support

The WNBPA started with a small request in its negotiations: stop talking down the league.

"Why would any league do that?" you might reasonably ask. Why would a league take a property to which it hopes to lure fans and sponsors and either overtly or subtly denigrate it? Would Roger Goodell start an NFL CBA negotiation by talking publicly about how tedious it is to watch a football game? Would Rob Manfred lament that MLB players today just aren't as talented as Hank Aaron and his generation as an argument to reduce the size of their contracts?

Of course not.

And those are established leagues that aren't fighting to overcome generations of disrespect as a matter of survival.

But look at how leagues with a male and a female component talk down the women's side of the game. In their enthusiasm to pay less in the negotiation, they undercut their own product, threatening the reputation of the games and players they are responsible for marketing. U.S. Soccer actually used this self-defeating tactic in court as recently as 2020, saying that the four-time World Cup gold medal–winning, victory-parading, television-ratings-record-breaking women's team was less skilled than its male counterparts.

It's not always in a court of law, either. It can happen at the negotiating table.

Leagues confront women with an existential question at the start of a negotiation over pay: "Why should we, the entity that stands to promote and profit off you, care about your game?"

"That's like, the U.S. Soccer Federation when they said in their brief the women's game is an inferior game because their lungs have less air and they run slower, women are inferior," the sports broadcaster Sarah Spain said. "Then they're like, 'But also, are you interested in buying tickets and merchandise for our women's team?' . . . The number of ways that this shit is cut off at the knees while trying to succeed can't really be measured when we have these conversations, and yet we try to simplify them into, like, fucking ratings."

Rethinking these issues in terms of collective bargaining is finding other applications. Commissioner Jessica Berman said that the NWSL is listening to players and rethinking assumptions about everything, even teams' away uniforms. Recall the Orlando Pride's experience advocating for uniform design that took menstruation into account. How does that issue look when it's time to negotiate policy at the bargaining table?

"One of our teams, the Orlando Pride, they met with their players before the season, and the players gave feedback individually . . . about not wanting to run in white shorts," Berman said. "And they just didn't think twice. They were just like, 'We are. It's done.' It's a pretty reasonable request. 'I get nervous when I'm running if I have my period. Is this something you can do something about?' It's like, 'Oh, OK. We can do something about that. We should do something about that.'"

And leagues such as the NWSL can take the issues to brands. There might be a larger performance market for, say, leak-proof athletic shorts. But it starts with the open dialogue, where players don't have to accept the smaller and pinker version of men's professional kits and contracts.

"It's just creating a safe environment for players to be able to say, 'This is what I need in order to be successful,' and trusting that either . . . if it can't be done, like, there won't be repercussions for having asked the question, [or] you'll just get a reason as to why, which is, like, totally fine," Berman said. "We have to be comfortable saying no sometimes, but saying why or getting it fixed."

But there is a new generation of women ready to assess the value of professional women's sports properties and argue on behalf of that value. It harks back to the days when Billie Jean King confronted tennis over the peanuts in prize money the women were told to be grateful for.

Negotiating Solo

Players for individual sports are also advocating for greater benefits. The two-time Grand Slam winner Victoria Azarenka had a son in 2016 and returned to the WTA Tour in 2018. It was a difficult comeback, professionally and personally, but in 2020 she reached the U.S. Open final.

"You do have to pause your career, and it is a lot of responsibility," Azarenka explained to the audience at the espnW summit. "For me, it was really scary at first. I was just, like— I was top five in the world when I was pregnant with Leo. And I was like, 'Does it mean I'm not going to play tennis again?' I had all these questions, but then I . . . thought, this is a blessing."

With $36 million in career prize money, Azarenka had the ability to pay for coaching support and professional infrastructure, as well as for additional care for Leo. She's become an advocate for thoughtful policy in her own sport, where players are independent operators.

When she started to plan, she gathered her coach and support team together to ask for their patience while she figured out a timeline, and then she started to see how little was in place for pregnant players. It started, as Ogwumike noted, with the idea that recovering from giving birth is often discussed using the language of injury or short-term disability. That's language that has been used in the American workplace for years to account for paid or partially paid leave. For professional athletes, however, it was especially pernicious.

"What I started to understand . . . [was that] we didn't even have a maternity rule. You can freeze your ranking, basically, but it's like one of your long-term injuries," Azarenka said. "And I said, 'How come? How is my pregnancy a long-term injury?' That's something [that] sounds ridiculous. So we started to look into the policies of how it can be changed; how it can change a stereotype that you can't have kids, even though we had already people who have done it."

In 2009, Kim Clijsters retired but then launched a comeback after having her daughter. Many sports fans will remember the photos of a radiant Clijsters after again winning the U.S. Open in 2012, bringing her daughter Jada onto the court to check out the trophy after that match.

"Kim Clijsters was one of the most recent examples who had a child, came back, and played [at] a really, really high level—[at an] even higher level than she was before," Azarenka said. "But the stereotype was just, like, 'No—you have to pick one or the other.' And I was like, 'OK, we're going to have to break that.' I had great help [from] one of my biggest rivals and one of my favorite athletes, Serena [Williams], who got pregnant a year after."

With Williams, the best player in the world, set to pause her career to have her daughter Olympia, there was greater pressure to really examine what the policies were.

"We have, I think, fifteen-plus or even more women who are mothers now playing tennis," Azarenka said. "It happened within a span of five years. So I'm very happy to see that."

This is what it looks like when women can negotiate for their own ends and not just get the pink version of a contract built for men.

The Stakes

When athletes band together to advocate for their health care, their bodily autonomy, their full human experience in and out of their sport, it can sound to some listeners—perhaps used to an older set of norms—like a pie-in-the-sky wish list. But the demands of bargaining athletes are written in the suffering and trauma the status quo has brought to other athletes.

Mary Cain was a high school phenomenon coming out of Bronxville, a small and affluent community just north of New York City. It's a town not much bigger than a postage stamp, but its elegantly massive Tudor-style homes are filled with ambassadors and chief executives. NFL Commissioner Roger Goodell lives there. Families in an income bracket to send their offspring to the best private schools are comfortable with the insular public school that looks like a British castle, where the boys wear white tuxedos and the girls wear white gowns to graduation.

Cain was a runner with speed and intellect. At sixteen, while competing in the Wanamaker Mile race at New York City's Millrose Games in 2013, she broke the record for the fastest mile. The venue was the 168th Street Armory in the Bronx, a little more than ten miles from her home but a world away by so many other metrics.

Cain broke her own record, to be clear, by a full four seconds, running the mile in four minutes and 28.25 seconds. This was the future of American distance running. The year after winning the Wanamaker, Cain went to Oregon to train with Nike's running team, led by Coach Alberto Salazar.

"America loves a good child prodigy story, and business is ready and waiting to exploit that story, especially when it comes to girls," the former Nike athlete Lauren Fleshman told the *New York Times* for a story about Cain in 2019. "When you have these kinds of good girls, girls who are good at following directions to the point of excelling, you'll find a system that's happy to take them. And it's rife with abuse."

In November 2023, Nike settled a $20 million lawsuit with Cain, in which she alleged abuse and public weigh-ins. Salazar was banned by the U.S. Center for SafeSport from working with track and field athletes and was implicated in a doping scandal.

Cain was another athlete broken by a system that doesn't care about the whole person, just the competitor. But she has shaped the ashes of that experience into something new.

Cain founded Atalanta, a nonprofit professional running group for women. It pays them to train, and in return they serve as mentors and coaches for runners at under-resourced high schools in the Bronx. The group aims to mint not just Olympic runners, but also coaches who understand a new way of interacting with athletes that doesn't seek to "break them down" before coaching them to championships.

Efforts such as this are scalable and could shift a coaching paradigm. Women's and girls' sports are rife with abuse, but a coaching philosophy that centers the athlete and not the system could change that and develop young men and women who use those sports as a springboard into later success. One of the worst examples of abuse arising from prioritizing the system over the athlete is the scandal in women's gymnastics in which years of abuse by a physician, Larry Nassar, were ignored by officials. It took the raised voices of Olympians to bring him to justice, but there was a system that failed its athletes, as well.

There is still a risk that landing with the wrong coach or in a toxic system can shatter lives and destroy careers. Reducing that risk is essential, and Cain's efforts address it.

As Cain told Erin Stout for a story in *Women's Running*: "Although it's been overwhelming and a lot to do, it's been so rewarding going through this entrepreneurial process and knowing that I'm going to ultimately walk the walk instead of just talk the talk around all the advocacy work I've wanted to do for a long time."[2]

Cain has come through that experience eager to build the kind of supportive training structures that she would have benefited from. She is one of many athletes refusing to let the old systems stand.

11

TAKING A STAND

There are some things money can't buy.

When Sue Bird started playing basketball for UConn in 1998, she was not given to political demonstration. A gifted point guard out of the New York City Catholic high school powerhouse Christ the King, Bird was everything the public could want in a player. She won championships and, with a round face, curly ponytail, and pixie smile, she looked every bit the part of the highly marketable basketball player.

But over the years she saw that playing sports meant playing a role that didn't authentically fit. There was pressure to behave and present herself in a way that comported with the norms at the time, and if she didn't, she feared she might lose opportunities.

"When I was twenty-one coming out of college, I had to worry about, 'Oh, God—if I tell people I'm gay, am I going to lose endorsements?'" she told me during an interview for the *Ladies Room* podcast with Julie DiCaro. "I would love to not have to think about that. That was awful."

Fast forward to 2020. The pandemic forced the players into the WNBA's season-long bubble. Bird was the longest-tenured player in the WNBA. A leader on the court, on the union board, and in the public, she was no longer trying to hide. Bird was out and part of the biggest power couple in sports, with the soccer star Megan Rapinoe.

You could say being a professional athlete had radicalized her.

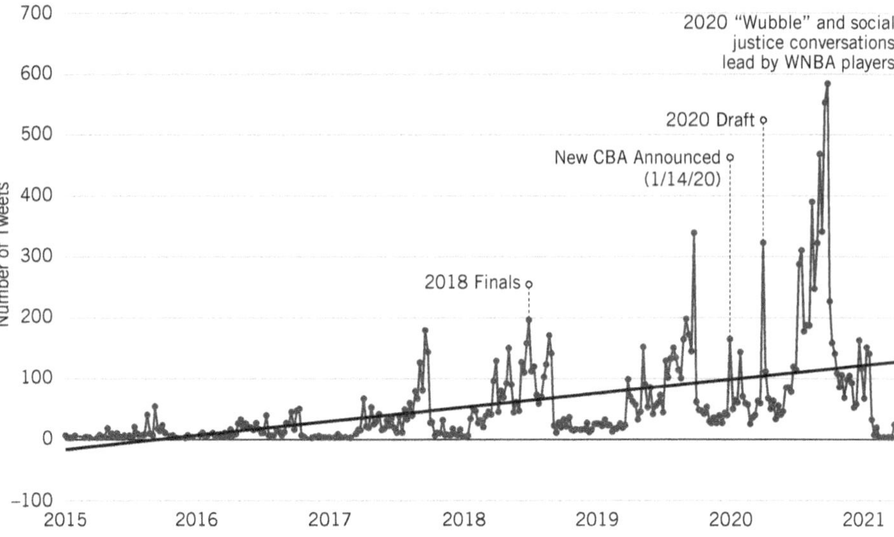

Figure 11.1 Players' demonstrations during the WNBA's pandemic-safe tournament, the "Wubble," brought increased attention to the league, as measured by social media engagement. (Sports Innovation Lab)

"For a very long time, female athletes—and specifically, I can speak for basketball players—we've not been allowed to just be basketball players. That's never been the story line around us," Bird said. "Not many people talk about the amazing three-pointers we hit or the dimes we drop. It's always about what we look like; what we don't do. We're judged based on everything, so we've really developed this fight about us and this backbone about us."

So when the first responder Breonna Taylor was killed in her own home during a police raid in 2020, Bird joined with other players in the league who couldn't stay silent. And this was not a normal year. Where players once might have been with their own teams, going out to dinner and meeting with outside friends, no one could do that in a pandemic. They were in the Wubble as protests were happening all over the country, talking about the murder of George Floyd while in police custody. And those basketball players were together as a group, as a family. They lobbied the WNBA to join them, and the league painted Black Lives Matters on the courts.

"I think when people become fans of our league, there are, of course, categories of people where it's just about the basketball. But I do think when people start to follow our league, you know exactly where we stand—on issues, on different things happening in society. You know exactly who we are and what we stand for," Bird explained. "So when you become a fan, you're already bought into that. So this summer wasn't different for any of our WNBA fans. And I'm sure we got more fans and more eyeballs because we were on TV a lot more. Shout out for that: when you're on TV, people watch. We didn't lose our fan base. If anything, we gained, because people started to see more of us and to either get into the basketball or how we're using our platform."

Then they looked to see what else they could do that would go beyond the symbolic. And that summer, WNBA players made history.

Making Dreams a Reality

The Atlanta Dream's owner, Kelly Loeffler, who was appointed to fill a Senate seat, was running her first campaign to be elected to the U.S. Senate as a Georgia Republican. She was a forty-nine-year-old former chief executive and the immaculately groomed wife of a wealthy businessman. An excellent profile from Candace Buckner in the *Washington Post* detailed Loeffler's own basketball-playing days, and she took a huge interest in the Dream's Xs and Os when she first bought the team.[1]

As she became more politically active, however, Loeffler's views were becoming increasingly opposed to what her players were advocating for from their perspective in the Wubble. After the election of Donald Trump in 2016, Loeffler morphed into a strident soldier in the culture wars, even adopting the sartorial style of the Georgia voter—wearing what appeared to be freshly ironed plaid shirts to political events as a notable departure from her usual designer wardrobe.

Loeffler wrote a letter to WNBA Commissioner Cathy Engelbert that implored her to rein in the activism taking place in the league: "I adamantly oppose the Black Lives Matter political movement, which has advocated for the defunding of police, called for the removal of Jesus from churches and the disruption of the nuclear family structure, harbored anti-Semitic views, and promoted violence and destruction across the country."[2]

You can imagine how this landed with Bird, and with Loeffler's own players. Elizabeth Williams was a longtime member of the Dream and one of the team's leaders off the court when it came down to deciding what path to take. It's one thing to be angry; it's another to take collective action.

"What stands out are the difficult conversations, because we didn't know exactly which plan we wanted to take or which route we wanted to take," Williams told me. "So we had to talk about, 'Does this look like a boycott? Does this look like voting initiatives? What is the plan of action here?' And I think having those conversations, where it's not that everyone agreed at first, but because there was a collective, because there are shared ideas, that's what allowed us to come to the conclusion of, 'OK, this is the approach that we're going to take.'"

WNBA players, unlike the men who play in more lucrative leagues where teams can vie for the best players with fat contracts, had more to risk. The total 144 players in the WNBA would fit on three NFL teams. Good, deserving players get cut from the WNBA all the time. As we've seen, marketing has great influence on a player's value, but that's only if those players can keep a competitive spot on a team.

Angel McCoughtry was drafted by the Dream and at one time had a friendly relationship with Loeffler, but she was traded to the Aces when she began to speak out against injustice and the way communities of color are policed.

"This is what I believe, and one of the reasons I'm not in Atlanta, I'm not going to stand still and be quiet," McCoughtry told me for a December 2020 column for *Deadspin*.[3] "Think about it, the best player in Atlanta history is not there. It's not right, is it? When we stand up for ourselves, that's what happens."

McCoughtry, who went on to play for the Minnesota Lynx and played abroad during the offseason, knew she was risking paychecks by standing up.

But in a summer where anguish over the death of George Floyd was an echo across the country, WNBA players were moved to action.

Bird had an idea when it came to voicing opposition to Loeffler. She realized that the senator wanted the fight, wanted to package her actions to control the players on her team for the voters who weren't naturally drawn to her but who would welcome a Trump proxy. Georgia has ranked-choice voting, so Bird knew any name recognition would help Loeffler. Rather than just oppose Loeffler, the players started researching her opponents for a candidate whose profile they could lift. They met remotely with local politicians to find out about the issues and the candidates.

At the first nationally televised game for the Dream, the players appeared on the court to warm up in front of the cameras. On their T-shirts was a name and a message.

Warnock

That game introduced the candidate—now senator—Raphael Warnock to thousands in the WNBA and beyond. Every news report, Warnock. Every story written, Warnock. Every photograph, Warnock. Warnock. Warnock. WARNOCK.

The WNBA players made sure that his name was mentioned every time Loeffler's was. They had researched his views and arranged Zoom calls with Warnock and the Georgia political organizer Stacey Abrams, who was an adviser to the WNBPA.

"For women, it's always about the group," Bird said. "That's what's unique to the fight women take on. We usually do it together."

This wasn't even the first time WNBA players had mobilized at scale. Maya Moore took a season off to advocate for a wrongfully imprisoned man. The Lynx had been kneeling in solidarity with the NFL player Colin Kaepernick since 2016. Taking the floor in Warnock T-shirts was a moment years in the making.

"And I think what people did this summer [2020], it's something we've done for years," Bird said. "We were literally built for this moment in some ways, and it comes from having to fight. And now that we've had to fight our own fight for so long, we're very quick to extend and help others fight their fight."

But here's the thing: it also worked.

On January 5, Reverend Raphael Warnock was elected to represent Georgia. He replaced appointed Senator Kelly Loeffler.

Georgia actually elected two Democrats to the Senate. The Senate itself became tied, with fifty Democrats and fifty Republicans. A new Democratic administration gave Vice President Kamala Harris, the first woman and the first person of color to serve in that role, the tie-breaking vote.

"The WNBA literally saved the world," said Bird's wife, Megan Rapinoe.

"We have a very divided country, as you know, and sometimes view what players do is edgy," Englebert said. "But, you know, I'm just proud that they feel authentic in the W[NBA] and they feel authentically using their voice on their areas of passion, even if it's beyond the one we pick each year to really invest in from the league perspective, you know? They just continue to amaze."

That Wubble was just the beginning. Each year, the WNBA players pick a focus for their advocacy. In 2023, the issue was maternal health. Black women are far more likely than white women to die in childbirth in the United States, and the league centered those health issues in its advocacy. The WNBA front office never took Loeffler's letter seriously and now puts money behind player initiatives.

"This year, they picked maternal health with a focus on communities of color, and they're just so smart about what they pick and when," Englebert said. "Last year, it was civic engagement and voting rights, and I'm sure next year, with a general election, that'll be the same. So I think the players realize they have to have an authentic relationship with their fans."

What are the chances that the 144 players in the WNBA would be in one place, isolated from their friends and family, as they played a pandemic-shortened season? It created a moment of proximity and of motivation. Elizabeth Williams sees it as a moment of unexpected possibility.

"I think sometimes when you have a year like 2020, it's just like, it feels like, there's so much in the world that needs to be fixed," Williams said while playing in the offseason in Turkey in 2023. "Like, you can get kind of overwhelmed. And I think we as players and as a league have done a good job of taking a second to say, like, 'OK, we can talk about this issue now.' Like, we can address this, and it's equally important, and not feel like one is going on the back burner. Like, all of these things share importance, and all of these things can be talked about. I think we've done a good job of finding things that people are passionate about and then being able to share that."

Doing Well by Doing Good

And the kicker: the effort didn't drive off fans. In fact, more have been drawn to the game. Metrics have gone straight up, attendance and ratings—and the league is as popular as it was in the halcyon days when it was first launched.

"Let's use the Wubble as the real example. The way that those fans engaged on social [media] in response to values and cause-based marketing was, like, astronomical," the Sports Innovation Lab researcher Molly Tissenbaum said. "All of a sudden we had this chart in front of us where we saw when the WNBA was allowed, during the Wubble, to talk about human rights and George Floyd and standing up for Black lives. All of a sudden, their engagement rates are through the roof. . . . If you allow athletes to have a personality and to care about things, fans will recognize that, and they'll engage. They'll get on board with it."

So rather than just tolerating an athlete's voice, women's sports leagues can embrace the dialogue.

"It shows the power of sport and it shows the power of humanity," Thayer Lavielle of the Wasserman Collective said, "because 80 percent of that league is Black, and their white players also said, 'Those are my sisters that are feeling a certain way about this. And we are 100 percent behind whatever solution we can come up with to help alleviate what's creating this.'"

The infrastructure and courage built by that action in 2020 allowed WNBA players to act quickly to support Brittney Griner when she was arrested on February 17, 2022, in Russia for having a small amount of cannabis oil in her luggage.

Griner, an openly gay Black woman in a nation with anti-LGBTQ policies, was a valuable prisoner in President Vladimir Putin's country.

She was sentenced to nine years in prison before being traded for the notorious arms dealer Viktor Bout in a one-to-one prisoner swap between Russia and the United States on December 8 of that same year. Every day she was in jail, someone in the league posted to social media reminding the world of the number of days she was kept from her family and teammates.

"I think it helps that our league is smaller," Williams said. "It's a lot easier to create a group chat with 144 versus a thousand. I mean, we have player reps and stuff, but if there's ever a moment where it's like, 'OK. We actually need everyone,' it's a lot easier with 144."

There were people on the right side of the political divide who derided Griner, but they probably weren't fans of the WNBA to begin with. Being quiet to placate an unlikely audience hadn't grown the league, but standing up for an unlawfully detained teammate coincided with growth for the league.

"I think that's the big difference between traditional sports and what we see with fans of women's sports," Tissenbaum said. "Can you identify something that is not just geography that ties you to a sport or an athlete or a team?"

Something bigger.

Living Your Values

This kind of collective action has defined so many of the women's sports stories of the last decade. In soccer, the U.S. Women's National Team's fight for equal pay is one. The U.S. Gymnastics program is another. In the face of horrific abuse by a team-affiliated doctor, Larry Nassar, players such as Simone Biles and Aly Raisman stood together and publicly detailed his crimes. It was an incredibly brave way to call out their own federation as well, as players' complaints had gone unaddressed for years. As we've seen, opportunities and prosperity for women's leagues and players—whether in sponsorships or broadcasting—always feel precious and unstable to those who depend on them, so for these women to go against their sports' leadership to advocate for themselves and their successors represented an existential choice.

Many of those women spoke up early and in real time but were ignored. The gold medals were simply more important to the sport's organizers.

If Olympic gold is the only goal, then abuse is justified by success. But athletes are starting to realize that the victory is hollow if those champions have been broken by years of abuse and overtraining. When careers are longer, finding ways to train sustainably is vital.

In 2021, Naomi Osaka earned $60 million through tennis and endorsements, according to *Forbes*. She was the top female earner in sports and the twelfth-ranked athlete overall. But her record earnings weren't the most notable thing about Osaka that year.

The twenty-four-year-old had prompted a reassessment of the way we talk about athletes and mental health. When the French Open wouldn't alter the interview schedule and format, she withdrew from the tournament, citing mental health reasons. As unheard-of as this is for a top competitor in any sport, this didn't decrease Osaka's popularity. Again, the audience embraced the player's values in spite of organizers' trepidation about losing their market.

One thing Billie Jean King has always said about the greatest players: it's not enough to be technically excellent; you also have to love the spotlight and the pressure. That's been true for so many women over the years, perhaps none more than Serena Williams. But it's different for Osaka.

I covered Wimbledon in 2018 for *Newsday*. Right before the chaos of a Grand Slam starts, players talk to the media. It's a great way to settle in and get players on bigger-picture issues and get to know the newer pros.

Osaka was just starting to emerge as a real power player on the tour, but she was still green. I'd covered an earlier press conference and sat in the back of the room as it began. Most of the reporters in the front-row seats were from Japan, the nation for which Osaka plays and where her mother was born.

English-speaking press went first, and it was clear that Osaka was a star in the making. She was soft-spoken and a bit tentative but had a low-key, wicked sense of humor. Osaka charmed the English press that day without even trying, then took questions in Japanese. Raised in the United States, she was still learning the language, so she would revert to English mid-answer, but it was clear from the laughter and smiles that those reporters had enjoyed the exchange, as well.

Later that year, at the U.S. Open, Osaka reached the final against Serena Williams, who had been her icon growing up at Arthur Ashe Stadium. It's a tough dynamic for any young player. I called the match for the USTA's radio broadcast, and you could base an opera on what happened that night. Williams was docked a game for a rules violation and expressed frustration on the court. The crowd was behind the veteran, who was only one Grand Slam shy of tying Margaret Court's twenty-four titles, and there was Osaka, a newcomer in her first major final, bearing witness on the other side of the court.

Osaka won the match. The crowd booed the official. And Osaka broke down and was comforted by Williams on the court.

Williams hadn't intended any of this, of course, but Osaka was suddenly part of those high-volume sports conversations. Was Williams out of bounds? Had Osaka responded in the right way? Was Osaka's Grand Slam win legitimate, or was Williams robbed?

That win was just the start of Osaka's ascendance. She has become a truly great player but has expressed a reluctance to engage with the press and make her life available to the critiques that often come with success. For women, those conversations can feel intensely invasive and personal. Personal relationships, bodies, fashion, and everything else is rigorously scrutinized. Social media heightens the exposure.

Three years after that match, Osaka was at an impasse. She left Paris and missed multiple tournaments. She sparked a conversation about the format of press conferences and a culture that puts the performance over the person. As a global tour, the WTA has always needed its stars to show up for smaller venues in far-flung places. There are incentive structures to make that happen. There are requirements to maintain standing in the WTA Tour rankings.

But ultimately the WTA needs not be constrained by traditional ideas of how athletes should process and convey their emotions. Men's sports leagues have cultivated a game-first, human-second sensibility that has fostered all manner of arguably bad outcomes up to and including the prevalence of chronic traumatic encephalopathy (CTE) among professional football players. Plenty would contend that pushing athletes leads to championships and new records, but there's no way to know whether that kind of justification is actually true. And would those broken athletes have done *better* without the damaging pressure?

The WTA took a respectful position with Osaka and gave her the time she needed. In one sense, it couldn't afford not to. But in another, the league tried to put the player first in an individual sport.

The WTA was also the most forthright league when it came to dealing with China. As preparations were underway for the Beijing Olympics in 2022, the former WTA player Peng Shuai accused a government official of abuse on her Instagram page. The post was taken down within an hour, and Peng was detained for weeks.

"Peng Shuai, and all women, deserve to be heard, not censored," read the statement from WTA Chairman Steve Simon. "Her accusation about the conduct of a former Chinese leader involving a sexual assault must be treated with the utmost seriousness. In all societies, the behavior she alleges that took place needs to be investigated, not condoned or ignored. We commend Peng Shuai for her remarkable courage and strength in coming forward."

Simon had hundreds of millions of dollars at stake in tournaments and endorsements in China. Shenzhen was the site of the WTA year-ending finals, with $14 million in prize money for a single event. Peng and the two-time Grand Slam winner Li Na had opened the tour up to potentially billions of new fans. The NBA, when faced with a general manager who criticized China's actions in Hong Kong, balked at the prospect of supporting his critique over the business opportunities it threatened. China stopped showing NBA games temporarily, and it cost the league dearly. The Premier League similarly tried to quiet players' criticism of China. Even the International Olympic Committee (IOC) played the timid mouse in the Peng case, allowing China to have her appear on a video call, even though her home is in Beijing and the IOC's advance teams were in the country already.

But not the WTA. How could a league born out of a sense of injustice put revenue over a player whose autonomy had been threatened?

Osaka's experience sparked a conversation around mental health and wellness. And Peng's experience furthered a discussion around how to protect individual safety and well-being. Just as the athletes who play women's sports crafted collective bargaining agreements that responded to their needs, those same athletes might have different expectations of those leagues, as well.

Hard Decisions

In 2023, the WTA turned down money from Saudi Arabia to host the year-end finals there. Saudi Arabia has been investing heavily in sports such as golf, but not without controversy. On July 26, 2023, *The Guardian* estimated that Saudi Arabia had spent $6.3 billion on sports since 2021, and critics accused it of using sports to divert attention from human rights abuses.[4] Minky Worden wrote a piece titled, "Saudi Arabia's Newest Sportswashing Strategy: Sponsorship of Women's World Cup," for the Human Rights Watch website.[5]

It's a delicate balance for leagues: taking a stand on issues, especially if that means leaving money on the table. The PGA Tour, for example, took a different path when it decided to merge with the LIV golf tour, a competing league funded by the Saudi government that offered much larger contracts to lure PGA Tour golfers. Women's sports and leagues such as Professional Women's Hockey, the NWSL, and Women's Professional Volleyball are start-ups in many ways and need large investments to sustain themselves for years to come. It's worth remembering that the WTA Tour started with a cigarette sponsorship.

"As women's sport, we say no thanks and maybe no thanks to betting and maybe no thanks, we want to do it differently," said Sue Anstiss, the author of *Game On: The Unstoppable Rise of Women's Sport*. "However, does there come a point where that's where the money is? I have been thinking that recently with LIV [golf] and all that's happened. Actually, if we really want to grow it, do we need to go, 'We don't quite agree with your politics, but actually, that could make a massive difference'? How sad it will be if that's where we get to."

In 2024, the WTA announced the next three season-ending tournaments will be held in Saudi Arabia.

These are the kinds of conversations that the WNBA player Elizabeth Williams calls the hard ones. It's easy enough to say that people agree, but does that change when jobs are on the line, when the prize money might double, or when the cause means a lot to some in the league but not so much to others?

"People have realized that authentic sells," Williams said. "I think players, no matter what, should be true to themselves. And ironically, that's what people want to see. It's not like a fake image that a league creates for them."

Tissenbaum said the question may be *how* to use the platform, not whether to use the platform. Unlike with men's sports, fan bases are not put off by athletes using collective voices in women's sports for a cause.

"When you compare [fans of women's sports] to fans of traditional men's sports—potentially because they're younger, potentially because they're more tech savvy and they may be, again, more liberal, we don't know—the values alignment piece is massive," Tissenbaum said. "That's a huge reason why a lot of fans of women's sports say they become fans of women's sports. I care about the same things that these athletes care about. Admittedly, I am not a soccer fan, but when the U.S. Women's National Team said, 'We're not doing this,' you bet I was standing up and going, 'Yep. What they said!' To me it doesn't matter [that it's not my sport]. They're standing up for something that is larger than soccer."

Athletes have lived with the conventional wisdom that speaking out politically would alienate fans and anger team owners. Most important, sponsors have dropped athletes over controversial stances in the past.

When Jessica Berman was a candidate for the commissioner job at the NWSL, she had a lot of conversations with players. Keep in mind, this was a group of informed women, many of whom had become sensitive to inequity and abuse from the way they'd been treated in the past. Berman needed them to be able to bring their full selves to a league by which they may have felt burned.

"One of my questions to them is whether they're prepared—if I'm able to earn their trust, if I'm able to deliver what they want from the league with the board and our staff and everyone in our ecosystem—to lend their support and invest in us," Berman said. "Because I told them, and I would still say, they hold the keys to the future of this league, and that shouldn't ever be taken for granted. But we need them in order to maximize our potential."

The players weren't a problem to be managed. They were the solution.

Taking political stands may actually galvanize a fan base and draw more support. If team owners and a league are on the same side of those issues, which often center on the lived experience of the athletes themselves, then using the platform around women's sports is a net positive for leagues.

"Our players are just different. How they've been socialized to demand and build their own value proposition has been reinforced throughout their entire life," Berman said. "My strategy, or our strategy as a league, is to embrace that. There's huge value in that for us because their platforms that they own and operate are so authentic and connected to the people we want to connect with. So it's our responsibility to meet the players where they are."

CONCLUSION

Passing the Torch

The next generation isn't having it.

In 2021, the University of Oregon basketball player Sedona Prince looked at the small pyramid of weights the NCAA provided the women's tournament and got out her cell phone.

"I got something to show y'all," she began.[1]

One viral video later, many fans of the sport, and fans of equity, were just as outraged as she was.

This was the pandemic year, so the NCAA had erected two March Madness bubbles (although that trademarked name was to be applied only to the men's tournament): one for the women's tournament, and another for the men's. Others had posted images of the enormous palace built into a hotel ballroom that the men's bubble was using to lift.

The inequity was clear. There was no way to argue the NCAA was providing the same resources to these two groups of players.

"If you aren't upset about this problem, then you're a part of it," she said.

The NCAA protested that providing different fitness resources was completely fair because the women's contract didn't call for weights until the Sweet 16, so the inadequate pyramid at this stage of the tournament was actually a sign of largesse.

"It's 2021 and we are still fighting for bits and pieces of equality," Prince wrote as she introduced a video that grew to have 3.5 million likes.

If you want proof that the women were lifting, look no farther than Charli Collier, then a player on the Texas Longhorns team. As Collier was interviewed by ESPN's Holly Rowe after a late-round win, she stood with her hands on her hips, emphasizing two chiseled arms that could have been carved out of stone.

That kind of musculature doesn't come for free. It's earned in a weight room.

The inequity—that's an old tale. What's new here is the look on Prince's face. She wasn't grateful you were listening. She wasn't apologetic about the complaint. Hell, she didn't even comb her hair or put on makeup, as women historically have done for the camera. Prince had her hair pulled back and a look on her face that said, "Can you believe the shit we have to put up with?"

"Think of the perfect storm needed to get to that point," said the lawyer and women's sports advocate Kelsey Trainor. "Social media, a pandemic, two tournament bubbles, and younger players fed up with inequity. You see these women say, 'No, we're standing on the shoulders of everyone who came before us, but we're not going to be content with being happy to be here.'"

New Structures

Here's the thing about this generation: they know they deserve better. They also know they are worth more. Fifty years after the Virginia Slims tour and Title IX, sports are these girls' birthright as much as their brothers'. And lots of viewers agree. Enough to build a new house. A better house.

When many of the NCAA women's coaches saw Prince's video, they were also outraged, but their responses were filled with the fatigue of women who had spent decades fighting for resources within schools and the NCAA. Those coaches needed Prince's energy.

Prince's video ultimately prompted the NCAA to commission an external report on gender equity. The report, released by the law firm Kaplan Hecker & Fink LLP August 2021, found that the NCAA itself was holding women's basketball back through lack of investment and institutional apathy. In short, it found that the NCAA had not lived up to its commitment.[2]

It read: "The primary reason, we believe, is that the gender inequities at the NCAA—and specifically within the NCAA Division I basketball championships—stem from the structure and systems of the NCAA itself, which are designed to maximize the value of and support to the Division I Men's Basketball Championship as the primary source of funding for the NCAA and its membership. The NCAA's broadcast agreements, corporate sponsorship contracts, distribution of revenue, organizational structure, and culture all prioritize Division I men's basketball over everything else in ways that create, normalize, and perpetuate gender inequities."

It turns out that the small weights Prince noticed were just one manifestation of a system that deprioritized the women's game in many ways. And the argument that the market was voicing a preference for men's sports ignores the NCAA's neglect in how it measures that market.

The NCAA was leaving money on the table.

Had those inequities not been laid out side by side in a pandemic, Prince's viral video from the bubble tournament and the investigation it prompted might never have exposed the deeper, systemic issues. In fact, the report included an assessment by the media expert Ed Desser that the broadcast rights for NCAA women's basketball would be $82 million–$112 million in 2025. But the NCAA has never sold the women's basketball tournament on its own, the way it sells the men's tournament as an investment to be maximized. The NCAA had women's basketball rights bundled in with other NCAA championships, so the assessment found that the NCAA wasn't maximizing revenue. That adds up to money it wasn't able to reinvest in the sport because of institutional preferences for men's basketball.

When Megan Rapinoe talks about cinderblocks, this is what she means. These are the structural impediments that are quietly blocking success and making everything done to raise the women's game more difficult. The report found the NCAA wasn't even marketing the women's game. Packaging it with non-profit-generating sports became a self-fulfilling prophecy.

Professor Victoria Jackson of Arizona State University (ASU) pointed out how important it was to have the systemic issues on the record: "What we saw in the Kaplan Hecker & Fink *Gender Equity Review* is that there were all sorts of ways in which people were holding back women's sports and setting them up to fail and holding back the women to elevate the men and the way they were selling the media rights for the men's tournament versus the women's and all other sports. So even in those situations where we're going to allow you to thrive to a certain degree, there are still mechanisms in which women's sports are being held back."

The report made recommendations that included combining the men's and women's NCAA basketball tournaments, applying gender equity values to how revenue is distributed, and applying the brand "March Madness" to the women's tournament in addition to the men's.

The NCAA immediately adopted "March Madness" for both tournaments and has continued to authorize follow-up reports.

Nadia Rawlinson, the operating chairman of the Chicago Sky, said female athletes should expect resources and support.

"When you think about the future aspects of their career, you want women to be able to pursue sport at the highest levels," Rawlinson said. "They expect that they should be reaping those benefits, whether it's pay, whether it's support and resources, whether it's the fans that come and cheer them on. All that's available to them. And they should expect that there shouldn't be a difference."

New Media

Sedona Prince isn't the only one bringing a fresh set of eyes to these old systems and being horrified by what she sees.

Haley Rosen was baffled that she couldn't find information on her favorite teams in the conventional media. So when she was twenty-seven, the former soccer player launched the media outlet Just Women's Sports because she knows what she sees is inadequate. Her outlet covers women's sports, from the field to the front office, with the same regularity traditional sports outlets cover men's teams.

That historic number—that highlight sports shows devote 4–5 percent of space to women's sports—covers just part of the media ecosystem. But whether it's digital coverage, live games, or just opening up your local paper and looking beyond local high school coverage, there clearly just isn't the same level of coverage throughout that ecosystem. Rosen's site and newsletter look at women's leagues and events with the same thoroughness found in traditional men's coverage.

"For women's sports to be big, we need to make stars on the field, on the court," Rosen said. "These leagues need to run 365 days a year. The offseason and trades and what's happening—like, those need to be constantly running storylines. And I think that's all sports coverage for me. That's something we've really tried to push at Just Women's Sports. . . . Sports are good and bad and up and down, and there's joy and there's low points, and, like, we really try and cover that and be a part of that and push that forward."

Rosen secured $3.5 million in funding in 2021, including investment from women's players and the NBA star Kevin Durant.

"I feel so much urgency, almost to the point of anxiety, that we need to take advantage of this opportunity right now," Rosen said. "I think we can fundamentally change women's sports, and that leads to all these very positive changes around women in society. . . . Let's change it now. Like, I don't want to wait any longer. Let's change it now."

Candidly, I recognize Rosen's optimism and her frustration. I've seen it in so many people who wonder why certain things are easy and others are hard. I see my own fresh optimism when I left journalism school and started writing about sports. When I first met her in 2021, she was working on the problem in a way founders do, with a certainty that she had the key to fix it. Two years later, she had a perspective that came with the difficulty it takes to keep making those calls, keep pitching in meetings filled predominantly with men who may not see what she sees.

"I'm being very honest: the amount of sexism I've experienced has been crazy to me," Rosen said. "It drives me crazy, and it makes me sad. It's also very motivational and really makes you remember at the core why we are doing this and just how important it is."

Rosen has continued to attract investment and sponsors, including a $6 million raise in the summer of 2022 from investors such as the New York Nets and New York Liberty owners Joe and Clara Wu Tsai and Billie Jean King. Rosen has also become one of those connectors in the industry. People are drawn to her and want to see her succeed.

"And I will say: something very positive about working in women's sports has been that, like, the women and the men that work in women's sports, they're really different," Rosen said. "Like, the whole industry is so different than anything I've experienced. Like, it's a lot of people that have fought the bullshit and are done with it and want to go build something different and do things differently. There's, like, a lot of powerful women and personalities, and it doesn't feel nasty or, like, you know, any of that. And that is so exciting. You can see this new world that you've always imagined kind of, like, being built right in front of you, and there's something really, really fucking cool about being a part of it."

Rosen's frustration reflects a reality.

According to data from the University of Central Florida's Institute for Diversity and Ethics in Sports (TIDES), American sports departments are mostly composed of white men. Richard Lapchick, the institute's founder, has overseen *The Racial and Gender Report Card* for decades, tracking hiring practices in newsrooms and sports leagues. In 2021, 79.2 percent of sports editors were white, and 83.3 percent of sports editors were men. ESPN alone accounted for about a quarter of women who were sports editors, or five out of twenty.

Diversity has improved in the most coveted roles in sports media, but TIDES gave the industry an F when it came to gender hiring. Without ESPN, the percentage of women working as sports columnists would drop from 17.8 percent to 13.8 percent.

As an educator, I have taught dozens of young women who wanted to be sports writers, and several are in the middle of incredible careers. But the profession has been shrinking. The industry is undergoing seismic changes as the economic model around paying for coverage collapses. But this still doesn't account for the lack of women in this area.

Anecdotally, I have seen women in sports feel the tension between advocating to cover women's sports and knowing that their career success is defined by being assigned to cover a major beat, such as an NBA or NFL team. For men who wanted to cover women's sports, there could also be a stigma attached.

There have been excellent reporters who made women's sports their beat, such as the Associated Press's Mel Greenberg and Michael Voepel and Holly Rowe at ESPN, but they worked for decades without having their efforts and knowledge appreciated to the full extent it deserves.

Many major papers historically declined to regularly cover the major women's franchises in their area, with the notable exception of the *Hartford Courant*. UConn women's basketball was undeniable, and the *Courant* was an exception to major sports dailies. Some newspapers would argue against staffing the WNBA teams in their cities, even in the first few years, when the attendance and ratings were up. I covered the Liberty that first year, and you could see from the people in the Madison Square Garden press box on game day which papers cared enough to send a reporter, never mind a columnist.

Why on earth would Rosen or anyone else be satisfied with that status quo? And how could any reporter expect to upend these deeply entrenched systems as newspapers are fighting to stay afloat?

"We need to have coverage of women's sports," Rosen said. "And I think we see that there's these big breakthrough moments in women's sports when there is a World Cup; or we know the March Madness numbers were massive; or college softball, college volleyball outdrawing the men for multiple years in a row. And yet it [women's sports] is still 4 percent of sports coverage. And I think that that not only holds women's sports back from truly being mainstream, but it leaves a lot of value on the table. So we have to find solutions to that. I'm also more convinced than ever it's not going to be legacy media. Legacy media is built around, like, I was going to say, men's sports, but really it's built around the NBA and the NFL."

A new house.

Rosen isn't the only one trying to rethink the strategy.

"So often women are on the outside looking in, in particular BIPOC [Black, Indigenous, People of Color] communities, queer communities, etcetera, and that really is a shame because sports should be for everyone," Ellen Hyslop said. Hyslop and two college friends, Jacie deHoop and Roslyn McLarty, conceived of the Canadian sports media company *The Gist* in 2017. They were working in finance in Toronto, drinking wine and talking about sports in a way that felt organic to them but wasn't part of traditional sports coverage.

As Hyslop recalled: "I think for us, being mid-twenties at that time, thinking about the way that we engage with media and learned so much of it was through newsletters and social media and podcasts, and we weren't seeing any traditional media actually reaching folks in that way, and then traditional media at all, even thinking about women at the center of their fandom."

So often, the architecture of sports media is transposed from men's games to women's games. The sound of a broadcast, with deep-voiced announcers praising the "toughness" of opponents, seems to be a given. But does it have to be? *The Gist* looks and feels different as a website. It might start a piece with, "Happy Tuesday!" It takes itself less seriously while being serious about sports.

"[What] I'm proud of is that we really have proved that there's a new business model in sports and there's a new way to be successful within sports that doesn't have to be seeking avid male sports fans and working with advertisers that are only seeking men," Hyslop said.

The Gist went from an idea to a company in earnest in 2019. In that time, Hyslop and her partners have been witnesses to the pandemic surge in interest around women's sports and the ways athletes are connecting with fans via social media. Now they aren't looking just at content but at the ecosystem around an audience.

"I think what is going to be very interesting, just for the sports industry on the whole, is how technology is going to impact sports and, also, how different audiences react and relate to sports," Hyslop said. "We know that Gen Z has a totally different relationship with sports than Gen X and even Millennials. So I think that what has happened in the past is that women's sports have been left behind, not only from a coverage perspective, but also from a tech perspective."

Like Kelsey Trainor, Hyslop pointed to what has given the current conversation around women's sports its form: a viral video that showed inarguable inequity and the platform to distribute it. "Sedona Prince had the opportunity to actually get on TikTok and show it for herself and reach this whole new audience that would have never seen something like this on *SportsCenter*, or the *SportsCenter* audience wouldn't have cared," Hyslop said.

That's what's different. The decision making is coming not from the top down but from the bottom up. And if Prince can do that with her observation, why can't Hyslop and her investors?

"We've already seen digital marketing, digital media, be so good for women's sports," Hyslop said. "We've seen social media be so good for women's sports. But I think this next step of how we leverage technology to actually produce content around the games is going to propel women's sports even further and access a different type of audience and engage them in a . . . really, really different way."

Arielle Chambers is one of the strongest voices in the women's sports media space. She doesn't cover sports in a traditional way, as a detached observer; rather, she channels the perspective of many of the athletes she covers. She is an insider; she hosts red carpet events, such as the Women's Sports Foundation gala; and she's been on several lists of young Black entrepreneurs and influencers. Most of all, she understands the dynamics around this new iteration of women's sports.

"We're past fifty years of Title IX, so the generations that are coming up now have never experienced a life where pro women's athletics hasn't existed," Chambers said. "So it's becoming the norm. Social media allows you to consume women's and girls' sports highlights, so when you see that on your timeline every day, it normalizes it. It neutralizes your bias and allows you to consume it on the regular. So it becomes part of the culture."

Chambers points out not only that are there new technologies and new generations of athletes but also that there are new fans who aren't constrained in their imagination of how to enjoy sports. In 2019, Chambers started *HighlightHER* for Bleacher Report. Being able to directly amplify women's sports has been a game changer, and Chambers sees only growth in the space. She's been particularly engaged with coverage of the WNBA and was often courtside at Liberty games, given her New York City home base.

"Year over year, especially since 2020, it's been increasing, and it's no coincidence and that's because it's more visible and people are investing more into it," Chambers said. "So it shows that the upward trajectory of women's sports is a direct result of it being accessible and available to us."

Teams in the WNBA and NWSL aren't looking for an audience; they're looking for communities. The same can be said of new media sites. Barstool has done this very effectively on the men's sports side. It has Instagram accounts to go with college communities all over the country. Readers call themselves "Stoolies," and it's a whole thing. Even if brands for women don't want to duplicate the Barstool content, there is a model in terms of engagement.

"I just really hope that the way that we think about women's sports and the way that leagues and teams and properties are thinking about women's sports is actually more from a start-up and community-driven perspective," Hyslop said, "as opposed to a traditional advertising-based business model perspective, because I think we're seeing more from a macro perspective in the media landscape, those not even doing great for men's sports."

Certainly, the coverage environment around sports has not been as healthy and independent as it once was. The *New York Times* disbanded its sports section in 2023 after purchasing *The Athletic*, and many sports outlets have entered into partnerships with betting firms to pay for coverage that would have been unthinkable a decade ago. New models are coming.

"In the first five months of 2023, we had more impressions than [in] all of 2022 combined," Rosen said. "So, like, we have just also experienced a lot of growth. And I think for us, what's been exciting to see and what we have really tried to push as a company is true women's sports, and sports coverage is what it's going to take to push this industry mainstream."

New Will

Are these young sports entrepreneurs really on to something? If so, they aren't the only ones. Other young women are creating new structures and companies in areas where they see a lack of outreach. It's an area ripe for disruption.

"I . . . think women have been leading like they've been through adversity all the time," said Thayer Lavielle of Wasserman's The Collective. "So they're like, 'We'll figure this out. . . . This doesn't seem that hard. Come on.'"

Female athletes are reinvesting in women's games and teams. But there is a larger exasperation that things haven't been fixed already.

While discussing the activism playing out in sports, Professor Ellen Staurowsky of Ithaca College said she doesn't think it's limited to the field. Women who enter college programs to cover sports might also be among the few women in individual classes, but, she found, they are more likely than those in past classes to speak out.

"I think it's partly . . . the dynamic of what's happening with my women students at Ithaca," said Staurowsky. "I think the two are actually connected. I think that this generation of women coming up and the Wubble and WNBA women who, with their activism, have been so powerful over the past ten years, that this generation of women, they're just looking around, and they're just like, 'Are you kidding me? We are just not taking this.' If you do share the history with them, they're just like, 'Well, that's fine. But we're just not doing this anymore.'"

Remember the wave of the early 1970s, when Title IX and women's tennis created opportunities for women in sports? Then in the late 1990s, when there was another burst? Victoria Jackson of ASU has thought about what the conditions are that factor into these bursts of momentum around women and sports.

"You have to have the political, cultural, and economic [conditions]. The mix of those three have to be right," Jackson said. "So the economy has to be good and thriving, and there has to be, like, no economic anxiety. People have to feel optimistic about the forecasted economy going forward. You have to have political support and, kind of, all sorts of ways, whether that's traditional, actual politics, like who's in the White House, and then the cultural piece, where there's just widespread general public support around ideas of equity and inclusion.

"And then the other piece is that you have to win," Jackson continued. "It's so precarious and tenuous that, like, it might not even be that things are in declension. Just someone saying that things are in decline makes it true when it comes to women's sports. It might not even be, like, the evidence, and the receipts might suggest otherwise. But if there's a belief that things are in decline, then they are. You speak it into existence with women's sports in a way that doesn't happen with men's sports."

At this moment, there is a chorus speaking these opportunities around women's sports into existence. The energy is added to the growing wave around women's sports, and those who have been in the game for decades need the optimism and certainty of Prince, Hyslop, Rosen, Chambers, Rawlinson, and hundreds of others. Lavielle is one of them, and she thinks 2019 was the turning point.

"I don't think this is just a moment," Lavielle said. "I think that this is momentum that has been born over many, many years but is finally getting an enormous due. And this is my theory: I believe four years ago when we started this, there was this kind of start of a wave. The U.S. women had just won the World Cup. We were all coming off the World Cup. There was a lot of hype around it. There was a lot of hype going into the WNBA season. I think Cathy Engelbert had just recently been named [commissioner] the year before, and then all of a sudden we screamed into a pandemic and the world shut down. I remember reading an article that said, 'That's it. Women's sports is dead.' Like, nobody will give a shit, and nobody is going to give another dollar. Done, any momentum we saw done.

"And in reality, the absolute opposite happened," Lavielle said.

Have women's sports finally reached escape velocity from the precarity that Jackson details? Are they still so far behind, as Billie Jean King frankly pointed out?

As this book was being written, it seemed as though each week brought an announcement of a new development. For example, the long-awaited Professional Women's Hockey League (PWHL) started playing in January 2024, and just before it did, the Associated Press announced that it would provide ongoing game coverage for member newspapers. CBS signed a professional women's volleyball league to a rights deal. Financial analysts at the consulting firm Deloitte made news by projecting that women's sports would generate $1.2 billion in 2024, led by American women's soccer and basketball.[3] As if on cue, women's basketball and volleyball crowds then broke records and surged in ratings and interest.

In July 2024, the WNBA announced it had signed a new media rights deal worth $2.2 billion over the course of the next eleven years. That is game-changing money.

Women's sports are flourishing. Investment is flowing to leagues, and those athletes are redefining what it means to play sports. In just a few generations, Kathrine Switzer has gone from being pulled from the Boston Marathon to a world in which new leagues pop up like dandelions on a summer lawn.

Not all will last. But this generation of athletes will not face the malign neglect that their mothers and grandmothers did.

And, perhaps, an even greater promise of equity awaits their children.

ACKNOWLEDGMENTS

I'm writing this from a desk at a friend's house in Tisvildeleje, Denmark. My first day here, we walked to the Kattegatt Sea for a brisk June afternoon swim. My friend Lena and I had done this a dozen times before over the years and were waiting for enough warmth to soak in to make the water appealing.

Beneath the glare of the sun, I spotted a group of older women walking slowly from the edge of the beach to the water. One was quite elderly, her back sloped and her white hair pulled into a gentle bun. At each elbow was another woman to guide her.

I motioned to Lena, who had already seen them.

They reached the water and slowly waded in—all together, one entity. The elderly woman dipped her knees, and the water reached her waist, her companions pulling her back up. They went out farther. She dipped her knees again. When she'd had enough, the women led her back to the sand. And that's how a woman who had likely gone swimming unhindered many times in that sea felt its freshness once again.

This book would not have been possible without so many people at my elbow.

For some reason, as a writer I thought this would be easy. It was not.

First, I thank Julie DiCaro, my co-host for the *Ladies Room* podcast that was posted on *Deadspin*. For two years we got to speak to some of the most interesting people in sports, a topic about which we both care deeply.

DiCaro, who wrote *Sidelined: Sports Culture and Being a Woman in America*, was a mentor throughout the writing process. Thanks also to the veteran authors Howard Bryant and Dave Zirin, who offered early advice and insight into writing and publishing.

Before that, there was espnW, where I met my first two radio co-hosts and colleagues Sarah Spain and Kate Fagan. I adore them both still and hope all of their projects make them rich beyond their wildest imagining.

And I'm going to add the friends who have stoked my creativity and provided endless encouragement. Lena Skadegard invited me to her home and is my conspirator in adventure. She helped me parse the question, "Is your book woke?" from a well-meaning but tipsy Dane.

Her parents, Rashmi and Jakob, warrant my gratitude, as well, for engaging me on these subjects from a place with different associations and over the decades beyond mine. They raised two incredible daughters, and Mira Skadegard's antidiscrimination work at the University of Aalborg is another beacon in the darkness.

Nicola and David Jordan and Amy and Roland Diaz have also heard me work through the topics in the book for the past three decades. To Danni and Orion Michaeli, who took me in, and Gali Cohen for their friendship.

To Rowan Wilson, who took a chance on me at Cravath.

To editors who became friends in Ryan Hockensmith, Jon Scher, and Hank Winnicki, and to Rich Deitsch, Joanne Gerstner, and Kavitha Davidson, colleagues who have often worked through these issues with me.

To my roller derby pals Joanie Ramone, Jeri Fling'her, and Rita Wayward, who make me laugh so hard I need medical attention.

To two of the greatest mentors in the sports media business: first and foremost, Sandy Padwe, who raised me as a journalist, and Bob Ley, for all the conversations and strategy.

I owe thanks to Helen Benedict, whose book *Virgin or Vamp* alerted me to the way media narratives can worm their way into everyday coverage. I read it in graduate school, and it was particularly useful covering the issues around domestic violence and the NFL in the 2010s.

To Chris LaPlaca at ESPN for seeing the story I wanted to tell and connecting me to the people who could help me tell it. And I owe an enormous debt of gratitude to the dozens of people who gave me an hour, sometimes more, to work through the challenges and look around weird little corners of this subject with me. They are quoted throughout this book.

My agent, Chris Bucci at Aevitas Creative, believed in the story even as publishers wondered what the market for a book about women's sports might be. Wasn't there a single narrative about an inspirational athlete I wanted to tell?

Most important, I thank my daughters, Jean and Charlotte, and my husband, Steve. They have given me the time and support I needed to be thoughtful and focused as I wrote and reported this book.

When Jean and Charlotte were twelve and fourteen, we moved to London. I'd been laid off by ESPN in a massive shuffling of talent, and I had a non-compete agreement, as the remainder of my contract was paid. My husband got a job teaching high school at Marymount International, and our daughters attended while my contract remained in place. We visited Amsterdam, Athens, Berlin, Copenhagen, Dresden, Edinburgh, Marrakesh, Milan, Oxford, Paris, Prague, Rome, Santorini, Sorrento, Stockholm. . . . You get the picture. We documented the start with an appearance on House Hunters International.

I was endeavoring to write a book.

Now I have written a book.

So this is also a huge thank you to ESPN—not just for a job that I loved doing, but for an amazing landing. So many in media will not be able to choose how one or another job concludes, and not all jobs come with parachutes, but they are often hidden opportunities.

Finally, this book is dedicated to Nadgia James. Here is why.

When I was in my early twenties I was at an impasse.

I'd thought I wanted to go to law school, but after working for a few months at a big law firm, I realized it wasn't for me. I had met Nadgia working a temp job a year before that. Back in the 1990s, law firms hired temporary legal assistants for tasks that would make a modern iPad die from boredom: keywords, copying, counting, stamping. It was drudgery.

Six of us in a windowless room for three months got to know one another pretty well. Nadgia lived in Brooklyn, too, and when I went home with her one night, I realized she lived in the same apartment on 12th Street that my mother had lived in just a few years earlier—not the same building; the same apartment. In a city of eight million people, it was a coincidence too weird to ignore.

We became close quickly. Her dad had been a musician working with Harry Belafonte. She was creative and hilarious. I was at her apartment watching the Knicks when the game was interrupted by the OJ Simpson Bronco chase.

One day we were rollerblading in Prospect Park and I was lamenting about the Knicks and not wanting to go to law school and Nadgia said the thing that changed my life: "You should be a sportswriter."

I hadn't even considered this the kind of profession that was available to me. I read the *Daily News* and the *New York Times* sports on the subway. Back then the *Times* had a great section: Harvey Araton, Ira Berkow, Bill Rhoden, Selena Roberts, Mike Wise. How did someone even get to be a sportswriter?

I found a path. Nadgia and I stayed close for years. She came to my wedding; then I moved to Westchester, and we didn't see each other so much. She died of breast cancer at thirty-eight, an unbelievable loss.

From time to time I've met people she also impacted.

Nadgia, you are missed. This book is dedicated to your memory.

NOTES

INTRODUCTION

1. Rapinoe, Megan. Interview with Julie DiCaro and Jane McManus. "The One with Megan Rapinoe." *Ladies Room*, podcast audio, July 1, 2021. https://podcasts.apple.com/us/podcast/the-one-with-megan-rapinoe/id1543625034?i=1000527466462.

2. Pfister, Gertrud. "The Medical Discourse on Female Physical Culture in Germany in the 19th and Early 20th Centuries." *Journal of Sport History* 17(2) (1990): 183–198. https://www.jstor.org/stable/43611566.

3. Comstock, R. Dawn, and Sarah K. Fields. "The Eternally Wounded Athlete: How Medical Professionals and Sports Injury Researchers Have Limited Female Athletes' Sport Participation and Biased the Interpretation of Sports Injury Research." *Current Epidemiology Reports* 7(4) (2020): 327–333. https://doi.org/10.1007/s40471-020-00255-0.

4. McCarter, Christy. "Overlooking Her Shot: Women's Sports Need an Assist as Coverage Remains the Same as 30 Years Ago." *Purdue University News*, March 24, 2021. https://www.purdue.edu/newsroom/releases/2021/Q1/overlooking-her-shot-womens-sports-need-an-assist-as-coverage-remains-the-same-as-30-years-ago.html.

5. Foudy, Julie. Interview with Julie DiCaro and Jane McManus. "The One with Julie Foudy." *Ladies Room*, podcast audio, May 4, 2021. https://podcasts.apple.com/us/podcast/the-one-with-julie-foudy/id1543625034?i=1000520177619.

6. Allaster, Stacey. Interview with Julie DiCaro and Jane McManus. "The One with Stacey Allaster." *Ladies Room*, podcast audio, June 7, 2021. https://podcasts.apple.com/us/podcast/the-one-with-stacey-allaster/id1543625034?i=1000524511378.

7. Anstiss, Sue. *Game On: The Unstoppable Rise of Women's Sport*. London: Unbound, 2022.

8. Bonderson, Aaron. "92,003 Fans Set a Record for Women's Sports Attendance Watching College Volleyball." *All Things Considered*, National Public Radio, August 31, 2023. https://www.npr.org/2023/08/31/1197084285/92-003-fans-set-a-record-for-womens-sports-attendance-watching-college-volleybal.

CHAPTER 1

1. Center for Sports Media, Seton Hall University. "Equity, Influence and the Next Generation in Sports." Video, n.d., YouTube. Accessed February 19, 2024. https://www.youtube.com/watch?v=IKs9098NWuQ.

2. Murphy, Melissa. "Original 9 Trailblazers Stood for Tennis Equality in 1970." Associated Press, September 23, 2020. https://www.sandiegouniontribune.com/sports/national/story/2020-09-23/original-9-trailblazers-stood-for-tennis-equality-in-1970.

3. "Billie Jean King Reveals How a $1 Contract Shaped Professional Women's Tennis." *PBS NewsHour*, August 17, 2021. https://www.pbs.org/newshour/show/billie-jean-king-reveals-how-a-1-contract-shaped-professional-womens-tennis.

4. Badenhausen, Kurt. "The Highest-Paid Female Athletes 2018." *Forbes*, August 21, 2018. https://www.forbes.com/sites/kurtbadenhausen/2018/08/21/the-highest-paid-female-athletes-2018/?sh=30eaae98405f.

5. "The New Economy of Sports." Report, The Collective, n.d. https://www.wearethecollective.com/new-economy-of-sports.

6. Lieberman, Nancy. Interview with Kate Fagan and Jessica Smetana. "Shooting Stars," *Off the Looking Glass*, podcast audio, January 12, 2022. https://podcasts.apple.com/us/podcast/shooting-stars/id1592584251?i=1000547638485.

CHAPTER 2

1. Williams, Venus. "Wimbledon Has Sent Me a Message: I'm Only a Second Class Champion." *The Times*, June 26, 2006. https://www.thetimes.co.uk/article/wimbledon-has-sent-me-a-message-im-only-a-second-class-champion-f056h05hmzq.

2. King, Billie Jean, Johnette Howard, and Maryanne Vollers. *All In: An Autobiography*. New York: Alfred A. Knopf, 2021.

3. Smialek, Jeanna. "Claudia Goldin Wins Nobel in Economics for Studying Women in the Work Force." *New York Times*, October 9, 2023. https://www.nytimes.com/2023/10/09/business/economy/claudia-goldin-nobel-prize-economics.html.

4. Goldin, Claudia. Interview with Rhoda Metcalfe. "Claudia Goldin on Family Economics." *Women in Economics*, podcast audio, International Monetary Fund, June 9, 2023. https://www.imf.org/en/News/Podcasts/All-Podcasts/2023/06/09/claudia-goldin-on-family-economics.

5. Bird, Sue. "So the President F*cking Hates My Girlfriend." *Players' Tribune*, July 2, 2019. https://www.theplayerstribune.com/articles/sue-bird-megan-rapinoe-uswnt.

6. Eastman, Susan Tyler, and Andrew C. Billings. "Gender Parity in the Olympics." *Journal of Sport and Social Issues* 23(2) (1999): 140–170. https://doi.org/10.1177/0193723599232003.

7. Gregory, Sean. "How U.S. Soccer's Historic Equal Pay Deal Came About." *Time*, May 19, 2022. https://time.com/6178467/us-women-soccer-equal-pay-deal.

8. Draper, Kevin, and Andrew Das. "'Blatant Misogyny': U.S. Women Protest, and U.S. Soccer President Resigns." *New York Times*, March 12, 2020. https://www.nytimes.com/2020/03/12/sports/soccer/uswnt-equal-pay.html.

9. Peterson, Anne M. "U.S. Men's and Women's Soccer Teams Formally Sign Equal Pay Agreements." *PBS NewsHour*, September 6, 2022. https://www.pbs.org/newshour/economy/u-s-mens-and-womens-soccer-teams-formally-sign-equal-pay-agreements.

10. "President Biden Signs Cantwell-Capito Equal Pay Bill into Law, Historic Win for Women's Equality in Sports." U.S. Senate Committee on Commerce, Science, and Transportation, press release, January 5, 2023. https://www.commerce.senate.gov/2023/1/president-biden-signs-cantwell-capito-equal-pay-bill-into-law.

CHAPTER 3

1. "Luis Rubiales Suspended by FIFA over Women's World Cup Kiss." *BBC News*, video, YouTube, posted August 26, 2023. Accessed February 20, 2024. https://www.youtube.com/watch?v=UA13nn0CYy0.

2. Verria, Lawrence, and George Galdorisi. *The Kissing Sailor: The Mystery behind the Photo That Ended World War II*. Annapolis, MD: Naval Institute Press, 2023.

3. "Why a Female Athlete Should Be Your Next Leader." *EY*, September 23, 2020. https://www.ey.com/en_us/athlete-programs/why-female-athletes-should-be-your-next-leader.

4. Branch, Taylor. "The Shame of College Sports." *The Atlantic*, February 19, 2014. https://www.theatlantic.com/magazine/archive/2011/10/the-shame-of-college-sports/308643.

5. Martínez Fortuny, Núria, Alejandra Alonso-Calvete, Iria Da Cuña-Carrera, and Rocío Abalo-Núñez. "Menstrual Cycle and Sport Injuries: A Systematic Review." *International Journal of Environmental Research and Public Health* 20(4) (2023): 3264. https://doi.org/10.3390/ijerph20043264.

6. Barnes, Katie. *Fair Play: How Sports Shape the Gender Debates*. New York: St. Martin's, 2023.

CHAPTER 4

1. "The Fluid Fan Is Here." Sports Innovation Lab. Report, February 2020. Accessed February 20, 2024. https://www.sportsilab.com/free-reports/the-fluid-fan-is-here.

2. "The Growth of the Women's Sports Community—ABRIDGED." Sports Innovation Lab, n.d. https://www.sportsilab.com/free-reports/the-growth-of-the-womens-sports-community.

3. "Majority of Sports Fans Say Women's Sports Don't Get Enough Coverage." Poll, Marist Institute for Public Opinion. Marist College, Poughkeepsie, NY, November 2021. https://maristpoll.marist.edu/polls/marist-center-for-sports-communication-marist-poll-womens-sports-november-2021.

4. "Data Shows Highest Viewing Time on Record for Women's Sport as FIFA Women's World Cup Attracts a Younger, More Female Demographic." Women's Sport Trust, September 14, 2023. https://www.womenssporttrust.com/data-shows-highest-viewing-time-on-record-for-womens-sport-as-fifa-womens-world-cup-attracts-a-younger-more-female-demographic.

5. "How We're Making It Easier to Find Results on Women's Sports." Google, July 25, 2023. https://blog.google/products/search/how-were-making-it-easier-to-find-results-on-womens-sports/?fbclid=IwAR0avwymBtqZBrxIHxisBxxvSWgSrt9tnv0y1JFt6ZuMT1GiC7hv4cuqNS0.

6. Span, Emma. "The Book of Basketball and Staggering Casual Sexism." *Bronx Banter* (blog), December 17, 2010. Accessed February 20, 2024. http://www.bronxbanterblog.com/2010/12/17/the-book-of-basketball-and-staggering-casual-sexism.

CHAPTER 5

1. McCarter, Christy. "Overlooking Her Shot: Women's Sports Need an Assist as Coverage Remains the Same as 30 Years Ago." *Purdue University News*, March 24, 2021. https://www.purdue.edu/newsroom/releases/2021/Q1/overlooking-her-shot-womens-sports-need-an-assist-as-coverage-remains-the-same-as-30-years-ago.html.

2. Lewis, Jonathan. *Sports Media Watch*. https://www.sportsmediawatch.com.

3. Schneider, Michael. "100 Most-Watched TV Series of 2022–23: This Season's Winners and Losers." *Variety*, May 27, 2023. https://variety.com/2023/tv/news/most-popular-tv-shows-highest-rated-2022-2023-season-yellowstone-football-1235623612.

4. Perez, A. J. "Coco Gauff Powers ESPN to Record Viewership for Women's Final." *Front Office Sports*, September 13, 2023. https://frontofficesports.com/coco-gauff-powers-espn-to-record-viewership-for-womens-final.

CHAPTER 6

1. Perez, A. J. "Coco Gauff Powers ESPN to Record Viewership for Women's Final." *Front Office Sports*, September 13, 2023. https://frontofficesports.com/coco-gauff-powers-espn-to-record-viewership-for-womens-final.

2. "WNBA Finals Game Four Becomes Most-Watched on Record." *Sports Business Journal*, October 20, 2023. https://www.sportsbusinessjournal.com/Articles/2023/10/20/wnba-2023-finals-game-4-viewership.

3. "NWSL's Return Attracts Record-breaking Viewership." *Eurosport*, June 30, 2020. https://www.eurosport.com/football/nwsl-s-return-attracts-record-breaking-viewership_sto7790883/story.shtml.

4. "More Sports Fans Switching to Streaming." Poll, Marist Institute for Public Opinion, Marist College, Poughkeepsie, NY, May 4, 2021. Accessed February 20,

2024. https://maristpoll.marist.edu/polls/marist-center-for-sports-communication-marist-poll-results-and-analysis.

CHAPTER 7

1. "TEDxBoston @ the 'Quin." TEDxBoston livestream, YouTube, May 16, 2022. Accessed February 20, 2024. https://www.youtube.com/watch?v=RP0whSR2_cU.

2. "2022 Sports Participation Reports Available for the USA—Sports Marketing Surveys." *Sports Marketing Surveys USA*, n.d. Accessed February 20, 2024. https://www.sportsmarketingsurveysusa.com/2022-sports-participation-reports-available-for-the-usa.

3. Broughton, David. "Hoops Slam Dunk: Basketball Adds to Long Streak as Favorite Major Sport to Play." *Sports Business Journal*, September 26, 2022. https://www.sportsbusinessjournal.com/Journal/Issues/2022/09/26/Portfolio/Sports-participation.aspx.

4. "Mary Earps: Nike Knew 'They Got It Wrong' over Shirts." *Sky News* video, Facebook, December 13, 2023. Accessed February 20, 2024. https://www.facebook.com/skynews/videos/mary-earps-nike-knew-they-got-it-wrong-over-shirts/2345521355631129.

5. Murray, Caitlin. "Why Nike Didn't Have Enough USWNT World Cup Jerseys to Meet Demand—And What It Cost the Players and Fans." *Yahoo Sports*, October 10, 2019. https://sports.yahoo.com/why-nike-didnt-have-enough-uswnt-world-cup-jerseys-to-meet-demand-and-what-it-cost-the-players-and-fans-171933947.html.

CHAPTER 8

1. Wrack, Suzanne. *A Woman's Game*. New York: Faber and Faber, 2022.

2. "The N.W.S.L. and Players' Union Report on Women's Soccer." *New York Times*, December 14, 2022. https://www.nytimes.com/interactive/2022/12/14/us/nwsl-report-abuse.html

3. Young, Jabari. "Dwayne 'the Rock' Johnson Says the XFL Will Succeed. Who Wants to Tell Him He's Wrong?" *Forbes*, June 10, 2023. Accessed February 20, 2024. https://www.forbes.com/sites/jabariyoung/2023/06/10/dwayne-johnson-says-xfl-succeed-nfl-usfl-dany-garcia/?sh=4928a4bb57fe&utm_medium=social&utm_campaign=socialflowForbesMainTwitter&utm_source=ForbesMainTwitter.

4. Badenhausen, Kurt. "NFL Team Valuations 2023: Cowboys Worth $9.2 B[illion], Average Tops $5 B[illion]." *Sportico*, August 8, 2023. https://www.sportico.com/valuations/teams/2023/nfl-team-valuations-2023-cowboys-1234733495.

5. Toonkel, Jessica, and Rachel Bachman. "NWSL Set to Expand with Record-Setting $50 Million Franchise Fees." *Wall Street Journal*, January 27, 2023. https://www.wsj.com/articles/national-womens-soccer-league-san-francisco-boston-utah-11674857126.

6. "CBS Pays $1 Billion for NCAA Tournament Rights." United Press International, November 21, 1989. Accessed February 20, 2024. https://www.upi.com/Archives/1989/11/21/CBS-pays-1-billion-for-NCAA-tournament-rights/1138627627600.

7. "The Space Between." *Savanta*, February 2, 2023. https://savanta.com/case-studies/the-space-between.

8. Ricciardelli, Michael, and Marty Appel. "Sports Poll on Women's World Cup." Poll, Stillman School of Business, Seton Hall University, July 24, 2023. Accessed February 20, 2024. https://www.shu.edu/business/news/sports_poll_on_womens_world_cup.html.

CHAPTER 10

1. "WNBA Legend on Basketball, Motherhood, Success, and What's Next." TEDxBoston video, YouTube, June 7, 2022. Accessed February 20, 2024. https://www.youtube.com/watch?v=Jh-noQ-LGVE.

2. Strout, Erin. "Mary Cain: 'Creating a Super Healthy, Positive Dynamic is My Biggest Priority.'" *Women's Running*, June 28, 2021. https://www.womensrunning.com/culture/news/mary-cain-creates-atalanta.

CHAPTER 11

1. Buckner, Candace. "How Politics Transformed Kelly Loeffler from Hoops Junkie to WNBA Villain." *Washington Post*, August 29, 2020. https://www.washingtonpost.com/sports/2020/08/29/kelly-loeffler-wnba-black-lives-matter.

2. Bluestein, Greg, and Bria Felicien. "Loeffler Opposes WNBA's Plan to Spread 'Black Lives Matter' Message." *Atlanta Journal-Constitution*, July 7, 2020. https://www.ajc.com/blog/politics/loeffler-opposes-wnba-plan-spread-black-lives-matter-message/ybTbHIpzZx7dbRlz3sfLiM.

3. McManus, Jane. "The WNBA's Activism and How It Just Might Change the Country in a Matter of Weeks." *Deadspin*, December 21, 2020. https://deadspin.com/the-wnba-s-activism-and-how-it-just-might-change-the-co-1845926074.

4. Michaelson, Ruth. "Revealed: Saudi Arabia's $6 [Billion] Spend on 'Sportswashing.'" *The Guardian*, July 26, 2023. https://www.theguardian.com/world/2023/jul/26/revealed-saudi-arabia-6bn-spend-on-sportswashing.

5. Worden, Minky. "Saudi Arabia's Newest Sportswashing Strategy: Sponsorship of Women's World Cup." Human Rights Watch, February 16, 2023. https://www.hrw.org/news/2023/02/16/saudi-arabias-newest-sportswashing-strategy-sponsorship-womens-world-cup.

CONCLUSION

1. "Sedona Prince on TikTok." Video, posted March 18, 2021. https://www.tiktok.com/@sedonerrr/video/6941180880127888646?lang=en.

2. Kaplan Hecker & Fink LLP. *NCAA Gender Equity Review.* Report. https://ncaagenderequityreview.com.

3. Haskel, Jennifer, Paul Lee, Amy Clarke, and Pete Giorgio. "Women's Elite Sports: Breaking the Billion-Dollar Barrier." *Deloitte Insights*, n.d. https://www2.deloitte.com/us/en/insights/industry/technology/technology-media-and-telecom-predictions/2024/tmt-predictions-professional-womens-sports-revenue.html.

INDEX

Ackerman, Val, 141–144
adversity, overcoming, 3
Agasara, Nandini, 60
Allaster, Stacey, 12, 29
Ally Bank, 105–106
Amaechi, John, 23
Angel City, Los Angeles (NWSL), 11, 75; ownership structure of, 129–133
Anstiss, Sue, 14, 67–68, 136, 169
Aronowitz, Meg, 87, 92; strategy of, to raise visibility of women's sports, 101–108
Ashe, Arthur, 32
Association of Tennis Professionals (ATP), 19, 21–22, 26, 146–147
Augustus, Seimone, 58
Azarenka, Victoria, 27, 155–157

Barnes, Katie, 57
Bartkowicz, Peaches, 19. *See also* Original 9
Battle of the Sexes (tennis match), 8, 18, 146
BBC, 80, 93
Belth, Alex, 74
Berman, Jessica, 10, 105, 111, 155, 170–171; involvement of, in growth and broadcast negotiations of the NWSL, 121–131, 136–137
Berri, David, 7, 42; on emotional investments in men's sports, 125–126
Betos, Michelle, 55–57
Biles, Simone, 52, 71, 90, 166
Billings, Andrew, 38
Bird, Sue, 23, 36–37, 75, 101, 145, 159–162, 163
Boston Marathon, 1–4, 183
Bryant, Gigi, 146
Bryant, Kobe, 146–147
Buckner, Candace, 161
Bueckers, Paige, 118
Burrows, Charlotte, 24, 41, 43, 48–49; work of, on equal pay with USWNT, 33–35

Cain, Mary, 157–158
Caron, Emily, 148
Carter, Kathy, 37–38
Carvalho, Barbara, 66
Casals, Rosie, 19. *See also* Original 9
Chambers, Arielle, 179–180, 182
Chastain, Brandi, 9, 123, 129
Clarendon, Layshia, 58–59
Clark, Caitlin, 97
Clijsters, Kim, 27, 156
Cone, Cindy Parlow, 42–43
Cooky, Cheryl, 9, 46–47, 51–53, 57, 60, 81–82
Copa 71 (documentary), 6

Cordeiro, Carlos, 35–36, 42
Court, Margaret, 18, 167
Cullman, Joe, 20, 147

Dalton, Judy Tegart, 19. *See also* Original 9
Darvin, Lindsey, 40
Das, Andrew, 42
Davis, Amira Rose, 52–55, 59–60
Davis, Mark, 28–29, 141
Dawes, Dominique, 11
Deadspin, 162
Deitsch, Richard, 85, 91–92
de Varona, Donna, 38
DiCaro, Julie, 11, 115, 159
Djokovic, Novak, 26, 100, 146
Draper, Kevin, 42
Dream, Atlanta (WNBA), 99, 161–162
Driessen, Christine, 79
Dunn, Olivia, 50–51

Earps, Mary, 113
Ederle, Gertrude, 35
Ellis, Jill, 35
Englebert, Cathy, 63, 105, 144, 146, 153, 163–164
Equal Employment Opportunity Commission (EEOC), 33–35, 48
Ernst and Young (EY), 48
ESPN, 9, 13, 22, 23, 26, 39, 57, 61, 69, 71, 74, 75, 107, 126, 136, 146, 153, 173, 177; and growing coverage of NCAA women's sports, 96–105; ratings and historic women's programming of, 77–95; and *SportsCenter*, 79, 80, 82, 99, 135, 179
espnW, 48, 58, 69, 73, 80, 83–84, 87, 105, 112, 130, 153, 156
Evert, Chris, 26

Fagan, Kate, 11, 22, 74, 91, 93, 99, 107
Fair Play: How Sports Shape the Gender Debates (Barnes), 57
Federation of Association Football (FIFA), 28, 36, 41, 42, 46, 68
Ferro, Rita, 71–72, 107
Fightmaster, E. R., 58–59
Fleshman, Lauren, 157
Flores, Diana, 18
Forbes, 20–21, 114, 126, 166
Fortuny, Núria Martínez, 56
Foudy, Julie, 11, 22, 84, 129–130

Game On: The Unstoppable Rise of Women's Sport (Anstiss), 14, 67
Gauff, Coco, 12, 26, 27, 29, 100
Gentile, Laura, 69, 83–84
German Journal of Physical Education, 2
Giammanco, Michael, 62–63
Gibson, Althea, 32
The Gist, 81, 119, 178
Goldin, Claudia, 34
Google, 71–72, 99, 106, 139
Gotfredson, Sara, 106
Gotham, New Jersey-New York (NWSL), 11, 55–56, 66, 77–78, 106, 116–117
Graf, Steffi, 26
Greenberg, Mel, 177
Griner, Brittney, 165
The Guardian, 169

Hamm, Mia, 11, 22, 129
Hammon, Becky, 28
Harris, Ashlyn, 116–117
Harris, Franco, 75
Hartford Courant, 177
Heldman, Gladys, 19
Heldman, Julie, 19. *See also* Original 9
Hermoso, Jennifer, 45–47, 61
Hill, Jemele, 79–80
Hiltz, Nikki, 59
Hingis, Martina, 26, 60
Hogshead-Makar, Nancy, 57
Hyslop, Ellen, 119, 178–182

International Journal of Environmental Research and Public Health, 56
International Tennis Hall of Fame, 21

Jackson, Terri, 151–153
Jackson, Victoria, 6, 48, 69–70, 113, 174, 181–182
Johnson, Kate, 71

Kagawa Colas, Lindsay, 133, 153
Kaplan Hecker & Fink LLP, 173–174
Keys, Madison, 27

King, Billie Jean, 8, 10, 25, 27, 28–30, 40, 48, 53, 55, 90, 141, 146, 147, 155, 166, 176, 182; and development of the WTA Tour, 17–23; and mentorship of Venus and Serena Williams, 32–33; on transgender athletes and inclusion, 58
King, Rob, 88
The Kissing Sailor: The Mystery behind the Photo That Ended World War II (Verria), 47
Kloss, Ilana, 18–22, 28–29, 140–141
Kramer, Jack, 19, 22, 40

Ladies Professional Golf Association (LPGA), 21, 35
Ladik, Dan, 28, 134
Lapchick, Richard, 177
Lasry, Marc, 140
Lavielle, Thayer, 22–23, 99, 114–118, 133–135, 165, 181–182
Leslie, Lisa, 24, 149
Lewis, Jonathan, 85–86, 94, 97–98, 101, 104, 143
Ley, Bob, 39, 41, 82–83, 102
Li Na, 26, 168
liberation movement, women's, 17–20
Liberty, New York (WNBA), 11, 28, 62, 100, 176, 177, 180
Lieberman, Nancy, 22
Life Magazine, 47
Lobo, Rebecca, 24, 146, 149
Loeffler, Kelly, 99, 161–164
Lowry, Pat, 96–98, 101

Maddock, Dierdre, 112
Maher, Ilona, 101, 104
Major League Baseball (MLB), 23, 93, 103, 154
Major League Soccer (MLS), 9, 21, 42, 104, 123, 125
Manning, Eli, 11
Marciano, Stephanie, 105–106
Marist poll, on women's sports audience, 66–67
Mauresmo, Amelie, 60, 146
McCoughtry, Angel, 162
Medvedev, Daniil, 26, 100
Messner, Michael, 81
Metcalfe, Rhoda, 34
Miringoff, Lee, 66
Monarch Collective, 129–130
Moore, Maya, 163
Moore, Raymond, 146–147
Mosier, Chris, 57
Murray, Andy, 146–147
Murray, Caitlin, 113

name, image, and likeness rights (NIL), 13, 49–52, 109, 111, 118–119, 135
Nassar, Larry, 158, 166
National Basketball Association (NBA), 21, 23, 28, 38, 63, 73, 74, 85, 88, 94, 99, 104, 105, 123, 129, 131, 139, 141–146, 148, 149, 151–152, 168, 176–178
National Collegiate Athletic Association (NCAA), 13, 16, 25, 28, 29, 49–50, 58, 59, 63, 71, 74, 79, 81, 82, 90, 96–97, 99, 100–102, 104–105, 109, 118–119, 128, 142, 144, 147, 151, 172–175
National Football League (NFL), 17, 23, 26, 28, 38–40, 66, 70, 72, 73–74, 79, 80, 85–86, 88, 92, 123, 126–127, 128, 140, 141, 145, 154, 157, 162, 163, 177, 178
National Hockey League (NHL), 11, 22, 122, 127, 131, 142
National Women's Soccer League (NWSL), 9–11, 13, 18, 21, 28, 55, 65–66, 70, 73–74, 104–108, 111, 121–124, 128–136, 155, 169, 170, 180; pandemic viewership of, 100
Navratilova, Martina, 26–27, 57–58
New York Times, 34, 42, 101, 157, 180
Ng, Kim, 23
99ers (1999 gold medal–winning USWNT), 11, 22, 29, 38; ESPN documentary about, 22
Nortman, Kara, 129–130

O'Bannon, Ed, 50
Ogwumike, Nneka, 151–154, 156
Ohanian, Alexis, 8, 28, 121, 123
Olson, Lisa, 5
Olympics, 22, 25, 28, 54, 95, 101, 116, 168; ratings and percentage coverage of men's and women's, 38–39, 83; and success of American teams in 1996 Atlanta, 8, 41, 152

ON3 NIL, 50
Orender, Donna, 15
Original 9, 19, 21, 24, 26
Osaka, Naomi, 11, 20, 101, 133, 166–169
Ourand, John, 85–87, 91–95
Ovechkin, Alex, 11

PBS, 20, 43
Peng Shuai, 168–169
Pigeon, Kristy, 19–20. *See also* Original 9
Players' Tribune, 36, 101
Portman, Natalie, 11, 129–130
Prince, Sedona, 97, 172–175, 179, 182
Professional Golfers' Association (PGA), 21, 35, 136, 169
Professional Women's Hockey League (PWHL), 18, 169, 182

Raisman, Aly, 166
Rapinoe, Megan, 1, 36, 41–44, 65, 90, 120, 122, 145, 159, 163, 174; partnership of, with Victoria's Secret, 114–116, 118; at 2019 Canyon of Heroes parade and City Hall celebration, 35
ratings in live sports programming, men's and women's, 85–87
Rawlinson, Nadia, 11, 13, 63, 75, 127, 132, 175, 182; and search for investors for Chicago Sky, 138–141, 148
Reid, Kerry Melville, 19. *See also* Original 9
reproductive freedom and the foundation of women's sports, 49
Richards, Renee, 58
Richey, Nancy, 19. *See also* Original 9
Ricketts, Laura, 132, 148
Riggs, Bobby, 8, 18, 40, 146. *See also* Battle of the Sexes
rights packages, 104
Robinson, Jackie, 23
Robinson, Jasmine, 129–130
Roe v. Wade, 49
Rosen, Haley, 9–10, 66, 76, 99, 182; on building a new media framework for women's sports, 13; resilience of, since founding Just Women's Sports, 175–178, 180
Rowe, Holly, 173, 177
Rubiales, Luis, 45–47
Ruggiero, Angela, 64

Sabalenka, Aryna, 26, 100
Salazar, Alberto, 157–158
Scebelo, Steven, 145
Schilling, Emma, 65–66, 89, 128, 130–131, 135
Schofield, Kendall Coyne, 11
Semple, Jock, 1–3, 40
Seton Hall University, 17–18, 28, 82, 134
Simmons, Bill, 74–75
Simon, Gilles, 146
Simon, Steve, 168
Sky, Chicago (WNBA), 11, 13, 62–63, 73, 75, 112, 127, 132, 138–148, 175
Sky News, 113
Smith, DeMaurice, 145
Smith, Michael, 80
Spain, Sarah, 11, 73–75, 84–87, 91, 93, 132, 154–155
Sportico, 89, 126, 148
Sports and Fitness Industry Association and Sports Marketing Surveys, 110
Sports Bra (bar), 119
Sports Business Journal, 15, 85, 111
Sports Illustrated, 9, 51, 85
Sports Innovation Lab, 4, 67, 71, 93, 125, 141, 160, 164; and the "fluid fan," 64–65
Sports Media Watch, 85, 97, 100, 126, 143
Sportsology Group, 65, 89, 128, 135
Spotrac.com, 115
Staley, Dawn, 97, 120
Staurowsky, Ellen, 8, 9, 15, 16, 181
Stephens, Sloane, 21, 27
Stern, David, 131, 141–145
Stiff, Carol, 9–10, 88, 94, 101
Stout, Erin, 158
Sullivan, Tara, 5
Switzer, Kathrine, 1–2, 3, 183
Swoopes, Sheryl, 24; and Air Swoopes debut, 109–111; pregnancy of, in first year of the WNBA, 54, 149–151, 154

Thomas, Lia, 58
Through the Looking Glass (podcast), 22
TIDES (Institute for Diversity and Ethics in Sports), 177
Tigerbelles, Tennessee State University (track), 54
TikTok, 97, 101, 104, 179
Times of London, 27, 31, 32

Tissenbaum, Molly, 69–73, 93, 125–126, 141, 170; from hockey player to analyst at Sports Innovation Lab, 4; on lack of market data in women's sports, 64–67; on WNBA activism in the Wubble, 164–165; on women athletes investing in women's sports, 132–133
Title IX, 4–5, 8, 11, 15, 23, 29, 37–38, 41, 58, 66, 77, 80, 119, 128, 142, 173, 179, 181
Townsend, Taylor, 27
Trainor, Kelsey, 173, 179; on new investors to women's sports, 127–133
Tsai, Clara Wu, 11, 176

Uhrman, Julie, 129–130
U.S. Women's National Team (USWNT), 8–11, 63, 68, 81, 83, 100, 104, 113, 123, 131, 145, 166, 170; and the fight for equal pay, 35–44
U.S. Soccer Federation, 35, 42–43, 154

Vanstone, Erica, 77–79, 95
Verria, Lawrence, 47
Victoria's Secret, 114–116, 118
Voepel, Michael, 177
Volleyball Day, University of Nebraska, 15–16, 65

Wade, Dwyane, 11, 63, 148
Wall Street Journal, 118, 128
Wambach, Abby, 10, 99
Warnock, Raphael, 99, 163
Washington Post, 161
Wasserman's The Collective, 21, 22, 52, 67, 99, 114, 115, 133–135, 165, 181
Weaver, Karen, 9, 124
Weggemann, Mallory, 55
Whip It (movie), 78
White, Natalie, 110–114
Williams, Elizabeth, 161–165, 170
Williams, Jean, 40–41
Williams, Richard, 27, 32
Williams, Serena, 6, 8, 11, 12, 21, 26–27, 30, 31–32, 50, 52, 54, 94, 121, 129, 133, 147, 156–157, 166–167
Williams, Venus, 6, 12, 21, 26–27, 30, 94; opinion piece by, in the *Times of London*, impact of, 31–33, 44
Wimbledon, 25, 27, 31–33, 56, 146–147, 166
A Woman's Game (Wrack), 122
Women's College World Series, 13, 102
Women's Flat Track Derby Association (WFTDA), 14, 77–78, 95
Women's National Basketball Association (WNBA), 9, 11, 13–15, 18, 21, 24, 28–29, 36, 54, 58–59, 63, 65–66, 74–75, 79, 82–84, 94, 96, 98, 101, 104–105, 108, 109, 111, 113, 126–129, 132–133, 135, 138–139, 141, 143–146, 148, 149–150, 159–165, 170, 177, 180, 181–183; collective bargaining agreement of, 151–154; and difficulty finding games of on networks, 99; rising ratings of, 100
Women's Running, 158
Women's Sports Foundation, 1, 4, 29, 48, 55, 64, 68, 179
Women's Sports Network, 9, 88, 101
Women's Sport Trust, 68
Women's Tennis Association (WTA), 12, 20–27, 30, 32, 44, 58, 136, 156, 167–169
Women's United Soccer Association (WUSA), 9
Women's World Cup, 6, 9, 16, 22, 36, 61, 68, 71, 74, 81–83, 94–95, 123, 128, 134, 169; 99ers fight for large venues for, 38–41
Woods, Tiger, 27

Yahoo News, 145
Yogi Berra Museum, 17
Young, Jabari, 126

Ziegenfuss, Valerie, 19–20. *See also* Original 9
Zimbalist, Andrew, 11, 50–52, 93, 127; on economic success of women's tennis, 25–26; on historic short-term investment in women's sports, 123
Zimmer, Greta, 47
Zuckerberg, Mark, 2

Jane McManus is an Adjunct Professor at New York University at the Preston Robert Tisch Institute for Global Sport. She was the founding Executive Director of the Center for Sports Media at Seton Hall University and taught at the Columbia Graduate School of Journalism, Michigan State University, and Marist College. A former columnist for the *New York Daily News* and *Deadspin*, she spent nearly a decade covering women's sports and the NFL for ESPN. She was a founding columnist for espnW, appearing in multiple network shows and hosting two ESPN Radio shows. She is the guest editor of the 2024 edition of *The Year's Best Sportswriting.*